THE MASTER HANDBOOK OF
HOUSEHOLD
REPAIRS–

from
A-Z

Other TAB books by the author:

THE MASTER HANDBOOK OF
HOUSEHOLD REPAIRS—
from
A-Z

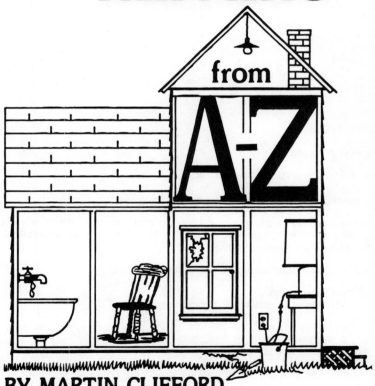

BY MARTIN CLIFFORD

FIRST EDITION

FIRST PRINTING

Copyright © 1982 by TAB BOOKS Inc.

Printed in the United States of America

Library of Congress Cataloging in Publication Data

Clifford, Martin, 1910-
    The master handbook of household repairs—from A-Z.

    Includes index.
    1. Repairing—Amateurs' manuals. 2. Dwellings—
Maintenance and repair—Amateurs' manuals. I. Title.
TT151.C55   643'.7   81-9108
ISBN 0-8306-0014-0   AACR2
ISBN 0-8306-1279-3 (pbk.)

Contents

To Ethel and David

Introduction

Maintaining a home is an unending process. If you think inanimate objects can be perverse, you are probably right. The problem is that many of us have a simplistic view about houses, looking on them as shelters only, structures with a roof, walls, and floors.

A house is much more than that. While it does have a roof, walls, and floors, these are just enclosures for a number of systems, all of which must function if home living is to be tolerable. Plumbing is one such system; electrical wiring is another. Painting isn't generally regarded as a system, but it is. And so are the roof, walls, and floors. Further, some systems can be fairly complex. The electrical wiring in a home can be a maze, and the plumbing may consist of pipes going off in all directions.

The difficulty with home maintenance is that it can become costly. It isn't the materials that are priced so high but the labor involved is expensive, with a ratio of 10 to 1, or higher, prevailing. A dimmer switch may cost about $3; the labor for installing it may cost $25 to $30.

Some home maintenance jobs are best left to competent plumbers, painters, paperhangers, electricians, carpenters or skilled handymen. But if you have the time and patience to do home maintenance and repair jobs yourself, you will have the satisfaction of having made substantial savings and, equally important, of doing the work yourself. Not all plumbers, electricians, or carpenters will rush to your aid when first summoned. And they will not always be willing to discuss your home maintenance problems with you, for they aren't teachers. Nor are they willing to dispense practical information based on their acquired experienced without charge to anyone requesting it.

The difficulty with home maintenance is that the solution to repair problems, although often very simple, may involve using strange tools, parts whose names are equally strange, and a lack of confidence on your part, plus a shortage of knowledge on how best to proceed. The lack of confidence is understandable, but it can be acquired. What is usually needed in home repairs is a willingness to try methods that may seem strange, new, or different.

An individual's sex is no part of in-home maintenance. For a long time the prevailing view was that in-home repairs were a man's world and man's world only. That is just so much nonsense. Anyone can learn to use tools; anyone can learn to do home repairs. Patience and the willingness to try are the essential ingredients.

This book is arranged alphabetically, so finding a particular topic is just a matter of knowing the subject name of the problem, with an assist from the table of contents. No one book could possibly cover every conceivable contingency in home repairs, and this book is no exception. What you have here are the most commonly encountered problems with suggestions on how to effect cures.

Cross references appear with almost every subject heading. These can act as a guide to supply you with supplementary information, and quite often you will find more information than you will actually need. No matter. It's all part of broadening your education in home repairs.

Electrical, plumbing, painting and other problems in the home never get better by themselves. A leaky faucet, unrepaired, can never improve but will only get worse. The failure to tackle an in-home repair can not only be expensive but can lead to other problems.

While repairs are emphasized, every home also requires a certain amount of maintenance, including sections that may at first seem imperishable. Cement is durable, but doesn't last forever. Pipes may seem strong, but they are subject to ruptures and leaks. Floors can develop squeaks. Mold may make its appearance on painted surfaces. Electric plugs may not fit into outlets. Painting is definitely an important part of home maintenance.

If you must call in outside help, do so, but try to learn as much as you can by watching and asking questions. Fortunately, salesmen in stores that sell parts for home repairs are not only knowledgeable, but helpful as well. Further, many kits are now being made. If a repair requires an assortment of nuts, bolts, screws, nails, or adhesives, you need not go scrounging. You have all the essential materials right at hand. Further, these kits often contain detailed instructions and drawings to help you, or may have the information printed directly on the container for the kit.

If you aren't experienced in a particular home repair job, you will find that a 10 minute task may take hours. Don't let that bother you. The next time around you will do much better. Ultimately you will be able to take all in-home repair jobs in stride. And that's the way it should be!

☐ Adapter Plugs, How to Use

An electrical *plug,* sometimes called a male plug, can have two or three prongs or blades. A two prong plug can fit into any outlet. A three prong plug can only fit into an outlet designed to receive such a plug. If your house or apartment is wired only with old style outlets made for two prong plugs, you will need to use an *adapter plug.* All modern appliances are equipped with three prong plugs.

The adapter has three holes to receive the three prongs of the plug connected to the appliance. However, the other end of the adapter has only two prongs or blades and can readily fit into any power outlet.

The adapter has a wire coming out of it with a grounding terminal connected to one end of this wire (Fig. A-1). Loosen the screw holding the wall plate of the outlet in position, put the grounding terminal under the screw head, and then tighten the screw once again. The purpose is to ground the appliance you are using and to protect you against accidental shock. By using an adapter you are modifying the outlet so as to accept two prong plugs or three prong plugs of electrical appliances. An adapter is a temporary expedient. The best arrangement is to replace all two hole electrical receptacles with three hole types.

It is possible to connect the adapter plug without using the grounding terminal, and this is sometimes done. However, this removes the safety feature; the electrical appliance is ungrounded and the user can get an electric shock in the event of a power short in the unit.

See Electric Plugs, *page 105*

Electrical Shock, How to Avoid, *page 107*

□ Aerator, How to Install

An *aerator,* as its name implies, is a device for adding bubbles of air to the water supplied by a faucet. Air contains oxygen and is a good, no-cost additive that helps in washing dishes. Some people claim that oxygenated water tastes better. An aerator also reduces splashing when the faucets are turned so as to supply a strong stream of water.

Faucets have three different types of spouts. Some are threaded on the inside, some on the outside, while some have no threads at all. In all instances, an aerator, an inexpensive little device, can be added.

The threaded portion of the *spout,* that part of the faucet from which the water flows, is right at the end of the spout. If the threads are on the outside you will be able to see them easily. All you will need to do is screw the aerator right on to the threads (Fig. A-2). To mount the aerator, turn it in a counterclockwise direction. The threads should engage easily and smoothly. If not, do not try to force them, but simply try to turn the aerator until the beginning threads connect.

If the spout has inside threads, the aerator you buy will have an adapter. Screw the adapter into the spout and then screw the aerator on to the adapter.

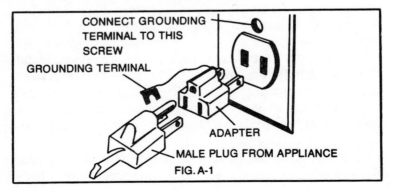

CONNECT GROUNDING TERMINAL TO THIS SCREW

GROUNDING TERMINAL

ADAPTER

MALE PLUG FROM APPLIANCE

FIG. A-1

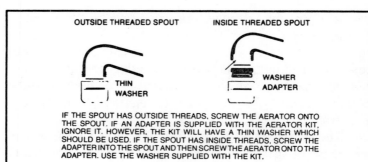

OUTSIDE THREADED SPOUT   INSIDE THREADED SPOUT

THIN WASHER   WASHER ADAPTER

IF THE SPOUT HAS OUTSIDE THREADS, SCREW THE AERATOR ONTO THE SPOUT. IF AN ADAPTER IS SUPPLIED WITH THE AERATOR KIT, IGNORE IT. HOWEVER, THE KIT WILL HAVE A THIN WASHER WHICH SHOULD BE USED. IF THE SPOUT HAS INSIDE THREADS, SCREW THE ADAPTER INTO THE SPOUT AND THEN SCREW THE AERATOR ONTO THE ADAPTER. USE THE WASHER SUPPLIED WITH THE KIT.

FIG. A-2

If the spout of your faucet isn't threaded, buy an aerator made for unthreaded faucets and follow the manufacturer's directions. You can also get an aerator for an odd-sized spout. Both types come equipped with adapters.

After the aerator has been installed and has been in use, possibly for several months, it may need to be cleaned. Remove the aerator, hold its mesh portion underneath the faucet, and let a stream of water flow through it. Hold the aerator up to the light supplied by an electric bulb, and you will be able to see if the water has cleaned the mesh completely. If not, repeat the cleaning process.

See Bathroom Faucets, Installing, *page 29*
Faucets, Compression Type, Leaking, *page 121*
Faucets, Repairing Non-Compression Types, *page 122*
Faucets, Types of, *page 128*
Faucet Handles, Replacing, *page 129*
Faucet Seat, Dressing a, *page 131*
Hose Faucet, Replacing, *page 186*
Leaky Packing Nut, *page 198*
Sink, Bath and Shower Faucets, How to Replace, *page 305*

□ **Air Conditioners**

An *air conditioner* does more than cool the air. It works as a dehumidifier, taking water out of the air. It also cleans and circulates the air.

Buying an air conditioner means getting involved in some elementary arithmetic and the use of measuring units that are probably strange. Air conditioners are rated in *British thermal units* or Btu. The Btu in this context is the cooling power of an air conditioner and is expressed in Btu per hour. The higher the Btu/hour rating, the greater the cooling capacity of the air conditioner. A conditioner with a capacity of 6,000 Btu is capable of removing 6000 Btu per hour from the air.

The Btu/hour rating is directly related to the size of your home or apartment. If the air conditioner cannot supply enough Btu per hour, it will not be able to do a proper job of cooling and will probably be overworked, increasing the possibility of a short air conditioner life. If the air conditioner is overrated, then you will have spent money unnecessarily in buying a conditioner that is too big for your needs. One that is too large may not operate long enough to dehumidify properly. Its operating costs will also be higher than necessary.

To determine the right size air conditioner to buy, measure the floor area in all rooms that are to be cooled. If just one room is to be air conditioned, then simply measure this one room. Do not include closet space. If you have several rooms but plan to close off these rooms, do not include them in your calculations. However, when using your air conditioner you will need to keep the doors to these rooms closed. All calculations are based on the idea that you will keep your windows and any vents closed when the air conditioner is turned on. These calculations are intended for rooms that have a ceiling height of 8 to 9 feet.

Measure the length of the room, in feet, and multiply this number by the width of the room in feet. You can ignore inches and round off the length and width to the nearest whole number. If you are measuring just a single room, multiply the area by 25 (you are going to allow 25 Btu per square foot of space). If you have room that measures 12 feet × 15 feet, it will need 12 × 15 × 25 Btu = 4500 Btu. Allow a safety margin and get a 6000 Btu air conditioner. If you plan to air condition more than just one room, add the areas of all the rooms and multiply the total area by 25.

Not all air conditioners are alike. Some are more energy

efficient than others. To determine the energy efficiency of an air conditioner, divide its Btu/hour rating by the wattage rating of the air conditioner. The wattage rating should be on a label on the bottom or back of the air conditioner. It may be stamped into the frame or may be on a metal tag attached to the unit. Thus, if your air conditioner is rated at 6000 Btu and has a wattage rating of 800, then its efficiency is 6000 divided by 800 or 7.5. The higher the energy efficiency ratio, the more cooling you will get per dollar. Conditioners having a high *energy efficiency ratio* generally have a higher initial cost. The higher the energy efficiency ratio, the more your air conditioner economizes on energy. An energy efficiency ratio of 10 or over is excellent, 8 to 9 is good, 6 or 7 is passable, while less than 6 is unsatisfactory. There is as much as 60% difference in the energy efficiency ratio of air conditioners.

If your air conditioner doesn't carry a wattage rating, it will probably have a current rating in *amperes*. Multiply this current rating by the amount of your house or apartment voltage, usually 117 volts, and you will have the wattage rating. If the conditioner has a current rating of 12 amperes, then 12 × 117 = 1404 watts. If you would rather not do the arithmetic, insist that your appliance dealer furnish you with the wattage rating. This information may also be contained in the instruction manual supplied by the manufacturer.

When you have an air conditioner turned on and then decide to turn it off, wait at least five minutes before you turn it on again. Turning air conditioners on and off in rapid sequence is a good way to blow the fuse protecting the ac line to the air conditioner.

If the conditioner is a window type, cover the outside of the conditioner during the off season. Clean the air filter regularly. Don't block the grilles from which you get a flow of cold air. The ideal temperature for conditioning is 78°F. Don't keep adjusting the thermostat and keep children's fingers away from it. An air conditioner is an expensive toy.

Keep drapes and blinds drawn to help keep sunshine out. If your entire house is air conditioned, use bathroom and kitchen exhaust fans to get rid of excess heat and moisture.

Do a minimum amount of cooking when your air conditioner is on. If you use a clothes dryer, make sure it is vented to the outside.

Schedule any ironing you need to do during air conditioner off time. Make sure you read the manufacturer's instruction manual. It will often contain excellent ideas on how to get the most out of your air conditioner.

Electric lights, broilers, and toasters all contribute to the heat level. Minimum use will help keep your home cooler.

Houses should be well insulated against outside heat as much as against outside cold. Keeping doors closed or open no longer than necessary is helpful. The greater the number of people in a house or apartment, the harder the air conditioner will need to work. People produce heat.

If you plan to leave your home or apartment for several days, turn the air conditioner off. When you return, do not set the air conditioner to a lower level than to which you're accustomed. Doing so will not cool the house faster, but it will make the conditioner work harder.

See Electric Bills, How to Save Money on, *page 103*

☐ Alligatoring (Paint)

An *alligatored* surface is so-called because of its fancied resemblance to alligator skin. It can happen if you are in a hurry and don't allow the first coat to dry thoroughly before applying the second. It can also happen if you use a low quality paint or if you change the paints for the various coats, such as applying a hard coating over a soft oil base paint.

It always pays to follow these two steps. Use a paint of good quality. Bargain paints, unknown brands, are no bargain. Also, follow the manufacturer's instructions. Don't aim for shortcuts.

If a surface is alligatored, you will have to scrape the old paint and then sand it smooth. You may also need to use a paint remover. If you do, allow adequate ventilation and avoid inhaling fumes. Make sure windows are open. If outdoors, do only a small section at a time. Give yourself frequent rest periods away from the job so you can inhale fresh air.

☐ **Aluminum, Joining**

Aluminum has a low melting point, around 1200°F. It does not change color when heated, so be extremely careful when using a torch to make an aluminum joint. It is possible to melt aluminum when heating, so it is a good idea to practice on scrap pieces before trying to repair a joint.

Clean all parts thoroughly and apply flux to the joint. play the flame on the joint near where the connection is to be made, but avoid exposing the flux to the flame directly. You may find it necessary to apply additional flux if too much burns off in the heating operation.

When the heated joint reaches its working temperature, apply the aluminum brazing rod. You can check the temperature of the joint from time to time by seeing if it is hot enough to melt the aluminum rod. After the joint has become completely cool, clean it thoroughly with a rag to remove any remaining flux.

☐ Aluminum Siding, Streaking

Streaking is caused by an accumulation of dust and dirt. The dust and dirt build up and then are partially washed away by rain, with the streaking effect caused by the way the rain moves down the siding.

To remove the streaks, make a hot water solution of *trisodium phosphate* (TSP). You can buy this chemical in paint stores and sometimes in supermarkets.

Scrub the area with a bristle brush. You will find it easier to do the cleaning by using a long handled brush rather than standing on a ladder. Do not give the cleaning liquid a chance to dry, so wash it away with water, using a hose, as soon as the brushing is completed.

See Fungus Stains on Wood Trim, *page 143*
Mildew (on Painted Surfaces), *page 210*

☐ Anchor Screws, Plastic

You can use plastic *anchor screws,* also called *rawl plugs,* for anchoring an object to walls made of Sheetrock, plaster, or wallboard.

Drill a hole through the wall so that the casing of the anchor screw will make a force fit. Do not make the hole too large. After drilling the hole, insert the casing of the anchor screw and drive it in with a hammer. The head of the casing should be flush with the wall surface. Put the screw through the object to be fastened and then into the casing. Tighten the screw with a screwdriver (Fig. A-3).

If you plan to drill into concrete, use an electric drill and a bit made especially for concrete. Wear goggles since the action of the drill bit can make bits of concrete fly out. These can come out with considerable speed.

The anchor of the plastic anchor screw consists of a ribbed portion which separates when the screw is driven into it. You can loosen or remove the bolt portion of the plastic anchor screw, but this action can weaken the grip the unit has on the wall.

See Molly Screws, *page 212*
Toggle Bolts, *page 332*

☐ Appliances, Do not Work

If an appliance doesn't work when you connect it to an outlet or when you turn its switch to the on position, make sure that the plug is actually in the outlet. Sometimes the two blades of the plug are pushed together and do not make good contact when inserted into the outlet. Separate the blades slightly.

Check whether you have power in the outlet. You can make this test by plugging in a portable lamp. If the lamp doesn't turn on, then power is not being delivered to that particular outlet.

If the outlet has no power, go to the fuse box. If you have a thermal reset type of fuse box, open and close the switch that controls power to the outlet and then check the appliance once again. If the fuse box contains screw in type fuses, examine each fuse. If you find a fuse whose window is smudged, you have evidence of an overload. Replace the fuse. If the fuse blows again, there is a short circuit somewhere in the line protected by that fuse.

If you must replace fuses regularly for a particular line, then that line is being overloaded. Too many appliances are being connected to the line via the various outlets.

The fault may be in the on-off switch of the appliance. Connect the appliance to another outlet known to be in good

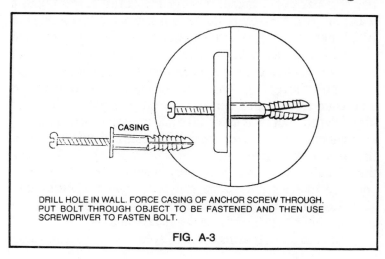

CASING

DRILL HOLE IN WALL. FORCE CASING OF ANCHOR SCREW THROUGH.
PUT BOLT THROUGH OBJECT TO BE FASTENED AND THEN USE
SCREWDRIVER TO FASTEN BOLT.

FIG. A-3

working order. If the appliance still does not work, the appliance is either defective or its on-off switch is broken. Most switches make a definite clicking sound when turned on.

See Circuit Breakers, *page 45*

☐ **Asphalt Tile, Replacing or Laying**

Plan the installation so you can work with the tiles with minimum cutting. Lay one row of tiles across the floor, across the length and another across the width, to get some idea of the final appearance and to plan for minimum cutting. The floor should be free of dirt and any nail heads should be removed. If the tile is to fit under molding around the room where the wall joins the floor, remove the molding and reinstall it after you have put down all the tile. If the floor is one that has been waxed, go over the entire surface with a wax remover. Make sure the floor is dry before installing the tile. When possible, use asphalt tile instead of linoleum since it can tolerate usage better and is also more impervious to moisture. Asphalt tile is best maintained by frequent waxing.

Apply the *asphalt* cement to one section at a time, using a notched trowel spreader. Do not put the tile on the floor immediately, but wait about 20 to 30 minutes until the adhesive gets tacky. To make the work easier and quicker, use a flat surface work table and cover it with newspapers. Apply the adhesive to a number of tiles, possibly a dozen. As you complete putting one tile down, cover another with adhesive. Keep the tiles in a row so you always lay down the tile that has been "curing" for at least 20 minutes.

You can use a brazing torch to help you do a better tiling

job. Heat the underside of each tile but do so gently. The idea isn't to make the tile hot, but simply warm enough so it becomes more pliant. This will help it conform much better to the surface of the floor, which may have some irregularities in it and also a slight slope.

It is important for the floor surface to be flat. Fill in any cracks with a wood dough filler, let it dry, and then sandpaper it.

To cut asphalt tile, draw a line on the top side with a pencil. If you want to make sure the line is absolutely straight, use a drafting T square. Using a sharp knife, score along this line. A *linoleum* knife, an inexpensive tool, is ideal for this purpose. After completing the score, heat the underside of the tile gently in the area along the scribe. Put the torch away for the moment and then, holding the tile along the scribe line, bend it. The tile should break cleanly without a rough edge.

Don't try to break the tile by holding it in your hands. Instead, put the tile on a table having a sharply defined edge. Lay the tile on the table so that the scoring coincides with the edge of the table, and then press down on that part of the tile that hangs over the edge. It is especially important to have a sharp edge if the cut tile is to butt up against another tile. Any irregularity along the break line will show as a crack or hole in the completed floor and will be a dirt catcher.

To remove and replace a defective tile, use a linoleum knife and score the four sides of the tile. Cut deeply so you get down to the subfloor. Try to avoid cutting or damaging any adjacent tiles since these will show as scratches or grooves when the repair is completed. Using a brazing torch, work the flame around the tile to soften the adhesive. Don't try to heat the entire tile at once. Instead, select one edge and work the flame back and forth along this edge. Using a putty knife, try to work the blade under the tile to lift it when the adhesive has become soft. Then continue using the torch, alternating with movement of the putty knife, until you have removed the complete tile.

Before applying adhesive to the replacement tile, test to see if it fits into place. If the floor has any small mounds of adhesive, heat these with the torch and then remove with a scraper or putty knife. The floor should be flat and clear of any old pieces of tile or adhesive. You can then apply adhesive to the replacement tile, wait for about 20 minutes, and then warm the underside of the replacement tile with a torch. Put the new tile into position, and then walk on it to apply pressure to the tile's surface. When putting adhesive on tile, do not apply so much that it will be squeezed out from the sides when the tile is put into position. If any cement is forced out from the sides, remove it before it has a chance to dry. Follow the manufacturer's instructions as to the kind of solvent used to remove any traces of cement which cannot be wiped away.

As tile gets older it gets darker due to washing, waxing, exposure to the light, and foot traffic. For these reasons, a replacement tile, even if it comes from the original batch of tiles used when laying the floor, will not make a perfect color match. In time, however, it will blend in more with the rest of the flooring.

See Bathroom or Kitchen Tiles, Loose or Broken, *page 30*

Floor Tiles—Loose, Broken or Damaged, *page 138*

B

☐ Basement, Waterproofing

A *basement* can become moist or wet by seepage through the floors and walls, or because of a leak due to a hole. Settling of a house can cause cracks in the basement, either in the floor or walls, or else water pressure on the outside can become strong enough to force water through the walls. Even if a wall has been dry for a long time, one or more strong rains can ultimately produce water seepage. Quite often you will first note seepage along the joint where the floor and the walls meet, or you may notice water coming out of a crack.

If the seepage is minor and occurs at the joint of the floor and walls, you can use a waterproof coating mixture. Special waterproof paints and mixes are available in paint stores. Wipe the joint until it is as dry as possible, and then apply a coating of the waterproofing paint. As soon as it dries, possibly in about two hours, apply another coat.

If the water seepage is heavy at the junction of wall and floor, you will need to cut a dovetail joint along the junction. Do this with a cold chisel and a hammer, chipping away enough material so as to form a groove that will hold the waterproofing mix.

After you have completed the groove, sweep it out with a bristle broom to make sure the groove is as clean as possible. For filling the groove you can use some ready mix cement or you can make your own by using one part of cement to two parts of fine sand. Do not make the mix too watery; rather it should be a thick paste. Wet the groove and then force the cement mix into the groove with a trowel.

Each day, apply some water to the cement to let it cure properly. After doing this for a week, let the cement patch dry thoroughly, and then paint it with a waterproofing paint. Apply two coats, but let the first coat dry before putting on the second.

If you have wall or floor seepage, you can sometimes solve the problem just by using waterproofing paint. The areas to be treated must be clean and free of paint. Waterproof paint will generally not adhere to a dirty, wet, or painted surface. Some waterproof paints can be applied directly to a moist surface, but it is always best to make the surface as dry as you possibly can.

If your basement is made of cinder block, you can make your own waterproofing compound by mixing cement and water. Stir the mixture until it has the consistency of a thick paint and then apply it with a stiff brush. Work with a circular motion until a small area of the wall is covered. Then, using a brush, paint the area with the mix, using horizontal and vertical strokes crossing each other. This will make sure you do not miss any area of the wall. The best place to start this waterproofing method is at the bottom of the wall and then work your way upward. After two or three days, apply another coating of the cement waterproofing mixture.

After the two mixtures have dried, possibly in a day, wash them down with a sponge and water. Let the coating dry for several days and then cover with a waterproofing paint.

If you have a hole in the wall or floor, enlarge the hole slightly and clean it out thoroughly. Pack in cement until the hole is completely filled. Let the cement dry for a day or two and then water it. Keep repeating the water treatment for several days and then let the cement dry. This will take another day or two. After the cement is dry, coat the repaired area with waterproof paint. Let that dry and apply a second coat.

See Gutters and Downspouts, Maintaining and Repairing, *page 154*
Damp Basements, *page 71*
Water Leaks, *page 361*

☐ Bathroom Faucets, Installing

One of the simplest bathroom faucets to install is the 4-inch type that does not have a *pop-up drain*. It is known as a 4-inch faucet because the spacing between its water supply pipes is 4 inches. If the sink has such a faucet, shut off the water supply to both pipes, one for hot water and the other for cold, by turning off the water valves for these pipes. There are two such valves and they are located beneath the sink.

Removing the old faucet is simply a matter of loosening the locknuts *which hold the faucet in place*. Use a box wrench or an open end wrench.

Before making the replacement, coat the complete rectangular frame of the new faucet with plumber's putty. This is the part of the faucet that will rest on the sink. The putty will help make a watertight seal between the fixture and the sink (Fig. B-1).

The replacement faucet has two shanks or threaded sections of pipe. At the end of each of these you will find a locknut. These locknuts will be fastened to the threaded hot and cold water pipes beneath the sink. Coat the threads of these pipes with pipe joint compound and then fasten the locknuts to the pipes.

Also on the shanks of the new faucet, you will find another pair of locknuts. Their function is to hold the faucet tightly in place against the sink. Turn these locknuts in a counterclockwise direction until they make contact with the sink. Tighten them with an open end wrench until they are secure.

Turn on both water valves and then try the faucet to make sure both hot and cold water are supplied. Remove any excess putty that may have escaped from the area where the faucet joins the sink.

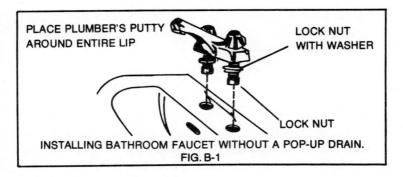

PLACE PLUMBER'S PUTTY AROUND ENTIRE LIP

LOCK NUT WITH WASHER

LOCK NUT

INSTALLING BATHROOM FAUCET WITHOUT A POP-UP DRAIN.
FIG. B-1

☐ **Bathroom or Kitchen Tiles, Loose or Broken**

Replacing bathroom or kitchen tiles is very much like putting in floor tiles. The difference is in the tile material. Bathroom and kitchen tiles are ceramic or plastic, but metal tiles are also used. The finish of plastic tiles can be damaged by the adhesive, so make sure to remove excess adhesive as soon as possible.

Remove old adhesive from the wall after taking off the old tile. If the old tile is just one that has become loose, remove the adhesive from its back. The solvent you use for this depends on the composition of the tile. Check with your local paint store.

When using new tile which needs to fit into place, cut it with a saw after making careful measurements. A way to make straight cuts on tile is by scoring it first. Then press the tile on the edge of a hard surface. Put the score mark right along the edge of the surface and then press down on the overhang part of the tile.

Apply adhesive with a brush or putty knife and press the tile firmly in place. Once the tile is in position, press against it every few minutes or so to make sure it doesn't move. Mix a small amount of grout powder with water until it forms a thick paste. Force the grout into the tile joints on all four sides using either a putty knife or your fingers.

Remove excess grout with a moist sponge or else use a damp cloth. Wipe the surface of tile to make sure no particles of grout remain. Clean all tools free of grout as soon as possible, before the grout gets a chance to dry (Fig. B-2). Do this by washing tools in a pail of water. Do not pour this water into the toilet or any sink; instead, pour it into the nearest sewer. If the replacement tile was in a shower, do not use the shower for about 10 hours to give the adhesive a chance to dry thoroughly.

See Asphalt Tile, Replacing or Laying, *page 24*

Floor Tiles—Loose, Broken or Damaged, *page 138*

⊐ Bathtub Appliques, Removing

Initally, scrape away as much of the *applique* as you can, but try to avoid scratching the finish of the tub. Apply rubber cement thinner, available in art supply stores. If this doesn't work as well as you would like, use acetone, sold in paint and hardware stores.

SCRAPE ADHESIVE AWAY. SCORE TILE AND BREAK TILE ALONG THE SCORE.

APPLY ADHESIVE TO WALL USING A NOTCHED TROWEL AND FIX TILE FIRMLY IN POSITION. APPLY GROUT TO ALL JOINTS WITH FINGER OR PUTTY KNIFE.

WASH TILE THOROUGHLY WITH WATER TO REMOVE ALL TRACES OF GROUT. CLEAN TOOLS AS SOON AS POSSIBLE.

FIG. B-2

□ Bathtub Drain, Clogged

Bathtub drains seldom become clogged, but when they do the cause is an accumulation of hair and soap in the bathtub trap. If there is a clog, first remove as much of the water from the tub as you possibly can, including any water that may be in the drainpipe leading down from the tub. Make a mixture of boiling hot water to which you have added some ammonia. Pour this mixture down the drain. If you note some movement of water down the drain, add some more of the mixture.

There are chemicals available in various stores and supermarkets for unplugging a bathroom drain. If you plan to use any of these, do not use ammonia in the hot water treatment just described, but use hot water by itself.

Another method is to use a plunger. Plug the overflow outlet with a rag; otherwise you will not be able to get any pressure from the plunger. If you do decide to use a plunger, it will not be necessary to remove accumulated water from the tub. If the plunger method works, you will notice its effect since water will begin draining from the tub.

To keep the tub drain pipes and trap clear, pour a pail of boiling hot water and ammonia down the drain once a week.

The tub has a drum trap, generally mounted beneath the tub (Fig. B-3). You will find it extremely difficult to reach this trap. If none of the methods suggested here do the job, it would be best to call a plumber.

See Clogging of Kitchen Sink, Preventing, *page 47*
Drains, Clogged, *page 81*
Kitchen Trap, Replacing, *page 194*
Sink Drain, Sluggish, *page 307*

□ Batteries, Prolonging Life of

All *dry cell type batteries* "get used up" whether you put them to work or not. Shelf life of a battery ranges from one to two years, depending on the amount of use in flashlights, portable radios, electric clocks, etc. To prolong battery life, store batteries in a refrigerator or freezer when you do not expect to use the battery operated appliance. Batteries allowed to remain in appliances corrode as they get older, becoming difficult to remove and spoiling battery contacts at the same time. Allow batteries to reach room temperature when you decide to put them back to work.

☐ Blistering (Paint)

Blistering of a painted surface is caused by moisture. The moisture can come from the outside due to poor house construction, poor ventilation, or inadequate insulation. In the inside of the home, excessive moisture in the air can be due to daily household activities such as cooking, bathing, dishwashing, and laundering. It is estimated that the daily evaporation in a home is about 25 quarts of water.

If your house has an attic, it should be equipped with louvers. If you are using your attic for storage, make sure the louvers aren't blocked. Don't put large pieces of furniture near the louvers so as to allow a free passage of air in the attic. It is helpful to install an exhaust fan. If blistering is confined to a particular room, consider installing a dehumidifier.

Do not paint directly over a blistered surface. Scrape all blisters and then use a blister-resistant paint. Never paint over a wet surface.

See Alligatoring (Paint), *page 20*
    Chalking (Paint), *page 44*
    Checking (Paint), *page 45*
    Doors, Painting, *page 79*

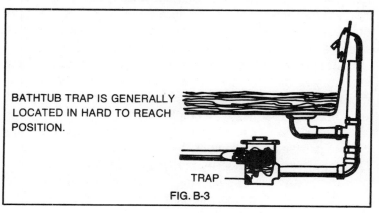

BATHTUB TRAP IS GENERALLY LOCATED IN HARD TO REACH POSITION.

TRAP

FIG. B-3

☐ Brazing

Brazing is a simple method of joining two metals, not necessarily the same metal, by using a third metal, a brazing rod, as a kind of "glue." It is an easy and effective way to make strong, permanent metal repairs on joints.

In the brazing process, the brazing rod or "filler or flux" used to join two metals is often a different material than the base metals. The correct technique is to get the joint hot enough so that the brazing rod melts from contact with the metals being joined and flows freely into the joint. This is the same technique used in soldering. The result is an alloying action which produces a very strong bond. Practically all brazing is done at temperatures above 1000°F and usually at about 1400° to 1700°F.

Bronze brazing rods are the most commonly used filler material for joining any combination of iron, steel, and brass. For joining aluminum parts, an aluminum rod is used. A stainless steel rod may be used for brazing two parts of stainless steel or two pieces of chrome-plated metal.

For copper pipe joints that do not have to be particularly strong, you can use solder. In soldering, the filler is commonly part lead and part tin and has a lower melting point than brazing filler, usually below 800°F.

Brazing is a useful technique to master for mending broken gardening equipment, toys, pots and pans, bicycles, lawn furniture, automobile mufflers, and fenders.

In brazing, as in soldering, the joint must be clean to secure a proper bond. Clean the metal parts to be joined by using emery paper or steel wool before making the joint. If the joint is painted, scrape the paint away and then clean with emery paper.

See Copper Pipe, Soldering, *page 60*
    Iron Pipes, Repairing, *page 189*
    Metals, Joining, *page 208*
    Soldering, *page 312*
    Water Pipes, Leaky, *page 364*
    Welding, *page 376*

☐ Bricks, Dirty

Brick around fireplaces may become discolored from smoke. Use a wire brush and then wash the brick with any of the commercial cleaning powders sold for home use. You can also use *trisodium phosphate* (TSP) available in department or paint stores. Clean the brick with the wire brush first and then use TSP. Follow instructions on the box for the amount of TSP to use. TSP dissolves very easily in water.

You may need to repeat the cleaning process several times. Wait until the brick is thoroughly dry before using the wire brush again.

See Cement, Ready Mixed, *page 43*
    Concrete, Repairing and Patching, *page 48*

☐ Buzzers, Chimes and Doorbells, How to Install

The simplest type of *doorbell* is one that is mechanical only. It requires no wiring, batteries, or transformer. However, electrically operated units are not only louder but often quite melodious. Some doorbells and chimes use batteries with the advantage that they are about as simple to install as the mechanical types. But the best and least troublesome are those that operate from the ac power line via a transformer.

Transformers used for doorbells, chimes, or buzzers have no moving parts and can be expected to give years of troublefree operation. These units are step-down types supplying 10 volts for doorbells and buzzers and 16 volts for chimes. If you plan to replace an ac operated doorbell or buzzer with chimes, make sure that the existing transformer is capable of supplying the correct amount of voltage. If you are doubtful, measure the voltage of the secondary winding of the transformer with a volt-ohm-milliammeter or else have an electrician do this for you. The secondary winding has two leads which lead directly to the buzzer, doorbell or chime.

The transformer has two windings, a primary which is connected to an ac outlet or directly to a junction box that supplies 117 volts ac, 50 Hz or 60 Hz, and a secondary connected to the sound making device. The two wires of the secondary are often connected to the bell, buzzer or chimes using No. 18 gauge insulated wire. The overall length of the wire isn't important. The transformer can be mounted in any position on any convenient joist. Neither the two leads of the primary winding nor those of the secondary winding are connected to plugs for these wires are attached permanently into position. It isn't necessary to solder the connections.

The simplest installation is that of a single bell or buzzer. The primary winding of the transformer is connected permanently to 117 V ac from any convenient junction box. One secondary wire of the transformer is wired to a screw connection on the door push button. The other secondary wire is connected to a terminal on the bell or buzzer. Finally, you must connect the push button to the remaining terminal on the bell or buzzer. Depressing the push button connects the transformer across the bell or buzzer, causing it to ring. The distance of the push button from the bell or buzzer or from the transformer isn't critical. Naturally, the closer the push button, bell or buzzer, and transformer are to each other, the less wire that is required to connect them.

The bell or buzzer can be operated from either the front door or back simply by adding another push button. The same transformer can be used and just a single bell or buzzer is required. The bell or buzzer can be mounted in any convenient place in the home. While the wiring arrangement is easy, the listener does not know which push button has been activated—front or back. To overcome this difficulty, you can use a buzzer for the back door and a bell for the front. The only requirement is that the bell and the buzzer must be designed to operate from the same amount of ac voltage. You can also use a combination bell-buzzer for this purpose.

Unlike a bell or buzzer, the combination unit is a three terminal device. Bells, buzzers and bell-buzzers are generally supplied with wiring and connection diagrams, or you can use the diagrams shown here (Figs. B-4 and B-5).

Chimes can be wired in the same way as bell-buzzers. Most chimes are designed to supply a single tone to indicate use of the back door push button and two or more tones for the front door. Unlike bells or buzzers, many chimes are made to be decorative. They are often mounted where they can be seen.

When buying chimes, make sure to get a transformer designed to work with a particular chime. The wiring for a four note chime is a bit more complicated, but it is easily handled if you connect one push button at a time, testing the first push button before going on to the next.

Push buttons are on-off switches. If a push button doesn't produce bell ringing, buzzing, or chiming, short the

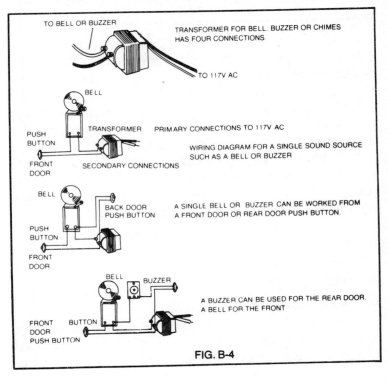

FIG. B-4

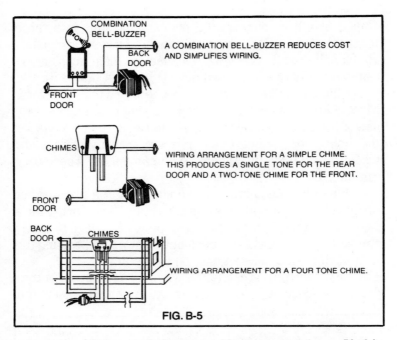

COMBINATION BELL-BUZZER

BACK DOOR

FRONT DOOR

A COMBINATION BELL-BUZZER REDUCES COST AND SIMPLIFIES WIRING.

CHIMES

FRONT DOOR

WIRING ARRANGEMENT FOR A SIMPLE CHIME. THIS PRODUCES A SINGLE TONE FOR THE REAR DOOR AND A TWO-TONE CHIME FOR THE FRONT.

BACK DOOR   CHIMES

WIRING ARRANGEMENT FOR A FOUR TONE CHIME.

FIG. B-5

terminals of the push button with a screwdriver. If this results in sound, then the push button is defective. If the ringing system doesn't work at all, check the secondary winding of the transformer, using a volt-ohm-milliammeter (VOM) set to read low ac voltage. If there is no voltage across the secondary, the primary of the transformer may not be connected to the 117 volt, ac line.

To make sure a ringing device is receiving voltage, set the VOM to read low ac volts and measure voltage across pairs of wires reaching the ringer via the push button. The push button must be depressed when making this test.

See Electric Shock, How to Avoid, *page 107*
Electrical Connections, How to Insulate, *page 94*
Soldering, *page 312*
Splicing Wire, *page 324*

☐ BX Cable, Cutting and Installing

BX cable is just one of a number of different types of armored cable. The cable consists of a pair of insulated wires, one color coded black and the other white. A bare, uninsulated solid wire is also included inside the cable and is used as a ground wire.

Although there are special tools for cutting BX, you can also do so with a hacksaw. Use a hacksaw blade having 24 teeth per inch. Mount the blade so that the teeth point away from you. Allow about 8 inches from the end of the cable so that the wires, when exposed, will be able to reach any connecting points. If the wires ultimately prove to be too long, you can always cut them shorter or bend them out of the way.

You'll find the work easier if you mount the BX in a vise. Clamp it so that the edge to be cut is near the edge of the vise, which can then act as a guide for the hacksaw blade (Fig. B-6).

Make a starting cut in the BX. Loosen the vise, rotate the BX a few degrees, and make another cut. By doing this repeatedly, you will finally have a circle cut around the BX. Deepen each cut but be careful not to cut through, damaging the enclosed wires. Do not try to cut through the cable completely, just enough to make a good cut all around.

Remove the BX from the vise and then flex the cut. Use the hacksaw to cut away any part that still remains together. You will find that the wires are covered with some type of paper insulation. Using scissors or a razor, cut the paper away completely. If the edges of the cable appear to be rough, smooth them with a file. Put an insulating sleeve, available at electrical supply stores, over the wires. This insulating sleeve is a fiber bushing and will keep the sharp edges of the cut BX from damaging the wires.

You can now mount a connector on the end of the BX. The connector is equipped with a machine screw having a slot for a flat edge screwdriver.

At the end of the connector you will see a locknut. Remove this and then insert the connector with its wires into the electrical box you plan to use. Slide the locknut over the wires and then use the nut to fasten the connector and its wires to the box. You can now cut the wires if you think they are too long. Trim about ¾ inch of insulation from the wires, and you will be ready to make electrical connections. Attach

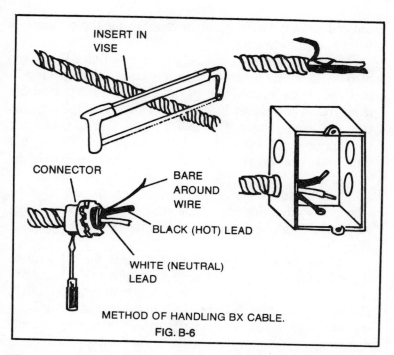

INSERT IN VISE

CONNECTOR

BARE AROUND WIRE

BLACK (HOT) LEAD

WHITE (NEUTRAL) LEAD

METHOD OF HANDLING BX CABLE.

FIG. B-6

the bare wire to a screw terminal inside the box. Using a pair of pliers, make sure the locknut is as tight as possible so there is no possible movement of the BX outside the box.

See Electrical Connections, How to Insulate, *page 94*
Electrical Wire Color Code, *page 102*
Electric Shock, How to Avoid, *page 107*
Romex Cable, Cutting and Installing, *page 287*
Soldering, *page 312*
Wires, Connecting Electrical, *page 385*

C

□ **Caulk**

See Weather Stripping, *page 369*
Window Glass, How to Replace Broken, *page 379*

□ **Ceiling Light, Basement**

For dark areas of a basement, you can easily add a ceiling light to eliminate the nuisance of using a flashlight. Obtain a porcelain socket made to mount on a junction box (Fig. C-1). Get one with a pull chain to avoid the need for mounting a wall switch and running a wire cable between the light and the switch.

The junction box will have several knockouts, circular areas that have been practically punched out. Remove any convenient knockout with the help of a flat blade screwdriver. Use a cable connector that will hold either the Romex or BX to the box. Make sure power to the cable is off. Before fastening the cable, allow about 6 inches of wire for the inside of the box. Strip the ends of the two conductors before inserting and fastening the cable to the socket.

Inside the box connect one wire to one terminal of the socket and the other wire to the other terminal. Although one wire will be color coded white and the other black, you can connect either wire to either terminal.

The electric box itself can be fastened to any basement cross beam and held in position by wood screws through two or three holes in the base of the box.

41

SIMPLE CEILING LIGHT FOR BASEMENT ONLY NEEDS PORCELAIN SOCKET EQUIPPED WITH A PULL SWITCH AND AN ELECTRIC BOX.

FIG. C-1

Usually pull chains are made of metal resembling a series of beads. The chain is fairly short and can be extended by a length of string. The string not only makes the pull more convenient but is safer.

See BX Cable, Cutting and Installing, *page 38*
  Ceiling Light, Defective, *page 42*
  Electrical Connections, How to Insulate, *page 94*
  Electric Shock, How to Avoid, *page 107*
  Romex Cable, Cutting and Installing, *page 287*
  Splicing Wire, *page 324*
  Wires, Connecting Electrical, *page 385*

☐ Ceiling Light, Defective

There are two problems associated with *ceiling lights*. Either they will not turn on at all or, if on, cannot be turned off. Ceiling light fixtures seldom become defective, so the problem is either in the bulb or the switch controlling the light.

If the bulb doesn't light, as a first step, change the light bulb. As a test bulb, use one that you remove from a lamp in working condition. If the test bulb doesn't light, then the problem is in the switch. If the ceiling light will not turn off regardless of the setting of the wall switch, the problem is in the switch. Replace it.

See BX Cable, Cutting and Installing, *page 38*
  Ceiling Light, Basement, *page 41*
  Electrical Connections, How to Insulate, *page 94*
  Electrical Wire Color Code, *page 102*

☐ Cement, Ready Mixed

Ready mixed *cement*, sold under various brand names, consists of premixed sand and cement. Theoretically, ready mixed cement can be used immediately. While cement and sand are mixed at the factory, they are of different weights. Vibration during transportation can cause the cement and sand to separate.

Before using ready mixed cement, pour the contents of the bag into a container, possibly a large carton or else on a cement floor covered with newspapers. Using a shovel, mix the cement thoroughly and replace the cement you do not intend to use back in its original bag.

If you do not store the cement properly, you will find yourself faced with cement that has hardened. The cement mixture must be held in an airtight container. This is difficult to do when using the original bag in which the cement was stored. Put this bag in a plastic bag, expel as much air from the plastic bag as you can, and then tighten it securely so no air can get in. If possible, store in a dry area.

☐ Chair Rungs, Tightening

The usual method of tightening a *chair rung* by adding glue doesn't always work if the end of the run fits too loosely. This is particularly true if you have cleaned the end of the rung, removing traces of old glue, paint, or varnish. For adhesives to be effective, the rung must fit tightly. Wrap the end of the rung with strong thread, apply the glue, and then force fit the rung into position. When forcing the rung back into place, turn it clockwise just as though you were screwing it in. Another method is to use slivers of wood from a matchstick. Mount these around the rung end with some thread, apply glue, and then force the assembly into the hole.

Before replacing a chair leg or a rung, clean out the hole in the chair using a small knife or a round file. If the glue is very hard, soften it with vinegar. Put glue into the hole and on the chair rung. Use a pipe clamp, rope, or twine to hold the glued parts together for at least 24 hours. If the glue you are using is thin, you can get a better bond by mixing in a small amount of sawdust into the glue.

If you want to rebuild an entire chair, take it apart but put tags on each piece, identifying it with a number so you will know exactly where it is to go when reassembling. Not all chair parts are interchangeable and that includes rungs and legs. Clean away all traces of glue from all holes and rung and leg ends. If corner braces and screws are used, remove these. You may find it necessary to replace the wood screws since these will probably have rusted. If the chair has corner braces, replace these if they have split.

☐ **Chalking (Paint)**

Chalking shows itself as a fine powder on the surface of the painted object. If you move your hand across the surface, the powder will cover it. Chalking can be caused by excessively humid conditions prevailing during painting. It can happen if you paint when it is raining and the air is moisture laden. Sometimes the problem is due to use of low grade paint. Make sure the surface is clean and dry and use a nonchalking paint. Clean the surface of chalk with a stiff bristle brush.

☐ Checking (Paint)

A checked surface has the appearance of numerous horizontal and vertical lines running through the painted surface. It can happen if you use oil paint over a damp surface or by using improperly mixed paint. When painting, you can avoid checking if you apply the paint evenly and avoid using an excessive amount. The whole idea in painting is to try to get as smooth and as uniform a surface as possible. Painting is sometimes used to cover a fault, and in such cases the tendency is to slop on as much paint as possible. Aside from possible runs and drips, this method can cause the area so treated to exhibit checking.

To remove, scrape paint until the bare surface is exposed. Use a good quality paint, the right brush for the kind of paint you are using, and a brush of the right size.

See Alligatoring (Paint), *page 20*
   Chalking (Paint), *page 44*
   Doors, Painting, *page 79*
   Exterior Metal Surfaces, Painting, *page 119*
   Masonry Surfaces, Painting, *page 207*
   Paint Brushes and Rollers, Cleaning, *page 229*
   Paint Brushes, Care and Maintenance, *page 234*
   Paint, Cracks in, *page 237*
   Paint, Removing, *page 238*
   Paint, Splattered, *page 245*
   Paint, Tips on How to, *page 250*
   Peeling (Paint), *page 273*
   Plywood, Painting, *page 280*

☐ Circuit Breakers

A *circuit breaker* is a fuse and, like plug or cartridge fuses, is intended to prevent an excessive flow of current through house wiring. The advantage of a circuit breaker is that you never need to look for a replacement fuse. Further, the circuit breaker is designed to supply the correct amount of fusing, so it isn't possible to replace a fuse with one having a higher or lower current rating.

Circuit breakers do not operate instantaneously. If a circuit breaker should happen to open, you may need to wait several minutes before pushing the circuit breaker back to its "on" position. No damage will occur if you do so at once; the breaker simply will not work.

If, no matter how often you keep resetting a circuit breaker it keeps tripping, then there is some fault in an appliance connected to the line protected by that particular breaker, or else there is a short in the line itself. There may also be a short in a wall switch.

On most circuit breaker boxes you will find a chart pasted to the inside panel. Each circuit breaker switch is numbered. Before you have any electrical problems, write on the list the number of each breaker and the rooms and hallways it controls. Then, when you have trouble in some room or hallway, you will know immediately which breaker switch is affected. It's easy to set up a chart of your own if your circuit breaker box does not have one.

If a breaker opens, wait a few minutes and then reset it. If power goes on for the wiring protected by that particular breaker and remains on, then you have had a momentary overload. It may be that you are operating too closely to the maximum current point. Circuit breaker switches often indicate their current carrying capacity. Make a list of all the appliances operating from that line. Add their current ratings to see how closely you come to the number shown on the breaker switch. This may not be possible since not all appliances indicate their current ratings.

Remove appliances from the power line one at a time, each time resetting the "blown" breaker, in an effort to learn which appliance is defective.

The circuit breaker box should not be used in place of wall switches (Fig. C-2). While the switching mechanism is satisfactory for turning power on and off to some branch ac power line, it is not intended for constant switching use.

In some circuit breaker boxes you may find two of the circuit breaker toggle switches joined by a small metal bar so that the two switches work together. This indicates that both switches must be turned on or off simultaneously.

See Appliances Do not Work, *page 23*

Electrical Outlets, Types of, *page 97*

FIG. C-2

☐ Clogging of Kitchen Sink, Preventing

Clogging of a kitchen sink can take place in the drainpipe between the trap and the sink, in the U-shaped trap, or in the drain pipe leading away from the trap.

To prevent clogging of the kitchen sink, use a perforated basket strainer. When the strainer accumulates food particles, clean the strainer into a garbage pail and not into the sink.

Sink clogging is often caused by liquid fats that are removed from dishes and pans being washed in the sink. These fats accumulate and solidify on the walls of the drain pipes leading to the sink and in the trap under the sink. Food particles and coffee grounds stick to the fat, forming a clog.

To keep the sink drain clear, pour boiling hot water down the sink drain once a day. If a layer of grease forms in the sink when washing dishes, skim this layer and put it in a garbage pail. Commercial sink drainers are available in supermarkets which will help keep the sink drain clear.

See Bathtub Drain, Clogged, *page 32*
Drains, Clogged, *page 81*
Kitchen Trap, Replacing, *page 194*
Sink Drain, Sluggish, *page 307*

☐ **Closet Auger**

See Toilets, Noisy, *page 336*
Toilet Bowl, Clogged, *page 337*
Toilet Repairs, *page 337*
Toilet Tank Overflows, *page 346*

☐ **Concrete, Repairing and Patching**

Defects in concrete surfaces can range from hairline cracks to large cracks to holes. If the crack is a hairline, don't try to enlarge it. Wash the entire area around it so it is clean. If the crack has any embedded dirt, remove it with a knife having a sharp point or any similar tool. Pour water along the length of the crack and keep repeating the moistening for several hours. Make a mixture of cement and water so that it forms a thick paste or grout. Apply the paste with a trowel or putty knife and, if possible, force the cement paste into the crack. Moisten the blade of the trowel or putty knife and run it over the cement so as to make a smooth surface which is level with the existing cement. Let the cemented area dry in the open for several hours and then cover it with a board. Put a few shims under the board so the board does not touch the cement. Water the cemented surface once a day for about five or six days.

Cracks that are larger than hairline should be undercut before applying cement. This means enlarging the crack with a cold chisel and a hammer with the crack made wider at the bottom than at the top. Undercut to a depth of at least 1 inch. Use a whisk broom to clean out the crack or you can wash away the loose dirt with a garden hose.

The problem with concrete repairs is that the patch has a tendency to form a solid block which separates from the surrounding concrete. To prevent this, use a concrete adhesive. Brush the cement adhesive into the crack and let it stand until it becomes sticky. Then apply the concrete patch. You can use ready mixed cement. Make a paste and force it into the crack which has been treated with the cement adhesive. If you prefer to make your own cement mixture, use one part of cement to two parts of sand. Mix thoroughly in a container, adding just enough water to form a thick paste.

The kind of finish you will get for the concrete patch depends on the finishing tool you use. If you want a smooth surface, use a trowel. Dip it in a bucket of water to make sure its surface is wet. For a rough surface, use a board (Fig. C-3). Before you do any finishing, make sure to tamp the cement in so that it fills the crack completely. Let the patch dry for several hours, then cover it with a board, lifting it only to wet the patch each day. Keep the board over the patch for about five or six days.

See Bricks, Dirty, *page 35*

Cement, Ready Mixed, *page 43*

☐ Condensation, Toilet Tank

Drops of water will often collect on the outside of a porcelain type toilet tank, particularly on the underneath portion. The drops can then form a continually wet condition on the floor beneath the tank. The water is due to condensation from the air surrounding the tank and is most troublesome during hot, humid weather.

There are two remedies. One is to line the inside of the tank with *styrofoam*. You can buy this material in sheet form and cut it to fit the inside of the tank. When doing so, flush the tank and then adjust it so water doesn't flow into it while you are working. The easiest way is to turn off the water cutoff valve leading to the tank. If you do not have such a valve, you can shut off water flow by lifting the float and holding it up

WIDEN THE CRACK USING A HAMMER AND COLD CHISEL.

JUST POURING CEMENT INTO A CRACK OR OPENING IS A POOR REPAIR AND WILL NOT LAST.

UNDERCUT THE CRACK. USE CEMENT ADHESIVE.

CLEAN THE CRACK THOROUGHLY.

WITH CEMENT YOU CAN GET A SMOOTH OR ROUGH FINISH. USE A BOARD FOR ROUGH; A WET TROWEL FOR SMOOTH.

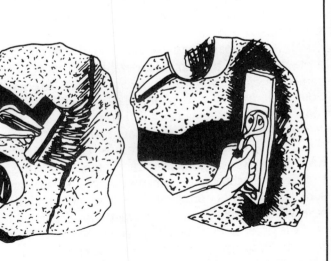

FIG. C-3

51

toward the top of the tank. You can get someone to hold this for you while you fit in the styrofoam, or put a stick beneath the rod connected to the float to hold it in position. Dry the inside of the tank thoroughly. A few dabs of a cement, such as *Elmer's Glue-All*, will hold the styrofoam in position. Do not use the toilet for about two to three hours.

You can also buy styrofoam kits in hardware and plumbing supply stores. Measure the inside dimensions of the toilet tank—width, depth, and height—to make sure you will get a styrofoam kit that will fit.

Another insulating method is to cover the entire outside of the tank with a tank cover. Made of fabric, the material can be obtained in a variety of colors and adds to the decor of the bathroom.

See Toilets, Dimensions of, *page 333*
Toilets, Noisy, *page 336*
Toilet Repairs, *page 337*

□ **Conduit**

Wires for carrying an electrical current are available with a metallic shield, as in the case of BX, or may be unshielded, as in the case of Romex. BX is more difficult to work with than Romex, but it does offer protection against a wire fire.

It is also possible to use unshielded wire and give it the protection of BX by using non-flexible thin wall conduit, also known as *electrical metallic tubing*, abbreviated as EMT. Conduit is available as plain, plastic covered, and as thin wall. You can also get conduit in flexible form, an advantage if you must bend the conduit at some angle.

EMT is available in sizes from ⅜″ to 2″. An advantage of EMT is that its interior surface is enameled, making it easier to fish wires through it. Enamel is an insulator and offers some added protection against electrical shorts in the event a bare wire happens to make contact with the conduit.

Flexible metal conduit is sometimes known as *Greenfield*. Its disadvantage is that it must be supported more than EMT. In some applications, Greenfield is superior to EMT.

If you must make a connection to some device that vibrates, such as a motor, flexible metal conduit is better.

Couplings are available for connecting EMT to EMT or EMT to Greenfield. Both types of conduit, non-flexible and flexible can be joined to electric boxes with connectors (Fig. C-4).

Conduit can be made of steel or copper. Copper will not rust and can be sweated (joined) to other copper conduit. Romex is sometimes run through conduit where the wires must be connected to a unit such as a hot water boiler.

☐ Copper Pipe, Connecting to Galvanized Steel

If, for some reason, you want to extend an existing length of steel pipe, you can use copper pipe with the help of a special adapter available in plumbing supply stores. There are many different types of fittings. However, the technique shown in Fig. C-5 does require that the end of the steel pipe be equipped with internal threads at its end. You will need to get an adapter whose threading arrangement corresponds to that of the steel pipe. The diameter of the adapter must be such that you should be able to thread it into the galvanized steel pipe. The other end of the adapter must be able to accommodate the copper pipe you plan to use.

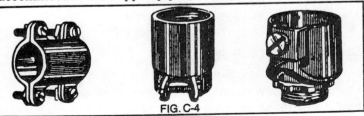

FIG. C-4

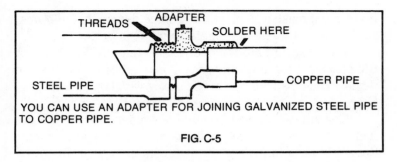

THREADS
ADAPTER
SOLDER HERE
STEEL PIPE
COPPER PIPE

YOU CAN USE AN ADAPTER FOR JOINING GALVANIZED STEEL PIPE TO COPPER PIPE.

FIG. C-5

To use the adapter, first thread it into the steel pipe. Use pipe joint compound on the threads. Make the adapter as tight as possible.

Clean the inner and outer surfaces of the other end of the adapter, the part which will hold the copper pipe, with sandpaper or fine steel wool. Do so until it is shiny. Use the same method on the end of the copper pipe. Using a paint brush, coat the adapter end areas, inside and out, with flux (not an acid type). Also, coat the end of the copper pipe with the flux. Insert the copper pipe and heat it with a brazing torch. Keep the flame away from the areas treated with flux. Apply solder to the area where the adapter meets the copper pipe. Do so completely around the pipe. Do not use the flame of the torch to melt the solder. Instead, the pipe must be hot enough to do so.

After completing the joint, allow it to cool and then wipe it clean with a cloth. Inspect to see if you have missed any areas and, if so, repeat the soldering process for those sections. Once again, allow to cool and wipe clean. Test by opening the water valve.

See Copper Pipe, Cutting, *page 54*
Copper Pipe, How To Repair, *page 56*
Copper Pipe, Soldering, *page 60*
Copper Pipe, Types of, *page 64*
Copper Tubing, Bending, *page 67*

☐ Copper Pipe, Cutting

There are various ways of cutting copper pipe or tubing. One of the more common techniques is to use a hacksaw. Select a blade having either 24 or 32 teeth per inch, nothing coarser. A blade with fine teeth will give a smoother cut with fewer burrs.

To hold the pipe while you are cutting it, mount it in a vise. If you want to protect the finish of the copper for any reason, cover the jaws of the vise with cardboard or wood. One method is to cut a V-slot lengthwise in the wood and then use this as a support for the copper (Fig. C-6).

You can also cut copper pipe or tubing in a miter box. Use C-clamps to hold the pipe at both ends. Put a strip of wood above the copper to keep the clamp from biting into it. The wood will also distribute the pressure and will keep the clamp from deforming the pipe. The miter box will let you cut at a 90° or 45° angle. And an adjustable miter box with a built-in protractor scale will let you cut the pipe at any angle you wish.

After you make the cut, use a flat file to remove copper burrs from the outside cut edge of the pipe (Fig. C-7). File gently since the burrs will come off easily. Then, with a round file or a tapered reamer, clean the inside edge of the cut.

Burrs on the inside will interfere with the free flow of water. Burrs on the outside are not only a hazard to fingers, but will make it more difficult to make connections.

Another method of cutting copper tubing is to use a special tool made for this purpose (Figs. C-8 and C-9). There is no reason for buying such a tool unless you plan to work

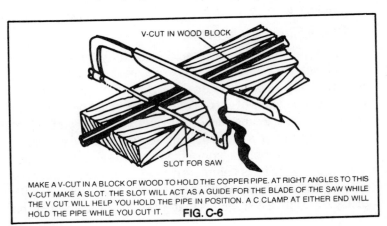

V-CUT IN WOOD BLOCK

SLOT FOR SAW

MAKE A V-CUT IN A BLOCK OF WOOD TO HOLD THE COPPER PIPE. AT RIGHT ANGLES TO THIS V-CUT MAKE A SLOT. THE SLOT WILL ACT AS A GUIDE FOR THE BLADE OF THE SAW WHILE THE V CUT WILL HELP YOU HOLD THE PIPE IN POSITION. A C CLAMP AT EITHER END WILL HOLD THE PIPE WHILE YOU CUT IT. **FIG. C-6**

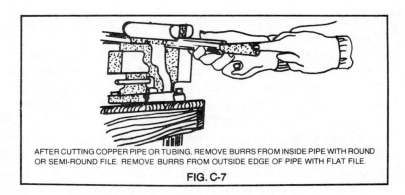

AFTER CUTTING COPPER PIPE OR TUBING, REMOVE BURRS FROM INSIDE PIPE WITH ROUND OR SEMI-ROUND FILE. REMOVE BURRS FROM OUTSIDE EDGE OF PIPE WITH FLAT FILE.

FIG. C-7

extensively with copper, rigid or flexible. However, you can get a cleaner cut by using a copper cutting tool. Insert the pipe in the tool, tighten the handle gently, and rotate the tool. Every time you make a complete turn, tighten the tool a bit more. Continue until the pipe is cut through.

□ **Copper Pipe, How to Repair**

A copper pipe can become damaged by being hit with some object, such as a tool. This can dent the pipe in, cutting down the easy flow of water through it. The pipe may develop a leak because of corrosion. It is often not necessary to replace the entire pipe since you can use either a standard copper coupling or a slip coupling to repair the damage.

A *coupling* is nothing more than a small section of copper pipe. A *slip coupling* is completely smooth inside; a *standard coupling* has a center ridge (Fig. C-10). The problem with putting pipe into a coupling is that it is difficult to know when

FIG. C-8

the two pipes being inserted occupy the same space. Ideally, the two pipes should meet in the center of the coupling. This lets the coupling give equal support to each of the pipes. The center ridge in a standard coupling lets you do just that. The ridge has the same approximate height as the pipes being inserted in the ends of the coupling, so there is no interference with the flow of water.

If you plan to repair a small leak in a copper pipe, turn off all water flow by shutting off the main water valve. Put a bucket beneath that part of the pipe on which you will be working. Saw the pipe directly at the point where the leak occurs, using a hacksaw with a fine blade, preferably 32 teeth to the inch. Even hard copper is relatively easy to cut through. Cut slowly and regularly on the forward stroke.

After you have cut through the pipe, let all water drain from it. Then wipe the ends of the pipe until it is as clean and dry as you can make it. Rub the ends of the pipe, completely around, with fine steel wool or sandpaper until the areas around the pipe ends are bright and shiny. Do the same with the slip coupling, sanding its ends both inside and out (Fig. C-11).

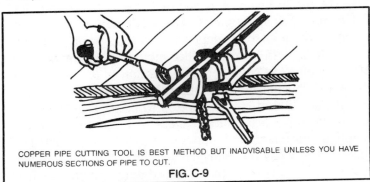

COPPER PIPE CUTTING TOOL IS BEST METHOD BUT INADVISABLE UNLESS YOU HAVE NUMEROUS SECTIONS OF PIPE TO CUT.

FIG. C-9

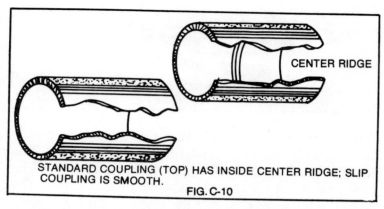

STANDARD COUPLING (TOP) HAS INSIDE CENTER RIDGE; SLIP COUPLING IS SMOOTH.

FIG. C-10

Apply flux paste to the ends of the copper pipe, coating both the interior and exterior areas. Treat the coupling the same way. You can apply the flux with a brush. Do not use acid flux since this will corrode the connection. You can heat the pipe with a brazing torch, but be careful not to apply the flame directly to those areas coated with flux. Do not use the flame to melt the solder.

Hold the solder directly in contact with the point where the pipe and coupling meet. When the pipe is hot enough to melt the solder, work the solder completely around the circumference of the coupling. Repeat on the other side of the coupling. Be certain that you do not omit any spots when going round on the pipe.

After you remove the torch, give the copper pipe a chance to cool and then wipe both joints with a clean, dry cloth. Examine the entire soldered area to make sure you have covered it completely and that there are no pin holes. You do not need much solder. The whole purpose is to make a watertight joint only, and so what you want is a thin, uniformly smooth layer of solder, not a big, lumpy buildup. After the pipe has cooled, test by turning on the main water valve and checking to see if there are any further drips.

If a section of copper pipe is to be repaired, you can follow the same procedure, except that you will need two couplings and a length of copper pipe to replace the damaged section. Cut away the damaged section and then use it as a "yardstick" to measure the required length of replacement

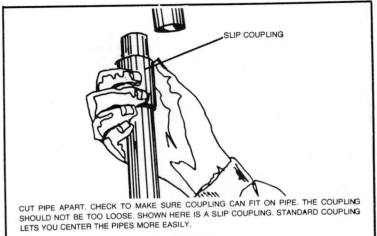

CUT PIPE APART. CHECK TO MAKE SURE COUPLING CAN FIT ON PIPE. THE COUPLING SHOULD NOT BE TOO LOOSE. SHOWN HERE IS A SLIP COUPLING. STANDARD COUPLING LETS YOU CENTER THE PIPES MORE EASILY.

FIG. C-11

pipe (Fig. C-12). Thoroughly clean both couplings, the ends of the replacement pipe, and the pipe being repaired (Fig. C-13). Use sandpaper or steel wool. Apply soldering flux (non-acid type) with a brush and then solder, using a torch, following the same techniques described earlier for making a single repair (Fig. C-14).

When using two couplings, you will find it easier to use the slip couplers instead of the standard type. To do a good job, center each coupling. You can do this by sliding the couplings and new pipe into position, and then marking the copper pipe with a pencil along the edges of each coupling. Then move the couplings out of the way to see how close you were to centering. Another method, possibly easier and faster, is to measure each coupling. Hold the new pipe in place without the couplings. Transfer your measurement to the old and new pipe and make pencil markings. It isn't necessary to get the slip couplings centered exactly, simply reasonably close.

See Brazing, *page 34*
    Copper Pipe, Cutting, *page 54*
    Copper Pipe, Soldering, *page 60*
    Copper Pipe, Types of, *page 64*
    Copper Tubing, Bending, *page 67*

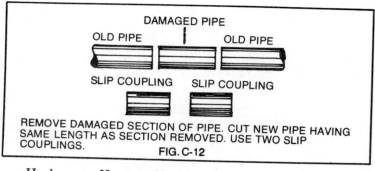

DAMAGED PIPE

OLD PIPE   OLD PIPE

SLIP COUPLING   SLIP COUPLING

REMOVE DAMAGED SECTION OF PIPE. CUT NEW PIPE HAVING SAME LENGTH AS SECTION REMOVED. USE TWO SLIP COUPLINGS.
FIG. C-12

☐ **Copper Pipe, Soldering.**

Also known as *sweating,* copper pipes used in home plumbing can be joined by *soldering.* Fittings are used to join copper pipe which must make turns at various angles. Before soldering, make a temporary union of the various lengths of pipe and their fittings to make sure you have cut each section of pipe to the right length.

Successful soldering depends on cleanliness. Clean the end of the pipe to be soldered with fine sandpaper or steel wool (Fig. C-15). The end of the pipe—the part to be soldered—must be sparkling bright. Wrap the sandpaper or steel wool around the end of the pipe and keep rotating the pipe, back and forth. Also, clean the inside of the fitting with

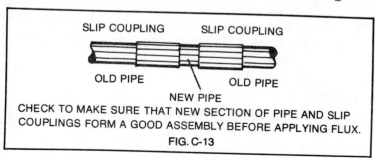

SLIP COUPLING   SLIP COUPLING

OLD PIPE   OLD PIPE

NEW PIPE

CHECK TO MAKE SURE THAT NEW SECTION OF PIPE AND SLIP COUPLINGS FORM A GOOD ASSEMBLY BEFORE APPLYING FLUX.
FIG. C-13

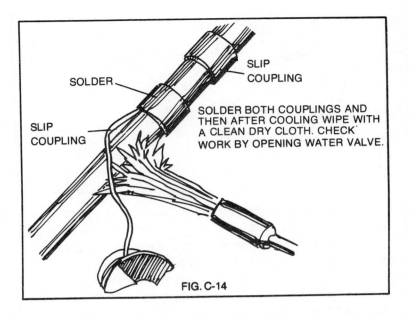

SOLDER

SLIP COUPLING

SLIP COUPLING

SOLDER BOTH COUPLINGS AND THEN AFTER COOLING WIPE WITH A CLEAN DRY CLOTH. CHECK WORK BY OPENING WATER VALVE.

FIG. C-14

steel wool—that part of the fitting which will come in contact with the pipe (Fig. C-16).

Copper oxidizes when it is heated. This film of oxide on the surface of the copper will keep you from doing a good soldering job. Coating the shined and cleaned areas of copper, both pipe and fittings, with flux or soldering paste will keep this oxide from forming and will help supply a good bond between the copper and the solder. Use a small brush to apply the flux, available in paint, hardware, and electrical supply stores (Fig. C-17). Caution: do not use acid flux since this will cause the pipe to corrode. A rosin flux is better.

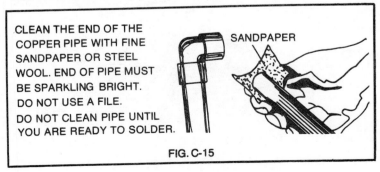

CLEAN THE END OF THE COPPER PIPE WITH FINE SANDPAPER OR STEEL WOOL. END OF PIPE MUST BE SPARKLING BRIGHT. DO NOT USE A FILE. DO NOT CLEAN PIPE UNTIL YOU ARE READY TO SOLDER.

SANDPAPER

FIG. C-15

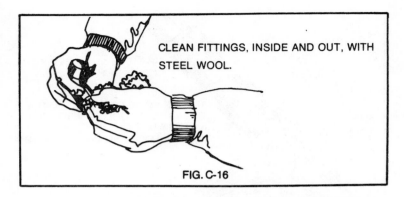

CLEAN FITTINGS, INSIDE AND OUT, WITH STEEL WOOL.

FIG. C-16

After you have spread flux on the pipe and its fitting, put the fitting in place on the pipe (Fig. C-18). When you have the fitting correctly positioned, turn it back and forth to get a more even spread of flux or soldering paste.

Unless you have a very heavy duty soldering iron, the best source of heat will be a brazing torch. A blow torch is also suitable but it supplies a tremendous amount of heat. It is capable of deforming the pipe if improperly used, especially with thin walled pipe.

Using the torch, heat the pipe, but do not direct the flame against any area to which you have applied flux. Do not

FITTING

BRUSH

FLUX

APPLY FLUX TO CLEANED END OF PIPE. USE BRUSH AS APPLICATOR.   FIG. C-17

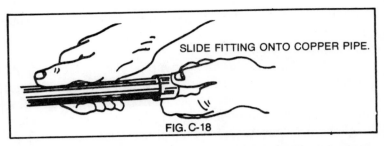

SLIDE FITTING ONTO COPPER PIPE.

FIG. C-18

apply the flame directly to the solder. The purpose of the torch is to make the pipe hot enough so it will melt solder without heating the pipe unnecessarily. Apply the solder to the joint. If it begins to run, the pipe is hot enough.

The solder will now begin to run into that part of the pipe joined by the fitting. Work the solder completely around the pipe until the entire circumference of the fitting and pipe has been filled with solder (Fig. C-19). Do not use acid core solder; use solid core solder only.

Do not try to cool the soldered joint by applying water. Let it cool by itself. Don't try shaking the pipe to see if the soldered joint is secure. Let the pipe cool before you touch it.

Obviously, soldering with a brazing torch requires some care. Solder can splatter, so as a matter of safety wear

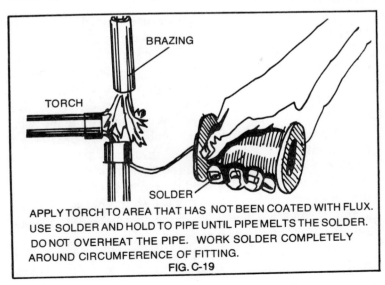

BRAZING

TORCH

SOLDER

APPLY TORCH TO AREA THAT HAS NOT BEEN COATED WITH FLUX.
USE SOLDER AND HOLD TO PIPE UNTIL PIPE MELTS THE SOLDER.
DO NOT OVERHEAT THE PIPE. WORK SOLDER COMPLETELY
AROUND CIRCUMFERENCE OF FITTING.
FIG. C-19

goggles and work gloves. Do not try to solder more than one joint at a time. Do one, make sure it is properly done, and then work on the next.

You can get fittings for copper pipe varying from a slight angle or bend to 90 degrees (Fig. C-20). You can also get fittings that will let you *branch*, that is, leading a third pipe into an existing pipe line (Fig. C-21). You can use a right angle branch connector, for example, to connect a third pipe to an existing copper pipe carrying water, so as to install a convenience faucet in your home.

See Aluminum, Joining, *page 21*

□ **Copper Pipe, Types of**

There are two types of copper pipe. One is *rigid* and the other is flexible. Rigid copper pipe is generally used in new work because it makes a neater, stronger installation. Flexible copper pipe is best for repair work around the house. It can be run around obstacles without making connections or cuts. Copper pipe is available in three different wall thicknesses; medium wall *Type L* is adequate for home use.

At one time, pipe used for plumbing was always made of galvanized steel. Copper is now preferred since it has a number of advantages. It resists corrosion and does not need to be painted. Its interior wall is smoother than galvanized steel and permits the easy flow of water. It is not as subject to *scaling*, a condition in which mineral deposits build up inside the pipe. And you can solder copper.

Copper pipe, also known as copper tubing, is specified by its *inside diameter* (ID). If you want to know the *outside*

FITTINGS FOR JOINING COPPER PIPE.
FIG. C-20

diameter (OD) of copper pipe, add ⅛ inch to the ID. This is just an approximation, but it does let you make a reasonable estimate.

The word "temper" is sometimes used in connection with copper pipe. This refers to its hardness. Hard temper pipe is always straight, just like iron pipe. Soft temper pipe is flexible. While hard temper copper pipe is more difficult to use, it does resist damage better than the soft temper variety.

The thickness of copper pipe is indicated by the letters K, L, M, and DKV. The thinnest of these is DKV. Type K is the thickest (Table C-1). Type L is a medium weight while M is a bit thinner (Table C-2). You should check with your local plumbing code to learn which type of pipe is permitted for pipe repairs in your home. There is a good reason for this. Water in your home is delivered under pressure and the pipe must be able to withstand it, in addition to any variations in the pressure.

If the repair you want to make does not involve a turn or bend, then either rigid pipe or tubing can be used. If the pipe must turn a corner or bend out of the way of an obstruction, the tubing is preferable. If you use rigid copper pipe, you will need to use a fitting.

Whether you use rigid or flexible pipe, remember that it is still softer than iron or steel. You can drop a heavy tool on

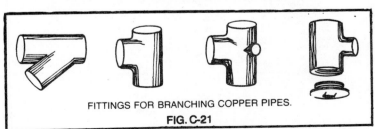

FITTINGS FOR BRANCHING COPPER PIPES.
FIG. C-21

TABLE C-1

Nominal Dimensions for Type K Copper pipe

(in inches) ID	(in inches) OD
¼	⅜
⅜	½
½	⅝
¾	⅞
1	1⅛

iron or steel pipe, but if you have the same accident with copper the pipe can be pushed in. When working with copper, remember that it can be deformed by too much pressure. Excessive pressure with a vise, for example, can damage the pipe enough to make it useless.

See Brazing, *page 34*
    Copper Pipe, Cutting, *page 54*
    Copper Tubing, Bending, *page 67*
    Hacksaws, How to Use, *page 160*
    Metals, Joining, *page 208*
    Pipe, Cutting, *page 274*
    Pipe, Electrical, *page 276*
    Pipes, Protecting, *page 279*
    Soldering, *page 312*
    Welding, *page 376*

TABLE C-2

Nominal Dimensions for Medium Weight, Type L Copper Pipe

Nominal Size	Outside Diameter	Inside Diameter
¼"	.375"	.315"
⅜"	.500"	.430"
½"	.625"	.545"
⅝"	.750"	.666"
¾"	.875"	.785"
1"	1.125"	1.025"
1¼"	1.375"	1.265"
1½"	1.625"	1.505"
2"	2.125"	1.985"

☐ Copper Tubing, Bending

Copper tubing is gradually being used more and more for home plumbing in place of galvanized iron pipe. Tubing is lighter and more easily supported. It can easily be joined by soldering. The ends of tubing can be flared, using a flaring tool, when it is necessary to attach a fitting to it.

You can bend copper easily around large diameter pipe. If you have a round *lolly* in the basement of your home, you can use it as a make-do copper tubing bending tool. The lolly is a cylindrical pipe support for the cross beams of your home.

A better method is to use a tool made for bending copper tubing. It is available in the shape of a spring, letting you bend the tubing into shallow or sharp bends (Fig. C-22).

See Brazing, *page 34*

Copper Pipe, Cutting, *page 54*
Hacksaws, How to Use, *page 160*
Metals, Joining, *page 208*
Pipe, Cutting, *page 274*
Pipe, Electrical, *page 276*
Pipes, Protecting, *page 279*
Soldering, *page 312*
Welding, *page 376*

☐ Corrugated Fasteners

See Wood, Fastening at Right Angles, *page 386*

☐ Cracks Around Bathtub or Shower

When *grout* between a bathtub or shower and the wall either cracks or falls out, you have a situation in which water can damage the house frame or walls. If the tub or shower are located on an upper floor, the water can reach a ceiling

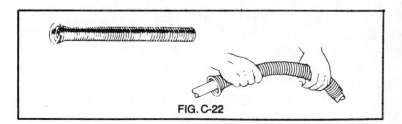

FIG. C-22

downstairs. A small amount of water can do a large amount of damage.

You can fill grout cracks or places where the grout has fallen out completely with either waterproof grout or plastic sealer. If you plan to use grout, make sure you select grout having a color to match existing grout. Bathtub and shower grouting is usually white, but colored grout is sometimes used.

Grout is available in the form of a powder. All you need do is to mix it with water until it becomes a paste. Plastic sealer is available in tubes, somewhat like toothpaste. It costs a little more than grout powder, but is a lot more convenient. Since you will probably be using just a small amount, the price difference doesn't amount to much.

As a first step, prepare the surface so it will hold the grout or sealer. Remove the old grout with the help of a knife or screwdriver. Be careful not to exert too much force since you may crack bathroom tiles. Using a sponge and some detergent or soap and water, wash the entire surface area to remove any soap film, dirt, or grease. Rinse thoroughly. Then dry the surface with an old, clean towel (Fig. C-23). Wait about an hour or two so that any moisture you cannot reach will have a chance to evaporate. In the meantime, no one should use the tub or shower.

If you have decided to use grout, mix a small amount of it. You can use a bowl, a small, clean tin can, or a tin can cover. Any clean surface will do, provided it will hold the grout powder and water. Mix the grout and water until you have a thick paste. Using a flat blade putty knife, force the grout into the crack. Don't worry about the fact that some of the grout gets onto the tile wall.

After you have filled in the entire cracked area, dip a small sponge or cloth into water and smooth the surface of the grout. Then wash the wall, but do not let any of the grout get into the shower or tub drain. It's a good idea to work with a pail of water, rinsing the sponge or cloth in the water occasionally.

When you are satisfied that the wall is clean and free of grout, empty the water from the pail into the street or a sewer. Before you do, though, clean the putty knife thoroughly and also wash the sponge until both no longer show any traces of grout. Don't do this washing in a sink or tub. Use the pail once again.

Plastic sealer requires no mixing, and you can apply it directly from the tube (Fig. C-24). As in the case of grout, apply with a putty knife pressing down on the sealer and forcing it to fill the entire length of the crack. Plastic sealer dries quite rapidly. After you have taken as much sealer from

CRACKS IN FROUT AROUND BATHTUB OR
SHOWER CAN CAUSE WATER DAMAGE

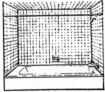

USE EITHER WATERPROOF GROUT OR PLASTIC
SEALER.

REMOVE ALL LOOSE GROUT.

WASH THOROUGHLY WITH DETERGENT AND SPONGE.
MOVE SPONGE BACK AND FORTH VIGOROUSLY.
RINSE WITH CLEAR WATER.

DRY THOROUGHLY.

FIG. C-23

PUT A SMALL AMOUNT OF GROUT POWDER
IN A BOWL AND MIX THOROUGHLY WITH WATER
UNTIL YOU HAVE A THICK PASTE.

 APPLY GROUT WITH PUTTY KNIFE.

PRESS GROUT IN UNTIL CRACKS ARE FILLED.

 WIPE THE SURFACE SMOOTH WITH YOUR
FINGER, A WET SPONG OR WET CLOTH.

APPLY PLASTIC SEALER TO CRACKS USING
SEALER DIRECTLY FROM TUBE.

FIG. C-24

the tube as you think you will need, be sure to put the cap right back on the tube. Smooth the sealer in the crack with a wet sponge or cloth and wash the wall. If the sealer you are using is an extremely rapid drying type, you will need to work quickly.

One advantage of grout powder over plastic sealer is that sealer has a tendency to dry in the tube over a long period of time. To keep grout powder for future use, make sure the cover has a tight fit. After you put the cover back on, tap around the edges of the cover with a hammer. Light taps will do the job.

Give the grout or sealer a chance to "cure." Although sealer will feel hard to the touch in much less than an hour, it is better to put an "off limits" sign on the bathtub or shower for one day.

☐ **Crescent Wrench**

See Wrench, Adjustable, *page 387*

☐ Damp Basements

A damp basement can be caused by the absence of gutters and downspouts, downspouts and gutters that have become clogged with dirt, leaves and branches, splash blocks that have been moved out of position, or the complete absence of splash blocks.

Check during a heavy rain to see if water is falling from the roof directly to the ground at any point. If this is happening, puddles of water can form near the basement walls of the house, letting water seep in even if there are no cracks or breaks in the basement walls.

If the house is built on a slope, surface water, either rain or melting snow, will flow toward the basement wall or walls. If the ground water level is high enough, water can seep through the basement floor.

A basement can have a damp or musty odor due to condensation of water vapor in the air on cold water pipes or floors. The basement can also be humid due to leaks in pipes.

Shrubs and plants positioned too near the house prevent good ventilation of the basement. A musty, damp odor in the basement can be relieved by increasing ventilation. If the basement has windows, open them, but make sure they are screened. At the same time, keep the basement door open to permit the movement of a cross current of air. A de-humidifier is helpful in keeping basement air dry.

Examine all pipes for evidence of leakage or condensation. Wrapping materials are available for pipes that sweat, that is, which condense moisture on their surfaces. Run your hands along walls to check for presence of moisture. You can use waterproofing paint to seal basement walls to prevent water seepage. Several coats may be needed to make a thorough seal.

See Basement, Waterproofing, *page 27*
      Concrete, Repairing and Patching, *page 48*
      Gutters And Downspouts, Maintaining And Repairing, *page 154*
      Musty Odor, *page 212*
      Water Leaks, *page 361*
      Water Pipes, Leaky, *page 364*

☐ Dimmer Switches

The usual type of electric wall switch is a go-no go device; it is either fully on or off. Consequently, lamps which are controlled by such switches are also either full on or off. A *dimmer* is an electric switch that lets you have any number of operating conditions between full off and full on.

One part of the dimmer is a switch that turns the light on or off. The dimmer section is generally controlled by a knob that can be turned clockwise or counterclockwise, increasing or decreasing the amount of light.

Dimmers are designed for use with fluorescent or incandescent bulbs. The advantage of using a dimmer is the saving in electrical energy. If you use a 150 watt bulb and set the dimmer for half light, then the power consumed is only about 75 watts.

Dimmers have power ratings. If you plan to control a single bulb rated at 200 watts, get a dimmer having at least a minimum rating of 200 watts.

You can install a dimmer in the same way as an ordinary wall switch. The dimmer control is housed in a small sealed box. Just connect the existing wires to the two terminal screws on the dimmer and put the dimmer control in the electric box that originally housed the wall switch.

The faceplate is the same as that used for an electric toggle switch, and it has a rectangular opening. The shaft of the dimmer goes through this rectangular opening and the faceplate is held in position by a pair of machine screws. The knob for the dimmer simply slides on or off.

The shaft of the dimmer works as a switch by pushing the dimmer knob in for on, and in again for off. When the dimmer knob is in its maximum counterclockwise position, there will be maximum light; rotate it counterclockwise for minimum light.

See BX Cable, Cutting and Installing, *page 38*
Electrical Connections, How to Insulate, *page 94*
Electrical Wire Color Code, *page 102*
Electric Shock, How to Avoid, *page 107*
Romex Cable, Cutting and Installing, *page 287*
Soldering, *page 312*
Splicing Wire, *page 324*
Wires, Connecting, Electrical *page 385*

☐ **Door Difficulties**

Doors can have a variety of ailments. They can squeak, stick, drag, get stuck, or may not close firmly or close at all. Quite often what is an aggravating nuisance is something that requires just a little attention and which can easily be repaired.

Doors Squeak. Open the door slowly and listen carefully as you do. If you hear a squeaking noise, the trouble is due to a dry hinge. Put a few drops of machine oil at the top of the hinge pin and along its length. Use the oil sparingly. Wipe off any excess oil with a cloth. Work the door back and forth a few times to give the oil a chance to move in to lubricate moving contacts. If the squeaking is reduced but not eliminated, try the oiling process again.

A better way to oil hinges is to remove the hinge pins. Remove and work on only one pin at a time. You can get the pin out by using a flat blade screwdriver and a hammer. Put the blade of the screwdriver beneath the head of the pin. Then tap the top part of the screwdriver handle with a hammer until the hinge pin comes out. If the pin is rusty or has paint on it, use sandpaper. The pin should be clean and free of rust, dirt, and paint.

Put a few drops of machine oil into that part of the hinge that holds the pin. Also, put some oil on the pin itself, rubbing the oil back and forth with your fingers until the entire surface of the pin is covered. Then replace the pin.

Follow the same procedure with the other pins. The door will have at least two hinges; some have three. If you work on only one hinge at a time, you will not need to worry about the door falling off its hinges.

When replacing hinge pins, make sure that the pin enters the hinge holes completely. Tap the head of the hinge pin with a hammer to make sure it does so. The head of the hinge pin should rest directly on the hinge and not extend out from it.

Sometimes, for some reason, a hinge pin may be missing, and a door with three hinges actually works with only two. Usually three hinges are put on heavy doors, and they are needed to support the door weight. If a pin is missing, get a replacement.

Sometimes the squeak isn't due to lack of oil. Instead, one or more screws holding the hinge may have become loose or have fallen out. This can put a strain on the hinge, forcing it to work in an awkward position. Replace or tighten the screws. To be sure, oil the hinge.

The door lock can also produce a squeaking noise. Check by turning the doorknob and also by closing the door. Listen carefully to determine if the squeaking does indeed come from the lock. Lubricate with machine oil or with graphite (Fig. D-1). You can get graphite in powder form in an applicator tube. Apply the lubricant to all moving parts of the knob. Turn the knob handle as you lubricate. When you finish, wipe all knob parts with a soft, dry cloth to remove any excess.

What may seem to be squeaking may just be the doorknob rattling. This can happen if the knob works its way loose. If the knob is held on by a setscrew, tighten it. If that doesn't help, remove the knob and put a small bit of putty or modeling clay in the knob. Put the knob back on and tighten it.

The faceplates for the knob, on both sides of the door,

are held in by screws. These screws are often phillips head types. You will need a suitable phillips head screwdriver to tighten them.

Door Sticks or Drags. Examine all the hinges and make sure all screws are tight. If screws are missing, replace them. If you turn a screw and it doesn't tighten, the hole for the screw has become too large. Remove the screw and pack the hole with a matchstick or else use wood dough (Fig. D-2). Give the dough enough time to dry and harden, following the instructions on the container. Sometimes, though, the screws are at fault and may have become bent or broken. Replace them but use screws of the same size.

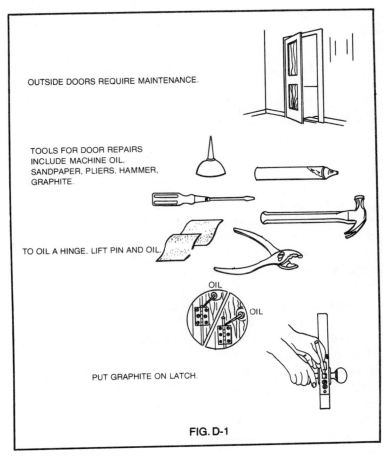

OUTSIDE DOORS REQUIRE MAINTENANCE.

TOOLS FOR DOOR REPAIRS INCLUDE MACHINE OIL, SANDPAPER, PLIERS, HAMMER, GRAPHITE.

TO OIL A HINGE, LIFT PIN AND OIL.

OIL

OIL

PUT GRAPHITE ON LATCH.

FIG. D-1

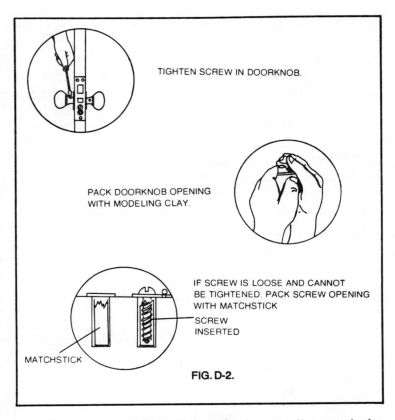

TIGHTEN SCREW IN DOORKNOB.

PACK DOORKNOB OPENING
WITH MODELING CLAY.

IF SCREW IS LOOSE AND CANNOT
BE TIGHTENED. PACK SCREW OPENING
WITH MATCHSTICK

SCREW
INSERTED

MATCHSTICK

FIG. D-2.

If the door sticks and doesn't close easily, watch the action of the door as you open and close it. Usually it is one small spot that causes the sticking problem. The difficulty may be with the door frame or with the door itself. Sometimes a shiny spot will develop at the sticking area caused by excessive friction between the door and frame. If the frame is painted, and this is usually the case, the sticking area will have the paint rubbed off.

To remove the sticking difficulty, sand the area that causes it. Sand both the frame and the door, using a medium grade of sandpaper. After sanding, try the door to see if it opens and closes more easily. The idea here is to remove just enough of the interference. If you sand excessively, the door may not fit as tightly as it should.

If the interference is along the side of the door, getting

the door to fit properly is no problem. It is much more difficult if the sticking is alongside the top or the bottom of the door.

If you have a saddle along the floor for the bottom of the door, the saddle may have worked its way up, or one or more of its screws may have become loose. Tighten all screws. Make sure no screw head protrudes above the top level of the saddle. If any screw is loose and cannot be tightened, remove the screw and pack the screw hole with soft wood. Matchsticks will do very well. No screws should be missing from the saddle. If they are, replace them.

If this doesn't help and if you have determined that it is the bottom of the door that is sticking, you will need to remove the door and either sand the bottom or use a plane. Before you do, try to locate the exact area where the sticking occurs. Mark the door in some way, perhaps with a pencil, to indicate just where the sticking occurs.

Remove the door by taking out the hinge pins. Examine the bottom of the door to see if you can find any shiny areas. Sand or plane the areas you suspect and then replace the door (Fig. D-3).

If the top of the door sticks, follow the same procedure as for the bottom of the door. Removing a door, putting it back on and removing it again is tedious. If the top of the door is causing the sticking, you may be able to cure it without removing the door. Instead, you can work across the top of the door by standing on a ladder or step stool.

The problem of sticking generally involves an outside door, a door that is subject to weather. If water gets into a door, it can cause the door to swell. If you note that your door sticks only after a heavy rain, then do something to protect the door against it. The door may need a coat of paint. Part of the existing coat of paint may have cracks, permitting water to get in. The top part of the door is especially susceptible. You may need to remove the door and either paint the top or coat it with some kind of protective sealant.

If the front door has become warped as a result of constant exposure to rain, the only solution is to replace the door.

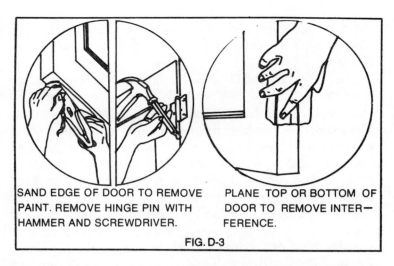

SAND EDGE OF DOOR TO REMOVE PAINT. REMOVE HINGE PIN WITH HAMMER AND SCREWDRIVER.

PLANE TOP OR BOTTOM OF DOOR TO REMOVE INTER— FERENCE.

FIG. D-3

Sometimes a door will stick because it has been painted. This is particularly true when a door is a tight fit and an excessive amount of paint has been applied to the door. Before painting, sand all three door edges: top, side, and bottom. If after painting you find the door sticks, examine all three sides carefully. You will be able to find the sticking area easily since the paint will be rubbed off. Sand that section strongly and then repaint.

Door Latch Doesn't Engage. The purpose of the door latch is to keep the door closed, not necessarily locked. When you close a door, you should hear the latch click as it engages the strike. The strike is simply a rectangular bit of metal mounted on the side frame adjacent to the doorknob. The latch of the door engages the strike. When it does, the door is closed properly.

To check if this part of your door is working properly, turn the knob while watching the latch. It should move in and out as you turn the knob. If it doesn't, it may be held in place through dirt, rust, or paint. Remove the paint or dirt and oil the latch. It should spring out every time you release the doorknob.

Check the strike. It is usually held in place by two Phillips head screws. If the screws are loose or missing, replace them. The strike should be firmly in place, and the latch should be able to fit in the rectangular hole of the latch easily and smoothly.

☐ Doors, Painting

To paint a door, first remove all hardware mounted on it. This includes the doorknob, the latch and any screws. Unscrew the door from its hinges and then stand the door against a wall so the door is as nearly vertical as possible. Put newspapers beneath the floor to protect the door. If you do not want any paint on the four edges of the door, cover these areas with masking tape. Unwanted paint on these edges may make it difficult to open or close the door where the door makes a close fit with the frame.

Always mix the paint thoroughly before using (Fig. D-4). Paint stores often supply a wooden paddle or an aluminum paddle with holes in it just for this purpose. Make sure no pigment remains on the bottom of the can. After you finish painting, remove all paint from the rim of the can. You can do this with a screwdriver and a small section of cloth, using the screwdriver to guide the cloth around the rim. To close the can of paint, put the cover in position and then put some plastic sheet, rags, or newspapers on top of the can (Fig. D-5). This will keep any paint from splattering when you hammer the lid back into position.

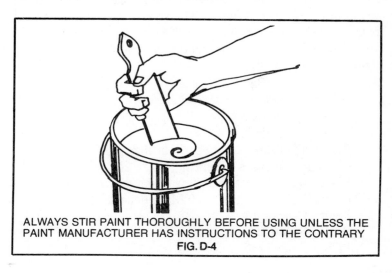

ALWAYS STIR PAINT THOROUGHLY BEFORE USING UNLESS THE PAINT MANUFACTURER HAS INSTRUCTIONS TO THE CONTRARY
FIG. D-4

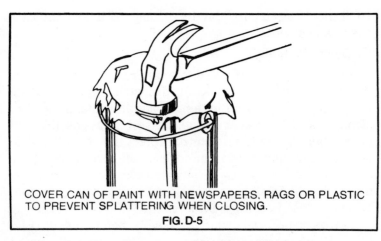

COVER CAN OF PAINT WITH NEWSPAPERS, RAGS OR PLASTIC
TO PREVENT SPLATTERING WHEN CLOSING.

FIG. D-5

If the door is bare wood, sand it with fine or medium sandpaper. Wipe the door with a clean rag to remove any traces of dust. If the door has been painted previously, you may want to remove the old paint. Do this with successive applications of paint remover, scraping and sandpapering the door afterwards. Then coat the door with a primer recommended by your paint dealer.

Ordinarily, doors are painted from the top down. A better procedure is to paint the door in a specific sequence. First paint the moldings between the panels and the frame, working from the top down. Then paint the panels. Next, paint the horizontal framing and then the vertical framing. If you plan to paint the casing, do this next and then finally the door jamb (Fig. D-6).

☐ Drains, Clogged

The drainpipe leading from the kitchen sink is the one that most frequently becomes clogged (Fig. D-7). If you are using a basket strainer, remove this and, using a long screwdriver, work it in a circular motion around the drain-

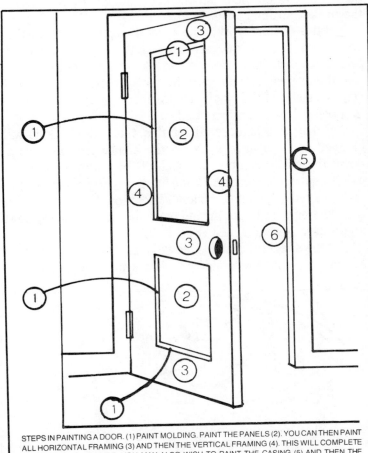

STEPS IN PAINTING A DOOR. (1) PAINT MOLDING. PAINT THE PANELS (2). YOU CAN THEN PAINT ALL HORIZONTAL FRAMING (3) AND THEN THE VERTICAL FRAMING (4). THIS WILL COMPLETE THE FACE OF THE DOOR. YOU MAY ALSO WISH TO PAINT THE CASING (5) AND THEN THE DOOR JAMB (6). DO NOT REPLACE DOOR UNTIL ALL PAINT HAS HAD A CHANCE TO DRY.

FIG. D-6

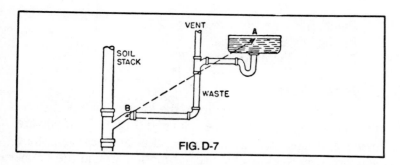

FIG. D-7

pipe. Quite often the drain becomes clogged directly below the basket strainer (Fig. D-8).

If this doesn't work, take a wire hanger, cut it, and then straighten it so it forms a straight length. With a pair of pliers form a U-shaped hook at one end. Put this end of the hanger into the drainpipe and rotate the wire. If you can manage to remove some of the clogged material this way, dispose of it in a paper bag or garbage pail.

Using A Plunger. If, at this time, the sink is still clogged and you have water in the sink which will not go down the drain, remove as much of the water as you can, using a sponge and a pail. Using a toilet type plunger, sometimes called a "plumber's friend," position the rubber end of the plunger over the drain and work the handle up and down vigorously several times (Fig. D-9).

If the sink still remains clogged, remove as much water as you can from the drainpipe. Add a little household am-

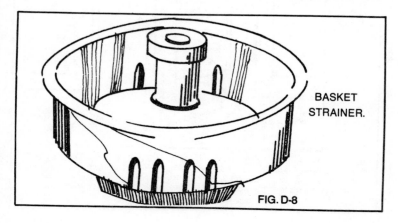

BASKET STRAINER.

FIG. D-8

monia to boiling hot water and, using a teakettle, pour this mixture down the drain. Wait a few minutes to give it a chance to soften the clog. Then use the plunger again to force the clog out of its position.

Using An Auger. If the plunger technique doesn't work, you can try using a "snake." This is a tool that is sold in home supply and department stores (Fig. D-10). The correct name for this tool is *sink auger*, but it is more often called a plumber's snake or simply a snake.

To reach the drainpipe, remove the sink trap and insert the head of the auger (Fig. D-11). Try to work the head of the tool down into the drainpipe. The auger consists of spring wire with a spiral gimlet head. The rotation of the gimlet

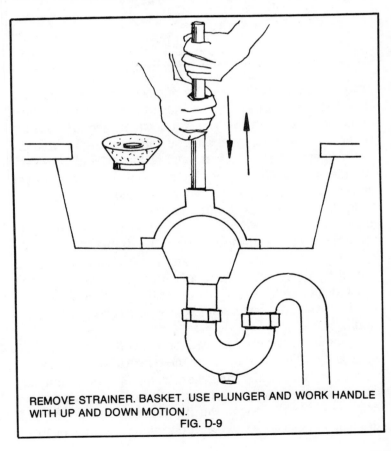

REMOVE STRAINER. BASKET. USE PLUNGER AND WORK HANDLE WITH UP AND DOWN MOTION.
FIG. D-9

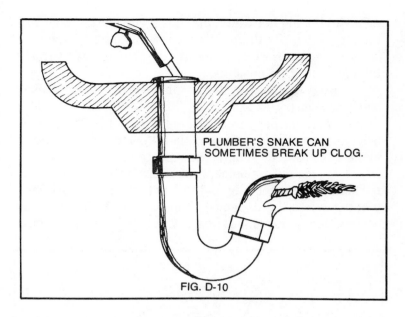

PLUMBER'S SNAKE CAN
SOMETIMES BREAK UP CLOG.

FIG. D-10

head cuts through the clog, forcing some of the debris into the head of the tool. After removing the auger, wash the head of the tool, preferably in a bucket of water, and then use the auger once again on the drainpipe until the clog is broken.

Augers are about 6 feet long, or longer, and have various kinds of heads for rotating the tool. Some augers are driven by hand; others are motor operated. For home use a hand driven auger is usually satisfactory. When using an auger, rotate the head of the tool, at the same time trying to force more of the spring wire into the drain.

If you have used *lye* or any commercial cleaner for removing a clog, and if the application of chemicals doesn't work, do not use an auger. Instead, call a plumber. Be sure to tell him what you have done before he begins work on the drain.

Some augers are designed for use with an electric drill (Fig. D-12). The drill should be the type whose speed can be controlled; otherwise, the auger, whipping around at a high speed, can be dangerous. The electric drill operated auger can be used in two ways. Put the auger as far into the sink drain as you can until you feel it encountering some obstruc-

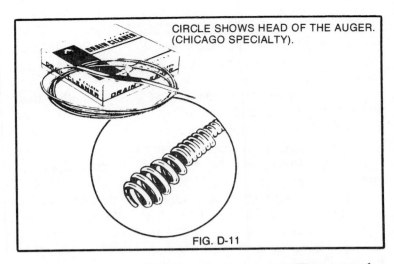

CIRCLE SHOWS HEAD OF THE AUGER. (CHICAGO SPECIALTY).

FIG. D-11

tion. Turn the drill on to its slowest speed. Then stop the drill and see if you can advance the auger. Repeat with the drill operating, all the time trying to move the auger forward.

If the trap and the drainpipe between the trap and sink are clear of clogs, it may be easier to work with the trap out of the way. Remove the trap, and working from beneath the sink, put the auger into the drainpipe. The work will be easier since you will not have the bend of the trap to overcome. The drainpipe leading away from the trap disappears behind the wall. It then turns down to connect with a larger

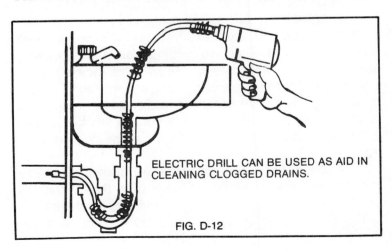

ELECTRIC DRILL CAN BE USED AS AID IN CLEANING CLOGGED DRAINS.

FIG. D-12

drainpipe. In making this turn it makes a sharp angle bend, so you will need to work the auger past it. Most often the clog will be in some horizontal section of drainpipe, not any vertical part.

Do not try to operate the drill at any speed other than very slow. You will find it easier to keep pushing the auger forward if you do so when it is rotating.

Sink Traps. Pipes leading away from sinks and toilets can become clogged by things falling into the drain like hair, undissolved soap, grease, and dirt.

Usually a clogged drain is due to the accumulation of waste in a sink trap. To clean out the trap, put a pail or bucket under the trap to catch any waste or water. The trap, a U-shaped section, is held in place by a pair of slip nuts. Loosen these with a wrench, turning the tool in a counterclockwise direction. Clean the trap and replace.

Kitchen sinks often become clogged when food particles are allowed to go down the drain. To prevent clogging, use a basket. This is a strainer that fits into the disposal opening of the sink. It is different from a flat strainer since its body extends down into the opening of the sink.

Sometimes a pair of adjacent sinks will use a common trap. Water from one sink will back up and fill the adjacent sink when the trap is clogged. Remove the trap and clean.

There are two basic types of traps used for kitchen sinks. One of these has a cleanout plug mounted directly beneath the center of the trap. With this type the trap need not be removed. Instead, turn the plug in a counterclockwise direction using a wrench (Fig. D-13). After the plug is removed, clean out the trap with a long screwdriver. You can make a cleaning tool from a wire coat hanger. Cut a straight section and bend one end into the form of a tiny hook. With this homemade tool you will be able to fish the clog out of the trap.

The other type of trap doesn't have a cleanout plug. The trap is held in place with two slip nuts (Fig. D-14). You will need to loosen these with a wrench and remove them (Fig. D-15). The entire trap will then come away from the drain-

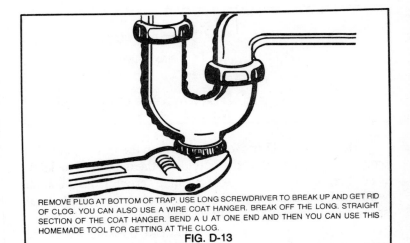

REMOVE PLUG AT BOTTOM OF TRAP. USE LONG SCREWDRIVER TO BREAK UP AND GET RID OF CLOG. YOU CAN ALSO USE A WIRE COAT HANGER. BREAK OFF THE LONG, STRAIGHT SECTION OF THE COAT HANGER. BEND A U AT ONE END AND THEN YOU CAN USE THIS HOMEMADE TOOL FOR GETTING AT THE CLOG.

FIG. D-13

pipe, and you can clean the trap by putting it into a pail of water.

If, after cleaning the sink trap, water still will not go down the drain, the problem is in the drainpipe leading away from the trap. The problem is often caused by an accumulation of grease and soap clinging to the inner walls of the pipe. This restricts the drain opening and in time will trap pieces of waste. The material can sometimes be removed by flushing with extremely hot water, preferably boiling. Various commercial cleaners are available in shopping centers for cleaning clogged drains. You can also use lye, but use cold water only. Lye is a rather dangerous chemical and should be used with extreme caution. Lye that spills on hands or clothing should be washed thoroughly and immediately with cold water. It is best to wear safety glasses, regular glasses, or goggles when working with lye.

See Bathtub Drain, Clogged, *page 32*

      Clogging of Kitchen Sink, Preventing, *page 47*

      Kitchen Trap, Replacing, *page 194*

      Sink Drain, Sluggish, *page 307*

☐ Drawers, How to Repair

Drawers in furniture can stick and come apart. Their handles or knobs can become loose, fall off or break.

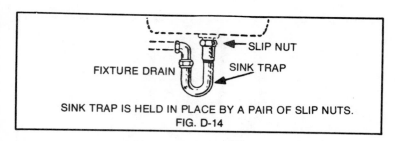

FIXTURE DRAIN   SINK TRAP

SLIP NUT

SINK TRAP IS HELD IN PLACE BY A PAIR OF SLIP NUTS.
FIG. D-14

How To Fix Handles. Quite often the drawer pull is a single knob centered on the outside of the drawer. The knob is held in place by a large head machine screw. Hold the knob with one hand and, using a flat blade screwdriver, tighten the screw from the inside of the drawer.

If tightening the screw doesn't make the knob as secure as you would like, remove the screw and wrap the screw threads with some thread. The thread will enable the screw to make a tighter fit.

Examine the screw hole of the knob. Sometimes, through regular use, it becomes too big to accommodate the screw. In that case you will need to replace the knob. If you cannot get a knob substitute, try using a larger screw. Another method is to put a dab of cement on the part of the knob making contact with the drawer. Give the cement a chance to dry thoroughly before using the drawer again. It is also helpful to put some cement on the screw threads.

It is often simpler to try to repair a knob than to find a replacement. You would need to find an exact match and that is often difficult to do. An alternative is to replace all the knobs on all the drawers, and this can be expensive.

Handles on drawers are held in place by screws or by force fit pins. In the case of a screw, simply tighten. A force fit pin is just a bit of metal resembling a nail, but quite small. If the pin (or pins) is loose, pack the pin hole with a small amount of newspaper. Force the paper into the hole using a large needle or pin. Then tap the force fit pin back into place.

Drawers may stick if they are accidentally interchanged. Although two drawers may look exactly alike, they do have small differences. Make sure each drawer is in its proper place.

Sometimes drawers don't move easily if they are overloaded. If the drawer has its contents forced into it, there may be enough drag between those contents and the frame around the drawer to prevent easy movement. The solution is to unload the drawer somewhat.

Kitchen drawers sometimes move on *bearings*. If these squeak or if the drawer doesn't glide smoothly and easily back and forth, a drop or two of machine oil on the bearings will do. If a drawer of any kind is stuck, it is quite possible that its runners aren't properly seated. In that case, try to work the drawer out. Examine the drawer and the drawer frame to make sure there is no damage. If there is, repair before replacing the drawer.

You should never need to force a drawer into position. It should always do so smoothly and easily. If there is an interference, locate the reason for it and remove the obstruction. Forcing a drawer doesn't solve the problem; it just aggravates it.

Sticky Drawers. Remove the drawer and examine it carefully. Look for shiny areas on the top, the bottom or the sides. Sand those areas for they represent high friction sections which keep the drawer from sliding easily.

Sometimes a drawer will stick when it is in the process of coming apart. If this is the cause, repair the drawer. Glue

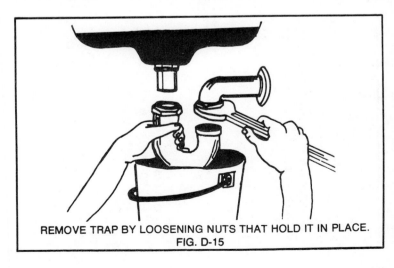

REMOVE TRAP BY LOOSENING NUTS THAT HOLD IT IN PLACE.
FIG. D-15

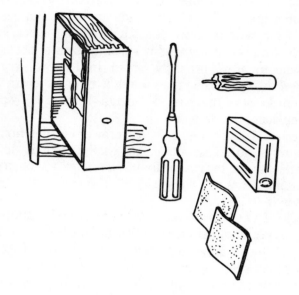

DRAWER SHOULD MOVE SMOOTHLY
AND EASILY

TO FIX DRAWERS YOU MAY
NEED SCREWDRIVER, SANDPAPER,
PARAFFIN OR WAX.

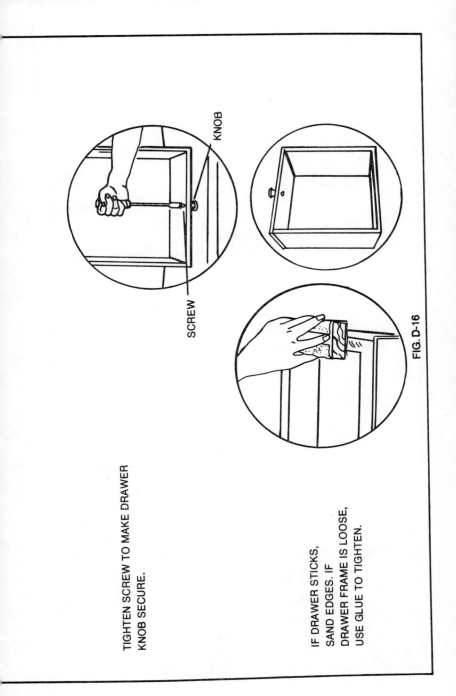

TIGHTEN SCREW TO MAKE DRAWER
KNOB SECURE.

IF DRAWER STICKS,
SAND EDGES. IF
DRAWER FRAME IS LOOSE,
USE GLUE TO TIGHTEN.

KNOB

SCREW

FIG. D-16

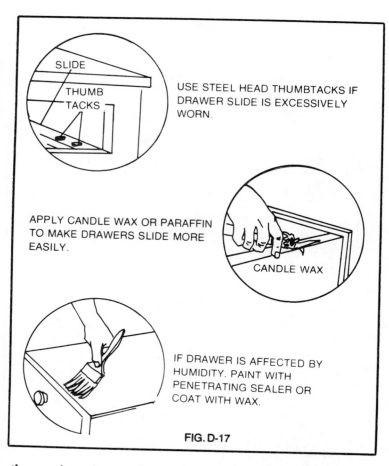

SLIDE

THUMB TACKS

USE STEEL HEAD THUMBTACKS IF DRAWER SLIDE IS EXCESSIVELY WORN.

APPLY CANDLE WAX OR PARAFFIN TO MAKE DRAWERS SLIDE MORE EASILY.

CANDLE WAX

IF DRAWER IS AFFECTED BY HUMIDITY. PAINT WITH PENETRATING SEALER OR COAT WITH WAX.

FIG. D-17

the sections that are loose, first making certain that they fit together tightly. It is also helpful to run some glue down the inside corners of the drawer where the edges of the drawer meet each other. Do one corner at a time. Position the drawer so that the edge to be glued is horizontal. Give the glue enough time to dry and then repeat with the other corners.

Some drawers have a center runner on the bottom of the drawer, from front to back. Make sure this runner is firmly in position. Glue it in place if it is not. Also, make sure that the frame that accommodates the runner is tight and in place. Glue it into position if it is not (Fig. D-16).

If there is nothing physically wrong with the drawer, the problem may just be one of excessive friction. Rub the drawer and its frame, wherever they touch, with soap, candle wax or paraffin. Make sure the soap is dry and just rub it over the affected areas. You can use the same procedure using a candle. Paraffin wax is available in supermarkets in small blocks. Do not use oil.

Sometimes the glides on which the drawer moves are badly worn. Get a thin strip of aluminum and cut it to fit the exact shape of the glide. Cement the aluminum in place on top of the glide. An alternative, quick method is to put three or more steel head thumbtacks into the glide.

Drawers will sometimes stick in damp weather. The humidity causes the wood to swell. To avoid this problem, wait until the weather is dry. Coat the wood with a penetrating sealer or with wax (Fig. D-17).

☐ Duplex Flush Receptacles, Replacing

See Electrical Outlets, Replacing , *page 95*

☐ Electrical Connections, How to Insulate

Bare wires, wires stripped of their insulation and connected to a source of electrical power, must be kept from touching any metal nearby. Aside from the fact that a short circuit can blow a fuse or trip a circuit breaker, it is both a shock and a fire hazard.

A quick way to insulate wire ends which have been stripped and joined is to use screw-on connectors (Fig. E-1). Before using the connector, twist the two bare wires together. To make a good electrical connection, use a pair of gas pliers to do the twisting. You'll find it much easier and better than trying to use your fingers.

After the wires have been joined, put on a screw-on connector, sometimes called a wire nut, available in electrical supply or home-repair centers. Turn the connector in a clockwise direction, and do so until you can no longer turn it.

Wire nuts are sold in different sizes. If you have any doubt about the size of the wire you are using, cut off a small piece and take it with you when buying the connectors.

The advantage of a solderless connector is that it requires no soldering. Should you wish to modify the wiring at some later time, it is easy to remove the connector.

As an alternative you can solder bare wires together and then cover the joint with insulating tape (Fig. E-2). The insulating tape can be a fabric or plastic type. The fabric has a

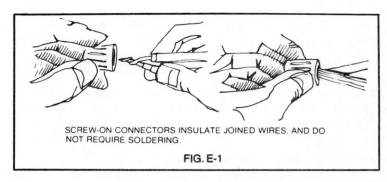

SCREW-ON CONNECTORS INSULATE JOINED WIRES. AND DO NOT REQUIRE SOLDERING.

FIG. E-1

tendency to unravel and dry out. The plastic type doesn't have these faults and, in addition, lets you make a tighter wrap.

Wires that are to be grounded, that is, connected to an electrical junction box, or to a metal pipe, need not be insulated.

See Buzzers, Chimes, and Doorbells, How to Install, *page 35*
Electric Shock, How to Avoid, *page 107*
Soldering, *page 312*
Splicing Wire, *page 324*

☐ Electrical Outlets, Replacing

Electrical outlets (also known as duplex flush receptacles) can and do become defective. If all the appliances you connect to a particular outlet seem to work intermittently or

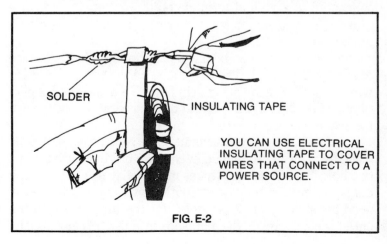

SOLDER

INSULATING TAPE

YOU CAN USE ELECTRICAL INSULATING TAPE TO COVER WIRES THAT CONNECT TO A POWER SOURCE.

FIG. E-2

will work only if you must move the connecting plug, or if the plug keeps falling out, it is possible the outlet needs replacement.

As a first step, shut off the power to the outlet by removing the fuse controlling its power or open the respective circuit breaker switch. To make sure power is definitely turned off, connect a lamp to the outlet and keep adjusting the plug until the light does go on. The light will go off when you remove the fuse or open the circuit breaker switch.

The faceplate is held in place by a single screw in the center. Remove this screw. You will see two mounting screws at the top and bottom of the outlet. Remove these. You will now be able to pull the outlet out of its metal box. Make a note how the wires are connected to the outlet and if you don't want to rely on memory, make a rough sketch.

Loosen the screws holding the wires in position, and you will then be able to remove the old outlet. All you need to do now is to reverse the steps you followed in getting the outlet out.

If you will examine your new outlet, you will see that it has two types of terminals or screws. Two of these have a silver or chrome color; two have a brass color. Connect the black wires to the brass terminals. Connect the white (neutral) wires to the silver terminals. You may have a green wire. If there is such a wire, it is a ground wire and should be connected to a ground terminal on the outlet. Instead of a green wire you may have one that is bare. This is also a ground wire.

Your new receptacle may use spring grip holes instead of screws (Fig. E-3). These are labeled to show which color wire goes into each spring grip hole. To make the connection, push back the insulation at the end of the wire and push the exposed copper wire into the hole.

When buying a replacement outlet, always buy the type made for a three prong plug even if the original outlet was a two hole unit. Many appliances made today use three prong plugs, so getting the correct outlet will help eliminate the need for an adapter. The "hole" for the third prong in the outlet is connected to the metal box in which it is mounted by means of the two screws which hold the receptacle to the box.

☐ Electrical Outlets, Types of

Electrical *outlets*, also known as receptacles or convenience outlets, are used to allow the quick connection or disconnection of electrical appliances equipped with a male plug, more often referred to simply as a plug.

Electrical outlets may be housed completely in a small, rectangular plastic container and supplied with lamp cord terminating in a plug. These are available in lengths from about 5 feet to 15 feet and are used when the power cord of an appliance, such as a small radio, cannot reach a power outlet.

For a permanent installation, receptacles are mounted in electric boxes which are mounted in a wall. The electric

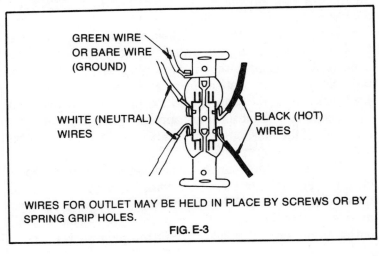

GREEN WIRE OR BARE WIRE (GROUND)

WHITE (NEUTRAL) WIRES

BLACK (HOT) WIRES

WIRES FOR OUTLET MAY BE HELD IN PLACE BY SCREWS OR BY SPRING GRIP HOLES.

FIG. E-3

box not only supplies support for the receptacle, but helps prevent the spread of fire in the event a short circuit develops in the receptacle.

Receptacles can be single or duplex types with the single accommodating one plug, the duplex able to handle two. Duplex receptacles are more convenient.

Receptacles can be two or three hole types (Fig. E-4). The three hole type is recommended since it automatically grounds the appliance being plugged into it, a good safety feature (Fig. E-5). Also, many appliances being made today are equipped with plugs designed for three hole receptacles.

All receptacles, whether single or duplex, two hole or three, have a pair of metal flanges, one each at the top and bottom of the receptacle. These have openings for machine screws to permit the fastening of the receptacle to the electric box.

Most in-home receptacles, such as those found along or near the baseboard in the home, are rated to handle a maximum of 15 amperes. To calculate the power handling ability of a receptacle, multiply the power line voltage by 15. If the line voltage is 115 volts, and that is usually the case, then $115 \times 15 = 1725$ watts or somewhat less than 2 kilowatts. This is the rating for the entire outlet. If it is a duplex type, each outlet of the duplex will be able to handle one-half of this amount of power or $1725/2 = 862$ watts approximately.

It is easily possible to overload an outlet by using cube taps. A *cube tap* is a combined plug and receptacle. If a pair of cube taps are used with a duplex receptacle, it becomes possible to accommodate as many as six appliances. If all of these are used at the same time, it becomes easy to overload the receptacle. What usually happens is that the fuse will blow, but if the fuse is the wrong size or is overrated, a fire can start in the receptacle.

Because of the connect-disconnect facility of receptacles, it is possible for them to become a source of trouble in the electrical system. When connecting an appliance, always make sure that the plug of that appliance goes as far into the outlet as possible. Partial entry of the plug means a poor

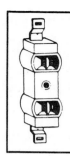

TWO HOLE DUPLEX RECEPTACLE (LEFT)
AND THREE HOLE (RIGHT).

FIG. E-4

connection with an inoperative or poorly operating appliance as a result. After an appliance has been on for some time, feel its plug. If the plug is very warm to the touch, the appliance is overloading the power line, the plug is making poor contact with the outlet, or the wire leading to the plug isn't heavy enough to carry the current.

Tug gently on the wire connected to the plug while the plug is in its outlet. If the plug falls out readily, the connection between the plug and the receptacle is poor. Bend the prongs of the plug outward slightly to see if you can get a tighter fit between the prongs and the receptacle. If not, replace the plug.

Sometimes the metal contacts in the receptacle separate. To check whether the fault is with the plug or receptacle, connect the appliance to a different outlet. If the plug makes a good, tight connection, then the suspected receptacle should be replaced.

The prongs of a plug are mounted in rubber or plastic. Sometimes these become loose especially if the plug is repeatedly inserted and removed from the convenience outlet. When this happens, replace the plug.

Some plugs are molded directly to their connecting lamp cord or cable. If the cable should become defective, if

SINGLE TWIST AND TURN RECEPTACLES.
THESE ARE THREE HOLE TYPES.

FIG. E-5

the insulation cracks, or if the plug becomes defective, get rid of the cable and its associated plug. They are potential troublemakers. If the cable seems to be in good condition, but the molded plug is defective, cut it from the cable and replace the plug. All you need do is strip the ends of the wires and attach the plug to them.

If a plug falls out of its receptacle readily and often, it can be helpful to replace both plug and outlet with a twist lock plug and associated twist lock outlet. Plugs of this kind require a twist and turn push action. As a result, the plug not only remains fixed in its outlet but makes better contact with it.

For the most part, convenience outlets are flush with their supporting walls. This means that when the plug of an appliance is inserted, the plug extends some small distance beyond the outlet. In some instances this can be a nuisance, as in the case of an appliance that must be mounted against the outlet. A kitchen clock is an example. Use a special outlet that is recessed, holding not only the plug and its extension but some extra wire attached to the plug, should that be necessary (Fig. E-6).

Outlets are also available which are mounted on a screw base, closely resembling the screw base of an electric light bulb. These can be put into lamp sockets just like an electric light bulb, and so the fixture becomes a combined lamp and outlet. Some of these lamp receptacles are equipped with a pull chain switch.

You can also buy a wall outlet that has a switch. With outlets of this kind the switch must be in its "on" position for power to reach the outlet. This type is referred to as a switched outlet; all others are unswitched types.

Some outlets are designed for use outdoors. These are more rugged than indoor types and are supplied with waterproof snap covers that automatically close over the face of the outlet when it isn't in use (Fig. E-7).

Some appliances in the home are designed for 220 volt operation instead of the usual 115. If an appliance is plugged into an outlet supplied with 220 volts and the appliance is intended for 115 volt operation, there is a good possibility of a

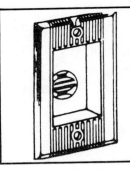

RECESSED RECEPTACLE IS CONVENIENT WHEN APPLIANCE MUST BE MOUNTED AGAINST IT.

FIG. E-6

burnout in that appliance as well as a fire. To prevent such errors, special outlets are designed for 220 volt use, usually single receptacle types with tandem blades. The blades in any receptacle are the metal parts that make contact with the blades of the plug when it is inserted.

There are several types of 220 volt receptacles (Fig. E-8). One type accepts tandem blades and a U-shaped ground connector. Another type has vertical and horizontal blades and a U-shaped ground. The purpose of the tandem arrangement is to prevent plugging in a 115 volt appliance into this 220-volt receptacle.

If you buy appliances, such as air conditioners, a washer or clothes dryer, you will need to make sure that the plug will fit the receptacle you may have already installed.

See BX Cable, Cutting and Installing, *page 38*

Electrical Connections, How to Insulate, *page 94*

Electrical Outlets, Replacing, *page 95*

Electrical Wire Color Code, *page 102*

Electric Shock, How to Avoid, *page 107*

Hacksaw, How to Use, *page 160*

Soldering, *page 312*

OUTDOOR RECEPTACLE HAS HINGED COVER TO PROTECT OUTLET AGAINST THE WEATHER.

FIG. E-7

SOME TYPES OF RECEPTACLES
FOR 220-VOLT APPLIANCES.

FIG. E-8

Splicing Wire, *page 324*
Wires, Connecting Electrical, *page 385*

☐ Electrical Wire Color Code

The wires used to bring electrical power to the various outlets in your home are color coded so you can identify them easily. A white wire is a neutral or ground wire, so-called because at some point it is connected to the earth. All the outlet boxes in your home are grounded—that is, they make an electrical connection with the white wire. The white wire should never be connected to a fuse or a switch; nor should it ever be attached to a wire of any other color, except if the wire is colored green.

Another wire is color coded black. This is the so-called "hot" lead. Black leads should never be connected to wires of any other color. The electrical pressure between the black and white wires is 117 volts; the frequency of the ac is generally 50 Hz (Hertz) or more commonly 60 Hz.

Electrical power is delivered to your outlets by a pair of wires, one white and the other black. A wire color coded red is used to carry current from a switch to an appliance. Sometimes you will also find a green wire. This is an extra ground wire.

See Electrical Connections, How to Insulate, *page 94*
Electric Shock, How to Avoid, *page 107*
Romex Cable, Cutting and Installing, *page 287*
Soldering, *page 312*
Wires, Connecting Electrical, *page 385*

☐ Electric Bills, How to Save Money on

Electric ranges can send your bills soaring. When making tea, coffee or any other hot liquid, measure the exact amount you are planning to use. Don't keep an electric burner on until liquid boils. When liquid looks as though it is ready to boil, turn off the range and let the heating element "coast." Use the right size pot or pan. A small pan on a large element wastes heat.

Wash and dry only full loads of clothes. Use a clothesline for drying, indoors or out when practical to avoid use of the electric dryer. Measure detergents carefully. Too much or too little detergent added to the wash load may not give good results. Remove lint from the clothes dryer after each use.

Do all your ironing at one time. Disconnect the iron as soon as it becomes hot enough to do its job. Iron items that require low levels of heat last, when the iron is in its cooling off stage and has been disconnected.

Repair leaky hot water faucets. They increase your electric and water bills. Make sure your hot water heater is set at the proper temperature. When leaving on an extended vacation, turn off the hot water heater. Set the hot water heater temperature gauge to the minimum reading that you can get away with.

Keep your electric light bulbs clean. Wipe them. If they've become greasy, wash them in detergent. Do not wash bulbs when hot. Clean glass or plastic fixtures regularly and keep reflective fixtures clean. Cleanliness helps you get more light and may enable you to get away with fewer "on" lights. Train children to turn lights and the television set off when leaving the room. Fluorescent fixtures, watt for watt, supply more light than incandescent bulbs, but fluorescent replacements cost more.

You can use lower wattage bulbs for decorative lighting. Use a three-way bulb to give you more light when reading or sewing, such as 100 or 150 watts, but turn the lamp to its lowest setting, either 30 or 50 watts, when the lamp is used for background illumination.

During daylight hours keep lights turned off, except if needed for safety purposes or for close work. When air conditioning is on, keep lights turned off as much as possible since the air conditioner must work harder to overcome the heat given off by the bulbs. When feasible, use fluorescent lights instead of incandescent types since these supply more light per watt.

When redecorating, use light colors for painted walls and ceiling since such colors are more reflective. Dark colors absorb more of the light supplied by electric light bulbs.

Turn off all appliances and electric lights when not in use. Use clock timers or photocells for turning night lights on or off during your absence instead of keeping lights on all night.

If you have an instant-on television set, remove the plug when you go on vacation. Instant-on means a current flows constantly into the set, even when it isn't in use.

Use your dishwasher only when it is fully loaded. A half load uses just as much hot water and electricity as a full load. Wash small load by hand, saving electricity and water.

Make sure the home is adequately insulated. Weather-strip windows and doors. This will keep your house cooler in summer and warmer in winter and will lower operating costs of air conditioners and heaters. Clean and replace filters regularly on air conditioners and heaters.

Keep heat out in the summer by using drapes, blinds or outside awnings. In the winter, uncover windows facing the sun to take advantage of the sun's radiant heat. Adjust the thermostat to lower temperatures at night or when you plan to be away. Heat comes into home in two ways: via air and from solar energy caused by sunlight streaming in through windows. Keep shades drawn in summer to keep sunlight out and up in winter to let sunlight in.

Replace worn gaskets on refrigerator doors. Air leaks cause excessive cold loss which increases electric usage.

Defrost regularly. Your refrigerator won't have to work as hard and will use less electricity. Try to avoid making repeated trips to the refrigerator or freezer. Keeping the refrigerator door open while trying to decide what to take out

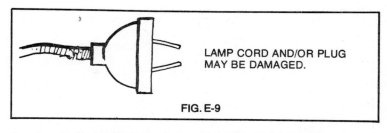

LAMP CORD AND/OR PLUG
MAY BE DAMAGED.

FIG. E-9

is one way to keep your electricity utility happy.

Small appliances can be more economical to use than your electric range. These includes electric grills, toasters, waffle irons, and frying pans. Try to use the toaster to full capacity. It operates at full capacity whether you use one slice of bread, two or more.

See Weather Stripping, *page 369*

□ Electric Fuses

See Appliances Do not Work, *page 23*
Circuit Breakers, *page 45*
Electric Plugs, *page 105*
Fuse Pullers, *page 145*
Fuses, Replacing, *page 146*
Fuses, Types of, *page 147*

□ Electric Plugs

Electric plugs, particularly those made of plastic, can be damaged if stepped on (Fig. E-9). If one or both of the prongs of a plug are loose, or if the shell of the plug is cracked, you have a potential source of fire or shock. If the plug is the type that is to be removed from its outlet fairly frequently, get a replacement plug that has an extension coming out of the back of the plug (Fig. E-10). This will let you hold the plug so

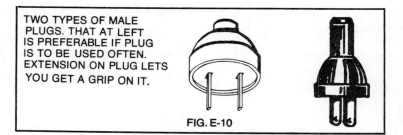

TWO TYPES OF MALE
PLUGS. THAT AT LEFT
IS PREFERABLE IF PLUG
IS TO BE USED OFTEN.
EXTENSION ON PLUG LETS
YOU GET A GRIP ON IT.

FIG. E-10

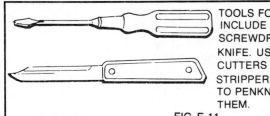

TOOLS FOR PLUG REPAIR INCLUDE FLAT BLADE SCREWDRIVER AND PEN-KNIFE. USE DIAGONAL CUTTERS OR WIRE STRIPPERS IN PREFERENCE TO PENKNIFE IF YOU HAVE THEM.

FIG. E-11

you can remove it easily. Never pull a plug out of its outlet by yanking on the connecting wires. Instead, get a grip on the plug. Only buy plugs that carry the *UL stamp* or tag.

For replacing a plug, you will need a flat blade screwdriver and possibly a pair of diagonal cutters or a penknife (Fig. E-11). You will only need the cutters or knife if the connecting lamp cord is damaged.

Never work on a lamp cord while the plug is in its outlet. Remove the plug from the outlet. If the cord is worn or abraded, cut away the damaged part (Fig. E-12). Examine the old plug and note how the wires are connected. There are two connecting wires with each wire fastened in position by a machine screw. The wire is stranded type and consists of five to seven strands.

After you have removed the old plug, insert the lamp cord through the center hole of the plug (Fig. E-13). Strip the insulation away from each of the wires. It does take a little practice to be able to do this without damaging or cutting away individual strands of wire (Figs. E-14 and E-15). The insulation to be stripped away should be about a half inch in length. After you have successfully stripped the insulation, twirl the wire ends so that all the strands form the appearance of a single wire.

The next step is to tie the two conducting wires into an Underwriters' knot (Fig. E-16) The purpose of the knot is to

CUT LAMP CORD TO ELIMINATE DAMAGED PORTION.

FIG. E-12

supply strain relief. However, you should know that homeowners often omit this step (Fig. E-17).

After you have made the knot, pull it firmly down into the plug (Fig. E-18). Take one of the wires and go around one of the terminals. Put the exposed wire around the screw in a clockwise direction. Now tighten the screw. Repeat this step with the other wire and the other terminal. As a finishing touch, replace the insulating cover over the plug (Fig. E-19).

The plug should fit firmly and tightly into its assigned outlet. If it does not do so, bend each terminal or the plug outward slightly. A loose connection between the plug and the outlet can mean intermittent operation of the lamp or appliance being serviced by the plug.,

See Adapter Plugs, How to Use, *page 15*
Electrical Connections, How to Insulate, *page 94*
Electrical Wire Color Code, *page 102*
Electric Shock, How to Avoid, *page 107*
Splicing Wire, *page 324*

☐ Electric Shock, How to Avoid

Make sure appliances, equipment, and wire that you buy are all stamped, tagged or marked with the UL (Underwriters' Laboratories, Inc.) marker.

REMOVE OUTER COVERING TO REVEAL
TWO INSULATED WIRES OF LAMP CORD.

FIG. E-14

STRIP INSULATION AWAY FROM WIRES. WIRE
USED IN LAMP CORD IS STRANDED. TWIRL WIRES
TO PRODUCE EFFECT OF A SINGLE, SOLID
CONDUCTOR.   FIG. E-15

Connecting cords to appliances of any kind should not be frayed. Lamp cords should not be cracked. Replace any wires that are damaged.

Don't try to install electrical appliances that require large currents—dryers and electric ovens. Get a licensed electrician to do it.

Make sure all fixed appliances are grounded. Have your electrician check for you.

Don't work with any electrical appliance while standing on a wet floor or with wet hands. Do not use electrical heaters or radios which must be plugged into the power line while you take a bath or shower. If you want to heat a bathroom electrically, do so before you let water into the tub or before stepping into and turning on a shower. Disconnect the appliance and remove it before bathing.

If you have pull chain lights, attach a string or cord to the pull. Do not use metal pull chains for lights or any appliances.

When cleaning electrical equipment, do two things. Make sure the on-off switch is turned to its off position and, more importantly remove the male plug from the power outlet.

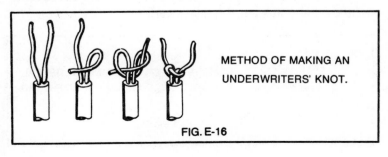

METHOD OF MAKING AN
UNDERWRITERS' KNOT.

FIG. E-16

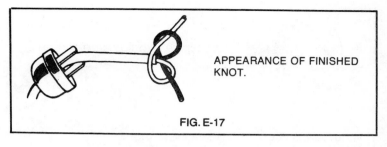

APPEARANCE OF FINISHED
KNOT.

FIG. E-17

Do not try to repair radio and television receivers that are line power operated unless you are experienced in doing so.

If you have small children in your home, put covers on the outlets to keep them from putting things into the receptacles. You can get such safety covers in hardware and electrical light and appliance stores.

Do not use an *extension cord* as a permanent installation. Extension cords are intended for temporary connections only. When disconnecting an appliance from an extension cord, disconnect that cord from the power outlet first.

When removing a lamp cord or any other pair of wires from an outlet, do not pull on the wires. Instead, disconnect by holding the plug and pulling on it. Plugs with extension handles are best.

If a plug has a loose or damaged connecting element, replace the plug. Plugs come with safety tabs, circular bits of

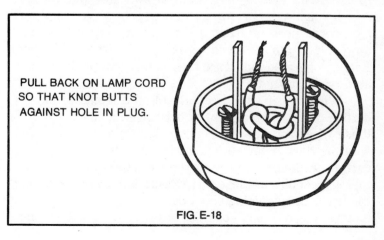

PULL BACK ON LAMP CORD
SO THAT KNOT BUTTS
AGAINST HOLE IN PLUG.

FIG. E-18

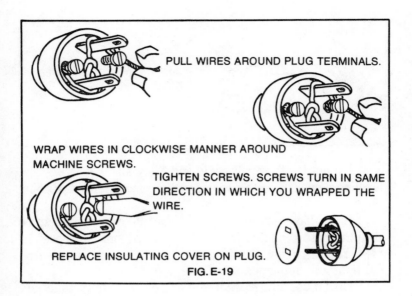

PULL WIRES AROUND PLUG TERMINALS.

WRAP WIRES IN CLOCKWISE MANNER AROUND MACHINE SCREWS.

TIGHTEN SCREWS. SCREWS TURN IN SAME DIRECTION IN WHICH YOU WRAPPED THE WIRE.

REPLACE INSULATING COVER ON PLUG.

FIG. E-19

insulating material that fit over the plug. Always make sure these are in place.

Plastic plugs can crack if stepped on. Replace.

Do not operate any appliance while you are grounded—that is, while you have your hand on a radiator pipe, (whether hot or cold water), faucet, sink, or any metal object that is fastened to your building.

Have defective electrical appliances repaired. Don't try to use them, even if they seem to work intermittently.

If you have your own swimming pool, never run extension cords near it. Keep electrically powered appliances away. Don't run overhead wires within 10 feet of the pool. Battery operated radios are okay to use near pools; ac operated types are not.

Wires are used to keep electrical currents confined to certain paths. Any current that is given a chance to leave those wires and flow to ground is known as a *ground fault*, with the flow of current via a ground fault called a leakage current. Although leakage currents can be very small, under the right conditions these currents can kill. Leakage currents can occur in swimming pool equipment such as filter pump motors, electric panel boards, or underwater lights. Fuses or circuit breakers should protect against leakage currents. If the currents are very small, they may not blow the fuse or trip the circuit breaker. However, they are still very dangerous.

You can protect against small leakage currents with the help of a *ground fault circuit interrupter*, abbreviated as GFCI. A GFCI will shut off electrical power in about 1/40 second even when the ground fault current is as small as 5 milliamperes.

Electrical appliances are switch operated. If the switch becomes loose, tighten it, but take the plug out of its outlet first. If a switch is intermittent, replace it. Never probe into an outlet or a light socket.

See Buzzers, Chimes and Doorbells, How to Install, *page 35*

Electrical Connections, How to Insulate, *page 94*

Splicing Wire, *page 324*

☐ Electric Switches, Installing

Put in a new electric wall switch if turning it on does not simultaneously turn on the appliance it is supposed to control. If you must jiggle the switch to get it to work, or if you hear a frying or hissing noise coming from the switch, replace it.

Most switches around the home are single-pole *toggle* types which make a definite clicking sound when turned on or off. However, in addition to the toggle switch there are also *mercury* and *silent* switches. You might want to consider either the mercury or the silent switch for installation in a nursery or an invalid's room where the click of a toggle switch cannot be tolerated. All three—the toggle, the silent, and the mercury—are interchangeable. The toggle type, though, is the least expensive.

The toggle switch consists of a metallic armature whose movement is controlled by the toggle. The switch also contains a pair of fixed terminals, also made of metal. When the toggle is in its down, or off position, the armature does not make contact with either terminal. Pushing the toggle to its up or on position forces the armature into direct contact with both terminals (Fig. E-20).

There are machine screws adjoining each terminal. These screws are used for attaching connecting wires. One wire is fastened to one screw, the other wire to the other screw. If, when making the connections, the working order of the switch is reversed, just transpose the wire connections.

The screws for switches are often *captive* types. This means the screw will not come completely out. Just turn the screw out far enough to let you wrap the connecting wire around it. The purpose of a captive screw is to avoid having the screw fall out. Finding them is often difficult, sometimes impossible.

Mercury is a metal which is liquid at room temperatures. Basically, the switch consists of a small hollow cylinder partially filled with mercury. The external part of the switch, the section you move when you want to turn it on or off, is connected to a small contact point inside the switch (Fig. E-21). When you turn the switch off, you move this contact out of the small pool of mercury. Conversely, when you turn the switch on, you immerse the contact into the mercury.

As in the toggle switch, there are two connections, one of which is to the mercury, the other to the moving contact.

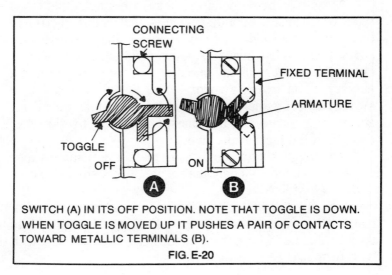

SWITCH (A) IN ITS OFF POSITION. NOTE THAT TOGGLE IS DOWN. WHEN TOGGLE IS MOVED UP IT PUSHES A PAIR OF CONTACTS TOWARD METALLIC TERMINALS (B).

FIG. E-20

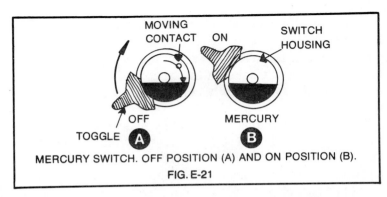

MERCURY SWITCH. OFF POSITION (A) AND ON POSITION (B).

FIG. E-21

Mercury is a highly poisonous substance. When a mercury switch becomes defective, dispose of it. Do not keep it around as an object of interest for children.

The silent switch is almost the same as the toggle. It contains a strip of spring steel. When in the off position, this strip is pushed away from its mating contact at the bottom of the switch. When you put the switch into its on position, the steel spring returns and contact is established between the spring and its contact point (Fig. E-22).

All three switches, the toggle, mercury, and silent, are known as *single pole, single throw*, abbreviated as SPST. There are other types of switches such as the *single pole double throw* (SPDT), the *double pole single throw* (DPST), and the *double pole double throw* (DPDT). However, for most applications around the home, the SPST is the one that is commonly used. The other switches are for special applications.

To replace a single pole toggle switch, shut off the power going to the switch as a first step (Fig. E-23). You can do this by opening the main power switch, in which case all power to your home will be turned off. The power switch is part of your main fuse box. If you have a reset type or circuit breaker, find the reset switch for the toggle you are going to replace. Open the reset switch. If your fuse box has replaceable fuses, remove the fuse that controls the toggle switch. While electricians can and do replace toggle switches without turning off power, they are experienced and know how to protect themselves against electric shock.

Remove the faceplate of the switch, held in position by two machine screws. Hold your hand under the faceplate when removing the screws so as not to lose them. When the two screws are out, take off the faceplate. You will not be able to see the junction box holding the switch and the switch itself.

To make sure that the switch is indeed disconnected from the power line, test using a small voltage tester. A voltage tester for line power consists of a tiny neon lamp and a pair of test leads. They are inexpensive, easy to use, and should be part of your in-home tool set up. Touch one of the leads of the test lamp to the metal junction box. Touch the other lead of the test lamp, in turn, to one of the connecting screws on the switch and then to the other. If the lamp lights, then power is still on and you should go back to your fuse box. You have apparently opened or removed the wrong fuse.

However, if touching the test lead to both screws results in a "no light" condition, then power is off and you can safely work on the switch. Note how the wires are connected (Fig. E-24). You will see one wire fixed to one screw of the switch and another wire fixed to the other screw. Both wires will have the same color insulation and will be black. You will also see a third wire, usually bare copper, connected to the metal frame of the junction box. If you want to be absolutely sure to remember how the connections are made, make a rough sketch of the switch and its attached wires before removing.

The switch is held in place by a pair of machine screws which fasten the switch to the junction box. Remove these two screws.

After the screws are removed, you will be able to pull the switch out of the junction box. Do so and examine the way in which the wires are connected.

Disconnect the two wires by using a screwdriver, turning the wire holding screws in a counterclockwise direction. Remove the wires and the switch will come out. Do not disconnect the bare wire (the ground wire) fastened to the junction box.

Put the new switch in the same position occupied by the

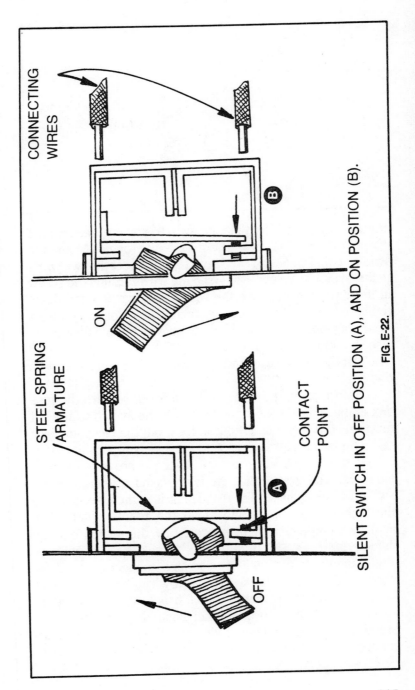

CONNECTING WIRES

STEEL SPRING ARMATURE

CONTACT POINT

ON

OFF

SILENT SWITCH IN OFF POSITION (A), AND ON POSITION (B).

FIG. E-22.

115

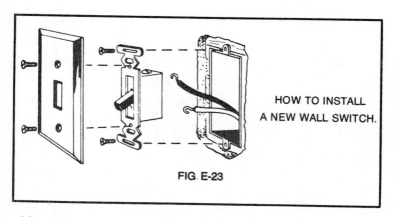

HOW TO INSTALL
A NEW WALL SWITCH.

FIG. E-23

old one. If you will examine the switch, you will see that the words "off" and "on" are cut right into the toggle. Mount the switch so that the word "off" is on top. Connect the two wires to their respective screws. Wrap the wires around the screw in the direction in which the screw will travel when being tightened. To tighten a screw, turn it in a clockwise direction. This means you should wrap the wire around the screw, also in a clockwise direction.

Put the switch back into the junction box and fasten with two screws.

Before putting the faceplate back on, restore the fuse box to its original condition. Then test the switch to see if it functions the way it should. If it does, put the faceplate back on using two screws.

If the switch does not work, there are several possibilities. The first is that the fault wasn't originally in the switch but elsewhere. The usual fault is in the fuse. Replace the fuse or else open and close the reset switch. The appliance or electric light operated by the switch may be defective.

Sometimes a switch is used as a connecting point for various wires in the home electrical wiring system. In that case it is better to make a sketch before disconnecting. Another method is to use small tags, the kind that have string, and use these tags to identify wire positioning. Tags for upper screw connection could be marked No. 1, for lower screw connection No. 2.

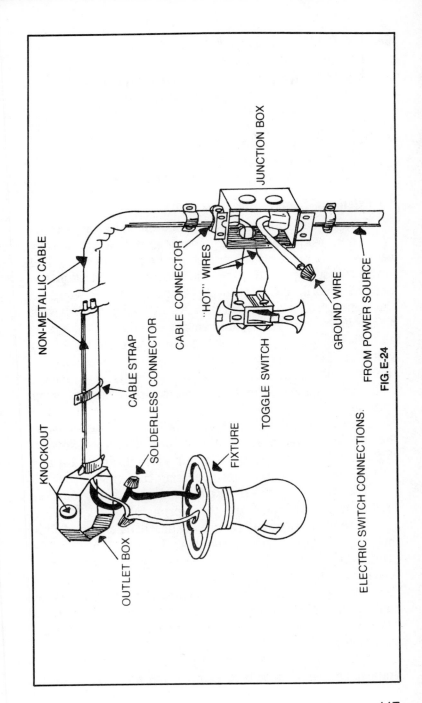

NON-METALLIC CABLE

KNOCKOUT

CABLE STRAP

SOLDERLESS CONNECTOR

OUTLET BOX

FIXTURE

CABLE CONNECTOR

"HOT" WIRES

TOGGLE SWITCH

JUNCTION BOX

GROUND WIRE

FROM POWER SOURCE

FIG. E-24

ELECTRIC SWITCH CONNECTIONS.

117

☐ Extension Cords

Tools, lawn mowers, and other electrical appliances will often work poorly, or sometimes not at all, if they receive their power through a skimpy extension cord. The current required by the appliance must flow through the extension cord, and so it is important that these wires be thick enough to carry the current. All extension cords have a *voltage drop*—that is, they decrease the amount of voltage. If an outlet has 115 volts and an extension cord produces a 10 volt drop, the amount of voltage available for the appliance is the difference, in this case $115 - 10 = 105$ volts. As a general rule of thumb, the maximum line voltage drop of an extension cord shouldn't be more than 10%.

The voltage drop along an extension cord depends on the length of the cord and the amount of current flowing through it. You can expect larger voltage drops for appliances which require more operating current.

You will need a three-wire extension cord for grounded tools that are equipped with three-prong plugs.

Extension cords will carry a tag or will be stamped with the gauge number and the number of wires. Thus, a 16-gauge, three wire cord will be identified at 16/3, or as 16/3 AWG or as 16AWG/3 or as 3 conductor 16 AWG. AWG is an abbreviation for American Wire Gauge. The larger the AWG number, the thinner the wire. Thus, AWG 16 is thicker than AWG 18. A "heavier" wire having a smaller AWG number always costs more.

Extension cords are made for inside and outdoor use. You can use an outdoor type indoors, but not vice versa. If

118

you plan to use an extension cord outdoors, be sure to get one market as suitable for outdoor use. The extension cord should carry the safety seal of approval by Underwriters' Laboratories and it will be marked as UL approved.

A 100-foot extension cord rated at 14 amperes could be used for all appliances having current ratings from 1 through 12 amperes. See Table E-1.

When using an extension cord, whether indoors or out, always make certain that the cord does not become entangled with the appliance. Always connect the extension cord to the outlet nearest to the appliance to be used. Don't handle any electric appliance or extension cord with wet hands. Wet feet, wet or damp floors, and electricity make a dangerous combination.

See Electric Plugs, *page 105*

Electric Shock, How to Avoid, *page 107*

☐ Exterior Metal Surfaces, Painting

If some part of the exterior of your home uses copper and you want to show a bright copper finish, clean the copper with a phosphoric acid cleaner. Buff and polish the copper until it is bright. Then coat it with a clear finish. There are various clear polyurethane finishes available. Copper oxidizes rather quickly, so use the finish as soon as the copper surface is ready. If you prefer not using phosphoric acid, try any one of the commercial copper cleaners you can buy in supermarkets.

If your house is equipped with copper gutters and downspouts, don't bother trying to clean or paint them. The copper will turn a naturally dark brown color or, over a period of time, will become green. The copper will not corrode if left unpainted. However, if the copper is adjacent to a painted surface, the change of color of the copper due to oxidation may tend to discolor nearby paint.

If you plan to paint exterior metal with an oil base paint, use a primer first. *Primers* for copper, aluminum, and steel surfaces are *zinc chromate* types, but other types of primers are also available. The exception is a galvanized steel surface, sometimes used for gutters and downspouts. For this

TABLE E-1

RECOMENDED WIRE GAUGES FOR EXTENSION CORDS

If tool or appliance has an ampere rating of	AWG for 25-foot cord	AWG for 50-foot cord	AWG for 75-foot cord	AWG for 100-foot cord
1 through 7 amperes	18	18	18	18
8 through 10 amperes	18	18	16	16
11 or 12 amperes	16	16	14	14

metallic surface you will need a zinc dust, zinc oxide type of primer. Some exterior latex paints can be used directly over galvanized surfaces, but not oil paints.

If you have iron metalwork, you can protect it against rust in two ways. Prior to painting, clean thoroughly using a wire brush. Remove all flakes of rust and loose paint. You can then paint the surface with an anti-corrosive primer and, after it has dried, paint with an oil base type. There are anti-rust paints on the market. They have the advantage of letting you do the entire paint job in one step since they require no prior primer.

See Alligatoring (Paint), *page 20*
    Blistering (Paint), *page 33*
    Chalking (Paint), *page 44*
    Checking (Paint), *page 45*
    Doors, Painting, *page 79*
    Masonry Surfaces, Painting, *page 207*
    Paint Brushes and Rollers, Cleaning, *page 229*
    Paint, Cracks in, *page 237*
    Paint, Removing, *page 238*
    Paint, Splattered, *page 245*
    Paint, Tips on How to, *page 250*
    Peeling (Paint), *page 273*
    Plywood, Painting, *page 280*

☐ Faucets, Compression Type, Leaking

Compression type faucets use washers for controlling water flow. If your faucet is a single type or is a double type with separate controls for cold and hot water, it is a compression type.

If the dripping faucet is noisy and you find the sound of the dripping intolerable, but you don't have time to give it the attention it needs, take a dish towel, soak it in water, and then wrap it around the faucet, holding it in place with a rubber band. It won't stop the drip, but at least you won't hear it. It is not a repair for the water still drips, but it uses the cloth as a guide.

See Aerator, How to Install, *page 16*
 Bathroom Faucets, Installing, *page 29*
 Faucets, Repairing Non-Compression or Single Lever Types, *page 122*
 Faucets, Squealing, *page 126*
 Faucets, Types of, *page 128*
 Faucet Handles, Replacing, *page 129*
 Faucet Seat, Dressing a, *page 131*
 Hose Faucet, Replacing, *page 186*
 Leaky Packing Nut, *page 198*
 Sink, Bath and Shower Faucets, How to Replace, *page 305*

The tools you will need for eliminating the drip from a faucet are a screwdriver, a monkey wrench or other adjustable type wrench, and a box of assorted washers and machine screws (Figs. F-1 and F-2).

Your first step is to turn off the water supply to the faucet. Usually there is a valve located beneath the sink. If not, then you will need to locate the main water valve, generally in some corner of the basement of the house (Fig. F-3).

After you have shut off the water valve, turn on the faucet until water stops flowing. Directly below the handle of the faucet you will see a packing nut. If the packing nut has a finish you want to protect, wipe it dry and then cover it with tape or with a bit of scrap cloth (Fig. F-4).

Adjust the wrench jaws so they have a firm grip on the packing nut, and then turn the tool counterclockwise. After you have made a few turns, you will find you can continue turning the nut with your fingers. You will then be able to remove the entire assembly (Fig. F-5).

Below the threaded stem of the assembly you will see the washer held in place by a machine screw. Remove the screw by turning it with a flat blade screwdriver (Fig. F-6). Replace the old washer with one having the same diameter (Fig. F-7). Insert the screw and tighten it (Fig. F-8). Put the stem assembly back into the faucet and tighten the packing nut. When first tightening the packing nut, do so with your fingers to prevent crossthreading (Fig. F-9). Then finish the job with a wrench. The final step is to turn on the water by rotating the water valve.

☐ **Faucets, Repairing Non-Compression or Single Lever Types**

A non-compression faucet has a single handle or knob to control the amount of water flow. It can also control cold water, hot water or supply a mixture. There are three types of non-compression faucets—*ball, valve,* and *cartridge.* In all cases, turn off the water valve before working on the faucets.

The non-compression valve faucet has a plug on one side. Turn this plug counterclockwise, and you will be able to

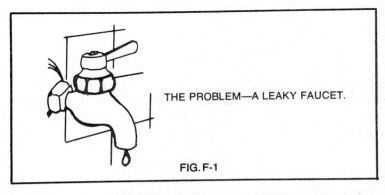

THE PROBLEM—A LEAKY FAUCET.

FIG. F-1

remove the entire valve assembly (Fig. F-10). Directly beneath the head of the plug you will see a gasket. Replace the gasket if it seems worn or is cracked.

Immediately beneath the gasket is a strainer and a valve stem assembly. If the faucet cannot seem to control the water flow or if there is dripping, replace the gasket, strainer, and valve stem. You can get these as a complete kit. The strainer is a small mesh screen, and it should be cleaned or replaced if damaged.

The ball faucet depends on the position of a ball inside the handle assembly for controlling water flow. The faucet will have an allen setscrew in the base of the handle. Loosen the screw (don't remove it) and work the handle back and forth. When the handle comes off, you will see a cap. The cap is threaded and screwed into position and holds the cam

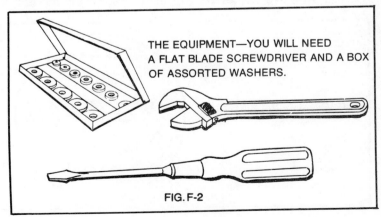

THE EQUIPMENT—YOU WILL NEED A FLAT BLADE SCREWDRIVER AND A BOX OF ASSORTED WASHERS.

FIG. F-2

123

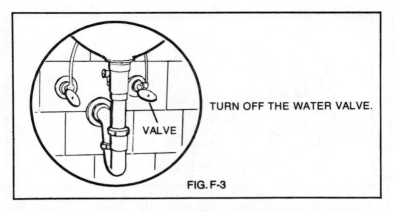

TURN OFF THE WATER VALVE.

VALVE

FIG. F-3

assembly and ball in place. Rotate the cap counterclockwise with a wrench, and you will then be able to take out the cam and ball assemblies (Fig. F-11).

You can get a complete kit of parts for ball faucets. It is always a good idea to replace the cam and the ball and seat assemblies. Mounting instructions are included with the kit, but assembly is simply disassembly in reverse order. Make sure the cap is tight after you have put the faucet back together again.

Of all faucets, the cartridge type is the most complicated. It uses a ported cartridge for controlling hot and cold water, or a mixture of the two. At the top of the faucet you will find a plastic snap-in insert. Remove this with the help of a flat blade screwdriver. Beneath the insert you will find a gasket. Remove it. There will also be a screw holding a

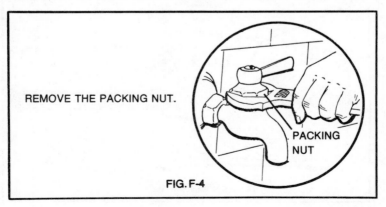

REMOVE THE PACKING NUT.

PACKING NUT

FIG. F-4

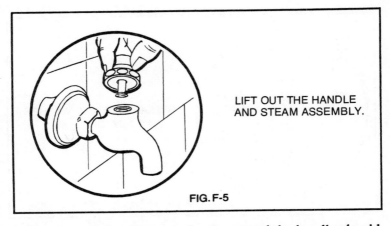

LIFT OUT THE HANDLE AND STEAM ASSEMBLY.

FIG. F-5

handle in position. Remove the screw and the handle should slide off. The screw helps hold the cartridge to the handle. The cartridge is held in place by a retaining clip near the bottom of the assembly (Fig. F-12). When you remove the clip you will be able, at the same time, to remove the cartridge. A repair kit should enable you to replace all or most of these parts.

See Aerator, How to Install, *page 16*
  Bathroom Faucets, Installing, *page 29*
  Faucets, Compression Type, Leaking, *page 121*
  Faucets, Squealing, *page 126*
  Faucets, Types of, *page 128*
  Faucet Handles, Replacing, *page 129*

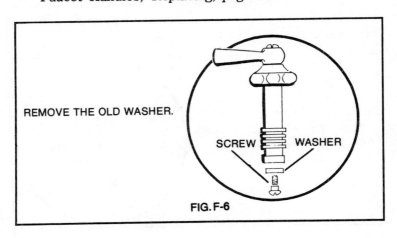

REMOVE THE OLD WASHER.

SCREW   WASHER

FIG. F-6

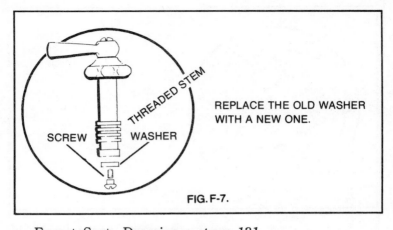

REPLACE THE OLD WASHER
WITH A NEW ONE.

FIG. F-7.

☐ Faucets, Squealing

Sometimes a compression type faucet will squeal or chatter when the faucet handle is turned toward the open position. Possibly this noise can be stopped by pushing the faucet handle to one side. The cause can be a worn washer or a wrong size washer. Unscrew the packing nut, remove the faucet stem, and replace the washer.

Sometimes the trouble is due to a stem whose threads are worn. In that case replace the stem. In some cases it may be necessary to put in a new faucet.

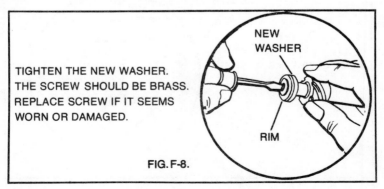

TIGHTEN THE NEW WASHER.
THE SCREW SHOULD BE BRASS.
REPLACE SCREW IF IT SEEMS
WORN OR DAMAGED.

FIG. F-8.

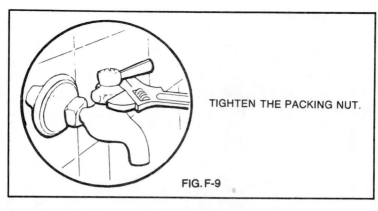

TIGHTEN THE PACKING NUT.

FIG. F-9

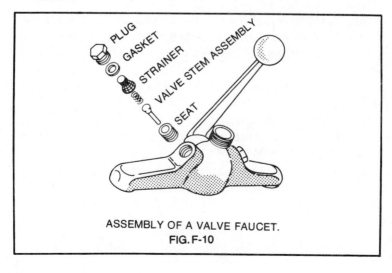

ASSEMBLY OF A VALVE FAUCET.
FIG. F-10

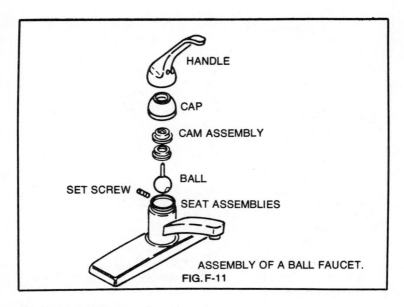

HANDLE

CAP

CAM ASSEMBLY

BALL

SET SCREW

SEAT ASSEMBLIES

ASSEMBLY OF A BALL FAUCET.
FIG. F-11

☐ Faucets, Types of

There are two basic kinds of faucets: *compression* and *non-compression* (Fig. F-13). Compression faucets are the more commonly used, and you will invariably find them in older homes, but they are also being installed in new homes as well. There are several ways of identifying compression faucets, for they have separate handles for hot and cold water supplies. However, you will also find individual compression type faucets when used with a laundry tub. A compression faucet is so-called since it uses a washer to control the flow of water.

A non-compression faucet has just one single knob or a lever for controlling the flow of both hot and cold water. The single control is also used for mixing the hot and cold water.

Faucet leaks never get better if unattended, always worse. Tightening the handle excessively to stop a drip may work termporarily, but can result in damage. A dripping faucet can waste a surprising amount of water. It can also result in sink stains which may be difficult to remove.

See Aerator, How to Install, *page 16*
Bathroom Faucets, Installing, *page 29*

☐ Faucet Handles, Replacing

At times faucet handles need to be replaced. In some cases they become loose. The plating may have worn away or the handle may have become damaged.

Faucet handles are kept in place in various ways. The handle may be a force fit type. In others the faucet handle is kept in place by a single screw located beneath a plastic insert on the top of the handle. In some, the screw is beneath the handle at the side.

Handles for faucets are either metal or a plastic material such as *Lucite*, or some combination of metal and plastic (Fig. F-14). To make sure the replacement handle will fit, take the old handle with you when you shop and get the advice of the salesperson.

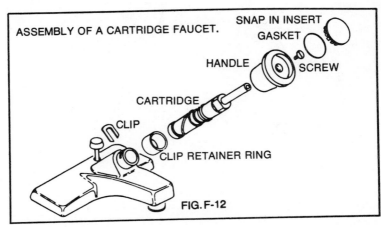

ASSEMBLY OF A CARTRIDGE FAUCET.

SNAP IN INSERT
GASKET
HANDLE
SCREW
CARTRIDGE
CLIP
CLIP RETAINER RING
FIG. F-12

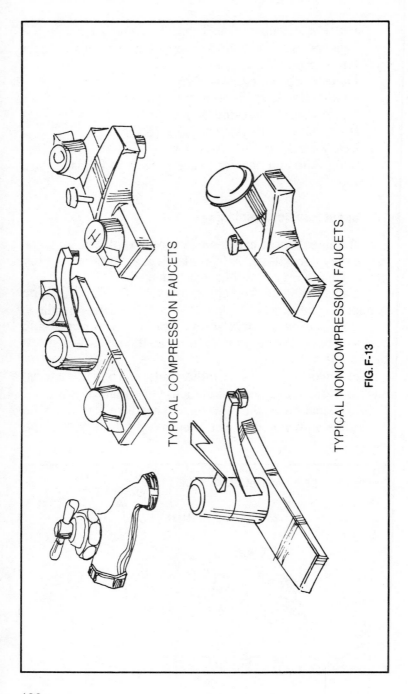

TYPICAL COMPRESSION FAUCETS

TYPICAL NONCOMPRESSION FAUCETS

FIG. F-13

130

☐ Faucet Seat, Dressing a

In compression-type faucets, water flow is controlled by a washer fitting into a faucet seat. When you turn the faucet handle to its "on" or "flow" position, the faucet is separated from its seat and water flows between the faucet and its seat, out of the faucet spout.

Ordinarily, if a faucet drips, the fault is due to a defective washer. Sometimes, however, you will replace the washer, effect a temporary repair, and then you will need to replace the washer again. If you must replace washers too often, or if putting in a new washer doesn't solve the water drip problem, then it will be necessary to "dress" the faucet seat. The flowing action of the water, the chemicals in it, and the rubbing of the washer may have produced a groove (or grooves) in the seat, supplying a channel for water flow. Since the water is under pressure, it will push its way through.

You can repair the faucet seat with a *faucet seat dresser*, an inexpensive tool available in hardware stores. There are various kinds, but they all work on the same basic idea (Fig. F-15). They consists of a rod with a grinder at one end and a handle at the other. To use this tool, shut off the water supply and remove the faucet stem. Getting the faucet stem out is just a matter of loosening a nut (Fig. F-16).

Mount the dressing tool so it is vertical and tight. It should not be able to move from side to side. Cutters used

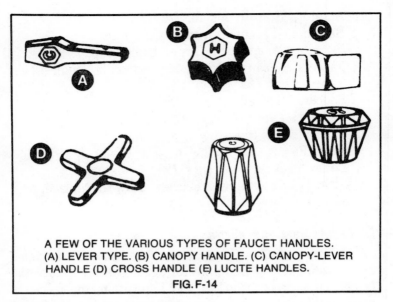

A FEW OF THE VARIOUS TYPES OF FAUCET HANDLES.
(A) LEVER TYPE. (B) CANOPY HANDLE. (C) CANOPY-LEVER
HANDLE (D) CROSS HANDLE (E) LUCITE HANDLES.

FIG. F-14

with faucet seat dressers range from ½ inch to 11/16 inch. After inserting the tool, turn the handle slowly in a clockwise direction. It should not be necessary to make more than a few turns of the handle. The idea is to remove grooves in the seat and not to remove too much seat material. Be sure to follow the instructions accompanying the tool.

See Aerator, How to Install, *page 16*
Bathroom Faucets, Installing, *page 29*
Faucets, Compression Type, Leaking, *page 121*
Faucets, Repairing Non-Compression or Single Lever Types, *page 122*
Faucets, Squealing, *page 126*
Faucets, Types of, *page 128*
Faucet Handles, Replacing, *page 129*
Hose Faucet, Replacing, *page 186*
Leaky Packing Nut, *page 198*
Sink, Bath and Shower Faucets, How to Replace, *page 305*

☐ **Fireplaces, Checking**

To test if a fireplace will draw well, open the damper, crumple some newspapers on the inner hearth and light

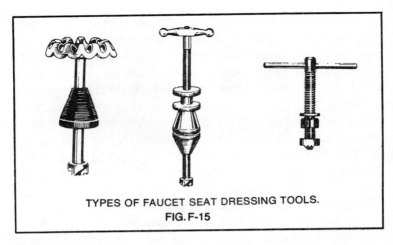

TYPES OF FAUCET SEAT DRESSING TOOLS.
FIG. F-15

them. If the fireplace is working properly, it will draw immediately; one that is simply usable will take about a minute to draw. If the paper burns poorly with considerable smoke hovering around or the fire goes out, the fireplace isn't drawing.

Make sure the fireplace has a damper. If not, install one to prevent the loss of heat up the flue. If the fireplace has a tendency not to draw well when burning logs, burn a number of newspaper sheets in it before starting the fire. This will help warm and dry the flue, improving the draft. You may also find it helpful to build the fire as far back on the inner hearth as possible.

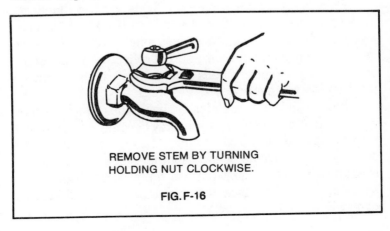

REMOVE STEM BY TURNING
HOLDING NUT CLOCKWISE.

FIG. F-16

If the fireplace is used regularly, it is a good idea to have the chimney inspected annually. Dirt and soot lower the effectiveness of the flue and can also cause a fire in the chimney. To check, look up or down the flue with a strong flashlight. If you can see deposits of soot, the flue needs to be cleaned. To clean the flue, load a burlap bag with old rags and lower it from the top of the chimney. Make sure you have the rope securely fastened to the bag and the bag securely closed to keep it and its contents from getting stuck in the flue. It is better to use the services of a professional chimney cleaner for he has vacuum cleaners capable of doing a better and cleaner job than homemade cleaners.

The top of the chimney flue may be covered with galvanized wire mesh to keep sparks and embers from blowing out and setting fire to your roof or possibly that of a neighbor. The wire mesh can become clogged with soot and dirt or with falling leaves, making it difficult or impossible to start a fire due to reduced draft. The mesh also serves to keep small animals, such as squirrels, mice, or other rodents from entering the chimney.

A *chimney cap* is more desirable than the wire mesh for it not only supplies protection from the danger of fire, but seldom requires attention. It also keeps rain from falling into the flue.

☐ Floodlights

Floodlights are high intensity lights used to illuminate an outdoor area. A *spotlight* is a form of floodlight but uses just a single bulb concentrated on a single area. Floods are generally equipped with some sort of reflecting shade; spots are not. Both types, floods and spots, can be obtained mounted on a swivel socket.

Floods and spots are electric light bulbs. Because they use considerable electric power, they become extremely hot after being on for just a short time. The wiring for floods and spots must be capable of carrying the total electric current required without getting warm in the process. Floods and spots also require fuses that can meet the total current demand.

You can calculate the current requirements of floods and spots by dividing their wattage rating by 115. Add the total power requirements of the spots and floods. Thus, if all the bulbs have a total power demand of 2 kilowatts (2,000 watts), then 2,000/115 = 17.39 amperes. This is a strong current. While a 20 ampere fuse would be satisfactory, the wires connected to the flood or spot sockets should be able to carry at least 20 amperes, but preferably 25. Do not use floods or spots with an extension cord, unless the cord has a current rating in excess of the total current requirements of the bulbs.

See Electric Fuses, *page 105*

Electric Shock, How to Avoid, *page 107*

☐ Floors, Sanding

You can remove shellac or any other floor finish by using a rented sander. Remove all furniture from the room and any rugs, including scatter rugs. Make sure all floor lamps have been disconnected and put into another room. If the floor is made of pine, it may not be worthwhile sanding since pine is soft and doesn't wear well. Oak floors are best. Make sure all floor boards are secure. If any are loose, nail them down. Measure the area of the room and take this information with you when you rent the sander. This will give your paint dealer some idea of the number of sandpapers you will need. At the same time, discuss with your paint dealer the kind of finish you should apply. Some are longer lasting (and more expensive) than others.

If you have never used a sander before, get your paint dealer to show you how to load sandpaper into the machine and how to do so correctly. The sandpaper must fit tightly into the machine. Never try to put sandpaper in with the machine running. Don't depend on the on/off switch; instead, remove the power plug from the outlet. Get into the habit of doing this every time you put fresh sandpaper into the sander.

Start with coarse sandpaper and move diagonally across the floor. Work back and forth and avoid going in circles. You will need to keep a strong grip on the handle of the sander, for it will have a tendency to move along by itself. Do not keep the sander in any one spot since this will gouge the floor. As long as the sander is running, keep it moving.

After the old finish is removed, replace the sandpaper with a medium grade and operate the machine once, going with the grain of the wood. Do so again using fine sandpaper.

You will not be able to get into corners with the large sanding machine; nor will you be able to reach that part of the floor that joins with the walls. For this you will need a hand sander. The hand sander will have a circular sanding element. As with the large sander, start with coarse paper, then use medium, and end with fine. Examine the floor carefully to see if there are any spots missed by the large sander or which seem to require additional sanding. You can take care of these with the hand sander.

It isn't always possible to use a machine to reach every area of the floor, particularly around pipes, radiators, or corners. For these areas you may need to sand by hand, use a scraper or possibly both.

After sanding is completed, vacuum the floor to make sure all wood dust has been picked up. In some areas you may need to use a broom, but you can sweep the dust out to where the vacuum cleaner can get at it. You can now brush on the finish you have selected. A single coat is seldom adequate. After applying the first coat, let it dry thoroughly and then sand the entire surface lightly using fine sandpaper. Vacuum the floor thoroughly, sweep if necessary, and then put down the second finishing coat.

Do not allow anyone to walk on the floor for several days. After the second coat of floor finish has dried, put down some sheets of plain brown paper if for some reason traffic in the room is necessary. While newspapers are sometimes used, there is always the chance that newsprint will be transferred to the floor. Brown paper bags, salvaged from supermarket shopping tours, can be cut apart and used. Such bags are also much stronger than newspaper and have less tendency to tear. Make sure any printing on the bag is on the upper side.

See Shellac, Applying Liquid, *page 301*

☐ Floors, Squeaky

A sqeaking floor is almost always caused by a loose board rubbing against an adjacent one. There are two problems involved in squeaking floors: finding the offending location and being able to get at the board to stop the noise. To pinpoint the squeaking section, have someone walk back and forth across the suspected area while you put your ear to the floor.

If you can get at the floor, that is if it isn't covered by a stair tread or wall to wall carpeting, you can make a temporary cure by squirting a silicone lubricant between the boards that are rubbing together. A better and more permanent solution is to use screws or nails on the loose section.

The squeak may come from the floor or from the subflooring. If the squeak is in the finish floor, use a pair of long finishing nails at the trouble spot and drive them in at a 45° angle to each other. Hammer the nails in so their heads are below the surface of the finish floor. The holes made by the finishing nails will be quite small and not noticeable, but if you prefer, you can fill the holes in with wood dough. Be careful when hammering in the nails as the head of the hammer can damage the floor finish. Drive the nails in almost all the way, and then finish the job by using a *nailset*. If you don't have a nailset, available in hardware stores, you can use a regular long penny nail for this purpose. Rest the point of the penny nail on the head of the finishing nail, and then hammer on the penny nail to drive the balance of the finishing nail into the wood.

The squeaky floor problem may be due to the floor joists which support the subfloor on which the finish floor rests. Again, it may be necessary to have someone walk on the finish floor while you listen with your ear close to the floor joists. Sometimes a floor joist will not be absolutely true— that is, the surface on which the subfloor rests will not be flat. There will be a space between the top part of the joist and the subfloor. In that case, just drive a wedge in between the joist and the subfloor. Drive the wedge in gently so as not to make a permanent fit but just a temporary cure. Have someone walk on the floor above. If the squeak has disappeared, remove the wedge and cover both sides with glue (Fig. E-17). Replace the wedge, but don't drive it in so far that it will raise the subfloor. You can also drive several nails through the wedge, but make sure the nails will not be so long that they will come through the finish floor.

If several of the subfloor boards are loose, nail a wooden block to the upper part of the joist so that the subfloor has a surface on which to rest. Make sure the block has a smooth flat upper surface so as to make maximum contact with the subfloor.

If the finish floor is covered with carpeting which cannot be removed, but you have located a squeak in the finish floor, you will need to work from below the floor. Use a wood screw and drive it through the subfloor. The screw must be long enough to reach the finish floor, but not to go through it.

See Floors, Sanding, *page 135*
   Hammers, *page 163*
   Nails, Types of, *page 214*
   Shellac, Applying Liquid, *page 301*

☐ Floor Tiles—Loose, Broken or Damaged

There are two basic kinds of tiles—those used for bathroom and kitchen walls and those for floors. Loose floor tiles, or damaged tiles, can be dangerous, while a similar situation for walls is unsightly.

Floor tiles can change color with age. They also change color because of floor traffic and the various cleaning agents that are used. Replacing a tile often means that the new tile is conspicuous. However, in time the new tile will blend in somewhat with the older ones. When having a tile floor put down for the first time, save excess tiles for repair jobs.

To remove the loose or damaged tile, you will need to warm the adhesive holding it. You can use a brazing torch or an iron, but put a cloth between the faceplate of the iron and the tile. Start with a corner of the tile and apply heat until you can pry up the tile with a putty knife. A putty knife is preferable to a screwdriver since the putty knife has a much broader working surface. After you have managed to lift one

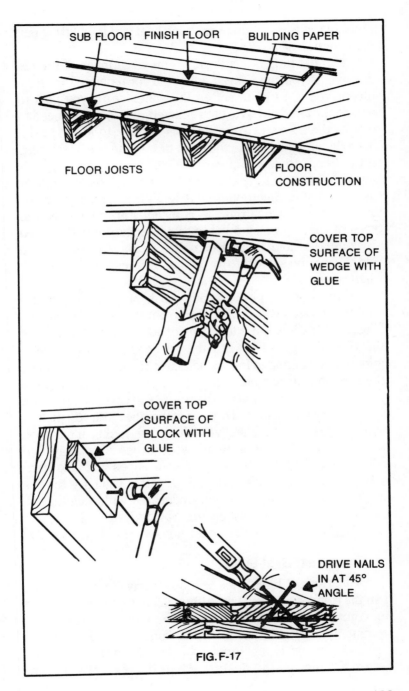

SUB FLOOR FINISH FLOOR BUILDING PAPER

FLOOR JOISTS FLOOR CONSTRUCTION

COVER TOP SURFACE OF WEDGE WITH GLUE

COVER TOP SURFACE OF BLOCK WITH GLUE

DRIVE NAILS IN AT 45° ANGLE

FIG. F-17

139

corner of the tile, continue applying heat and then lifting one small section at a time.

With the help of a scraper, remove as much of the old adhesive as you can. Check with your local paint store for a solvent you can use to soften the adhesive. If you plan to salvage the tile you have just removed, you will also need to remove the adhesive from its back surface to use it again. The solvent may damage the front face of the tile or the tiles on the floor, so use with care.

You can cut the replacement tile with a linoleum knife or shears or with a fine tooth saw (Fig. F-18). It all depends on the material of which the tile is made. For extremely stiff types of tile, you may be able to score the top side. Then break the tile along the score mark. Tile may be brittle when cold and may be subject to fracturing. It is less likely to break when warm.

Using a putty knife or a paint brush, spread the adhesive on the floor area where you plan to put the replacement tile (Fig. F-19). Also, put a few dabs of adhesive on the back of the tile and spread it with the putty knife. Wait several minutes, long enough for the adhesive to become tacky, and then set the tile in place. You can apply considerable pressure to the tile by walking on it. Be sure to cover the tile with a cloth, for two reasons. The first is that the cloth will pick up some of the excess adhesive. The other is that it's a good idea to keep the adhesive off your shoes. You may find adhesive difficult to remove, and your shoes will also track adhesive to other parts of the house. After you have the tile in place, wipe away any excess adhesive with a cloth.

See Asphalt Tile, Replacing or Laying, *page 21*

Bathroom or Kitchen Tiles, Loose or Broken, *page 30*

☐ Fluorescent Light Bulbs

Fluorescent light bulbs or tubes are available in various lengths from 15 to 60 inches, although longer tubes are made for commercial use. They are also available in circular form, commonly used in kitchens. White fluorescent tubes can be purchased in two types: *standard* and *deluxe* (Table F-1). The letter X indicates the deluxe. White fluorescent bulbs are

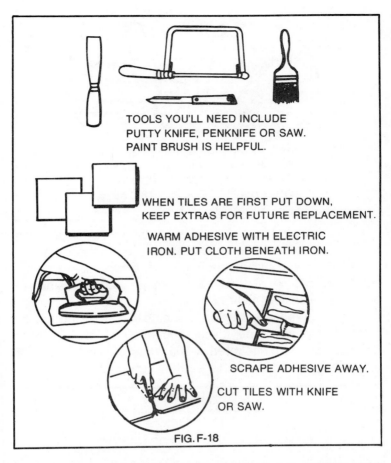

TOOLS YOU'LL NEED INCLUDE
PUTTY KNIFE, PENKNIFE OR SAW.
PAINT BRUSH IS HELPFUL.

WHEN TILES ARE FIRST PUT DOWN,
KEEP EXTRAS FOR FUTURE REPLACEMENT.

WARM ADHESIVE WITH ELECTRIC
IRON. PUT CLOTH BENEATH IRON.

SCRAPE ADHESIVE AWAY.

CUT TILES WITH KNIFE
OR SAW.

FIG. F-18

sold in "two colors," warm white and cool white. WW is used
as an abbreviation for warm white, CW for cool white. A
deluxe fluorescent is identified as either WWX or CWX. The
first of these is warm white deluxe; the second is cool white
deluxe. Various combinations of fluorescents, or fluorescents and incandescents are possible to get various kinds of
light.

Fluorescent bulbs supply more light per watt than incandescent light bulbs and are less costly to operate. However, fluorescent lights are electrical noise producers and, if
located near to an AM radio, will make that radio sound
noisy.

APPLY ADHESIVE TO FLOOR AREA WITH
BRUSH OR PUTTY KNIFE. WALK ON TILE
AFTER IT IS IN POSITION. ROLLING
PIN IS USEFUL TOOL FOR THIS ALSO.
FIG. F-19

Another problem with fluorescent fixtures is they can sometimes produce a flickering effect. For this reason it may be helpful to use such lights in groups of two, three or four. Since they will not all flicker at the same rate, the result will be a more constant light output.

With incandescent lights, one bulb may easily be substituted for another. Thus, it's no problem to replace a 50-watt incandescent with one rated at 100 watts. But in the case of fluorescent lights, the wattage rating determines the size. A

TABLE F-1
Selection Guide for Fluorescent Tubes
(All are T12 (1½ inch diameter) tubes)

Use	Wattage and color
Reading. writing. sewing:	
Occasional	1 40w or 2 20w, WWX or CWX.
Prolonged	2 40w or 2 30w, WWX or CWX.
Wall lighting (valances. brackets, cornices):	
Small living area (8-foot minimum)	2 40w, WWX or CWX.
Large living area (16-fot minimum)	4 40w, WWX or CWX.
Grooming:	
Bathroom mirror:	
One fixture each side of mirror	2 20w or 2 30w, WWX.
One fixture over mirror	1 40w, WWX or CWX.
Bathroom ceiling fixture	1 40w, WWX.
Luminous ceiling	For 2-foot squares, 4 20w, WWX or CWX 3-foot squares, 4 30w, WWX or CWX 4-foot squares, 4 40w, WWX or CWX 6-foot squares. 6 to 8 40w, WWX or CWX.
Kitchen work:	
Ceiling fixture	2 40w or 2 30w, WWX.
Over sink	2 40w or 2 30w, WWX or CWX.
Counter top lighting	20w or 40w to fill length, WWX.
Dining area (separate from kitchen)	15 or 20 watts for each 30 inches of longest dimension of room area, WWX.
Home workshop	2 40w, CW, CWX, or WWX.

142

15-watt tube is 18 inches while a 40 watt tube is 48 inches. Thus, you cannot substitute one for the other.

See Ceiling Light, Defective, *page 42*
     Electrical Connections, How to Insulate, *page 94*
     Electrical Wire Color Code, *page 102*
     Electric Shock, How to Avoid, *page 107*
     Incandescent Bulbs, Three Way, *page 188*
     Lamps, How to Fix, *page 197*
     Light Bulbs, Maintenance of, *page 202*

☐ Fungus Stains on Wood Trim

Try removing with a solution of warm, soapy water. If this doesn't work, scrub with a water solution of trisodium phosphate (TSP). TSP and commercial fungus stain remover products are available in paint stores.

See Aluminum Siding, Streaking, *page 22*
     Mildew (on Painted Surfaces), *page 210*

☐ Fuse Boxes

A home may be equipped with one or more *fuse boxes*, possibly a main box and a supplementary box. An apartment may have a small fuse box in a clothes closet or located near the entrance doorway (Fig. F-20).

Some fuse boxes are equipped with a handle type switch located on the outside of the box used for turning off all power going into that box. It's a good idea to turn that switch to its off position before replacing any fuses. This means you will need to have a flashlight handy, a blessing in disguise since its concentrated beam of light will enable you to spot a blown fuse much more quickly.

If some of your appliances seem to be temperamental and operate intermittently, make sure all fuses are screwed in tightly. Check by turning them clockwise.

If the fuse box has enough room, keep a supply of new fuses in the box for test and replacement purposes. Never replace a fuse with one having a higher or lower current rating. Most fuse boxes use plug fuses that are screwed into a socket very much like a lamp socket.

Don't try to salvage blown fuses. They are of no value, and you may add to your fuse replacement difficulties if the fuse gets mixed in with new ones.

You should know the room or rooms and hallways controlled by each fuse. Make a chart and put it alongside the fuse box. Then, when an appliance, light or switch doesn't work, you will know immediately which fuse to look for.

When replacing fuses, remember that electricity can be a silent killer. Your hands and feet should be dry. Don't let your feet make contact with the floor, particularly if it is wet. Wear shoes or slippers. If the cement floor has a tendency to be damp, cover it with a dry board big enough for you to stand on comfortably.

Each branch circuit should be protected by the correct fuse size (Table F-2). Branch circuits in the home generally use 14 gauge wire. The maximum safe load is obtained by multiplying the fuse current rating by the line voltage, generally taken as 115. Thus, if the fuse size is 20 amperes, $20 \times 115 = 2300$.

See Fuse Pullers, *page 145*

Fuses, Replacing, *page 146*

Fuses, Type of, *page 147*

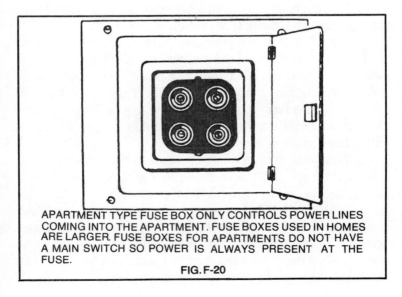

APARTMENT TYPE FUSE BOX ONLY CONTROLS POWER LINES COMING INTO THE APARTMENT. FUSE BOXES USED IN HOMES ARE LARGER. FUSE BOXES FOR APARTMENTS DO NOT HAVE A MAIN SWITCH SO POWER IS ALWAYS PRESENT AT THE FUSE.

FIG. F-20

TABLE F-2

Fuse Size (amps)	Maximum Safe load (Watts)	Wire Gauge
15	1725	14
20	2300	12
30	3450	10
50	5750	6

☐ Fuse Pullers

One type of fuse that may be used in the home is the *cartridge*. It looks like a small cylinder and is mounted and held at its ends by a strong spring action metal clip. Because of the strong snap-in action, such fuses are sometimes difficult to remove just by using fingers. Cartridge fuses are often wired directly into the main power service coming into the home. Since the fuses have metal ends, there is the possibility of an electric shock if they are removed by hand.

For this purpose you can use a *fuse puller*, also useful for bending fuse clips, adjusting loose cutout clips and for handling "live" electrical parts (Fig. F-21).

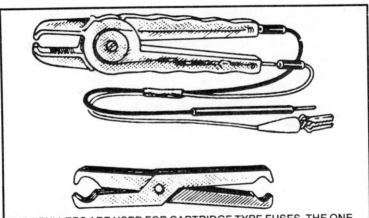

FUSE PULLERS ARE USED FOR CARTRIDGE TYPE FUSES. THE ONE AT THE TOP HAS A BUILT IN NEON GLOW LAMP WHICH CAN BE USED FOR TESTING FOR THE PRESENCE OF 117V AC. IT HAS A PAIR OF TEST LEADS WHICH CAN BE INSERTED IN THE ENDS OF THE HANDLES. THE PULLER AT THE BOTTOM DOESN'T HAVE THIS TEST FETURE.   FIG. F-21

Fuse pullers are made of some insulating material such as fiber or plastic so they can be used safely. One type, made of see-through plastic, contains a small neon glow tube which can be used for testing the ac power line. The fuse puller can be used at the service box to determine which, if any, of the cartridge fuses are defective. Fuse pullers are not needed with circuit breaker type fuse boxes.

□ **Fuses, Replacing**

A blown fuse can be caused by a short circuit in wiring, in an appliance or electrical fixture, or by a momentary current surge in the wiring. If the wiring is carrying the maximum amount of current protected by the fuse, a momentary demand for current by some appliance could cause the fuse to blow.

To replace a blown fuse, first disconnect all electrical equipment such as lamps, radios, televisions, and appliances serviced by that particular branch line. Examine the main fuse box and remove the blown fuse. This will be the one having a smudge across the top. Replace the fuse with one having the same amperage rating. When doing so, make sure your hands and feet are dry and that you are standing on a dry floor.

After replacing the fuse, check to see if it has remained in good condition. If it immediately shows a smudge across the top, you have evidence of a short circuit in the ac line protected by that fuse. If the fuse remains in good working order, replace each appliance, one at a time. Every time you do so, check the fuse. If, in replacing a radio, television, or some electrical appliance the fuse blows, then that radio, television, or appliance has a short circuit in it which needs repair.

If you can replace all the components and have them operate without blowing the fuse, then the cause of the original blown fuse was due to a temporary overload. It is sometimes caused by too many appliances working at the same time, all drawing electrical power from the same ac branch line.

See Circuit Breakers, *page 45*
Electrical Wire Color Code, *page 102*
Electric Fuses, *page 105*
Electric Shock, How to Avoid, *page 107*
Fuse Boxes, *page 143*
Fuse Pullers, *page 145*
Fuses, Types of, *page 147*
Underwriters' Laboratories, *page 348*

□ Fuses, Types of

Fuses are protective devices used to prevent excessive current flow in ac lines due to overloads and short circuits. They not only protect wiring but also appliances connected to outlets serviced by ac lines. In so doing they reduce the possibility of a fire in the wiring.

A fuse is a type of automatic switch either set or designed to open when the electric current exceeds a predetermined limit. Some types of fuses, such as the plug fuse, can be defeated by using a fuse with a larger rating or by shunting it by a conductor.

The size of a fuse has no relationship to its current carrying capacity. Thus, a 15 ampere plug fuse is the same size as one that is rated at 30 amperes. One of the most commonly used plug fuses is the 15 ampere unit for protecting 14 gauge wire. If the current flowing through the wire remains at 15 amperes or less, the fuse will remain in good working order. A momentary increase in current may not "blow" the fuse, causing it to open, but a sharp rise in current will. A good rule to observe is that the current rating of a fuse should never exceed the current carrying capacity of the wire it protects.

Fuses contain a short length of some metal designed to melt at a specific amount of current. In the process of melting, the fuse element can spatter, so the fuse is housed in some sort of small container made of glass, metal, fiber or some combination of these.

The plug fuse has a screw-in socket much like that used on a light bulb (Fig. F-22). It has a window across the top covered with a translucent material such as glass. The purpose of this glass, a sort of fuse window, is to let you see the fuse element. If the fuse is in good condition, this element will be unbroken. If the fuse has "blown," there will be a black smudge across the fuse window.

Fuse windows have two different shapes, round and hexagonal. If the fuse has a rating of 15 amperes or less, the window is hexagonal. If the rating is 15 amperes or more, it is round. You will find some exceptions.

Fuse ratings for plug types are 3, 6, 10, 12, 15, 20, 25, and 30 amperes. One of the easiest ways to check a fuse is simply to examine it for telltale signs of window smudges. Sometimes, however, a fuse will open without smudging. Another test is to substitute a known good fuse for one that you suspect. It is a good idea to keep test fuses in a box near the fuse box simply to be used for testing purposes.

The fuse rating is often stamped as a number on the base of the fuse, although it is sometimes placed on the window. If you cannot determine the rating of a fuse, discard it. When you buy new plug fuses, make sure that they carry a current rating somewhere on the fuse.

Whether or not a fuse will blow not only depends on the amount of excess current, but the length of time the current is in excess and the speed with which heat can escape from the fuse. For a short circuit condition the fuse will open immediately. For an overload, the fuse may or may not open depending on the amount of overload and how long the condition lasts. Generally, if the overload is 50%, you can expect the plug fuse to blow in 1 to 15 minutes. Hence, a 10 ampere fuse and a current of 15 amperes in its line may not open at once but will do so within a 15 minute period.

A fuse isn't a precision device and has a wide overload tolerance. Most have a 10% overload capability. A 20 ampere fuse will be able to carry a current of 20 amperes plus 10% of 20 amperes or 2 amperes. This represents a total current of 22 amperes.

Fuses have an indefinite shelf life—that is, they do not deteriorate and can be stored.

A fuse that blows isn't always a positive indication of trouble in the wiring or in the appliance connected to that wiring via an outlet. Sometimes power lines become overloaded gradually. Various appliances are used and then, with the help of a cube tap, more appliances are connected to the same line. When these appliances are used separately, there is no trouble, but sooner or later they will all be used at the same time. That is when the overload occurs. In this way a blown fuse is an indication that a dangerous working condition has been reached and that a particular pair of wires carrying current are being overloaded.

When a plug fuse is "blown," it is no longer serviceable and must be replaced. To avoid the nuisance of installing a new fuse, you can use a plug type that is actually a thermal reset fuse. This fuse looks like a plug fuse except that it has a center push button. To reset the fuse, just depress it.

Another type of fuse is the cartridge, available in two forms: renewable and non-renewable. The non-renewable type is housed in a small cylinder made of a hard, fiber-like material. As in plug fuses, the cartridge contains a strip of metal designed to melt at some predetermined value of current.

The fuse element, inside the non-conducting body of the fuse, is connected at both ends either to a metal ferrule or end cap (Fig. F-23). These end caps or ferrules are used for snapping the fuse into a pair of spring metal holders. Cartridge fuses having end caps made of metal in cylindrical shape are snap-in types which usually have a 30 ampere rating. Those with a knife blade type of ferrule are generally designed to carry larger currents, 60 amperes or more.

PLUG FUSE HAS BASE SIMILAR TO THAT OF LIGHT BULB.

FIG. F-22

FERRULE

 CAP

CARTRIDGE FUSES CAN HAVE FERRULE END OR CAP. THE
FERRULE OR KNIFE BLADE TYPE IS DESIGNED TO CARRY
HEAVIER CURRENTS THAN THE CAP TYPE.

FIG. F-23

Some of these are capable of passing currents of up to 600
amperes. Knife blade cartridge fuses from 60 to 100 amperes
are 7-⅛ inches long while those having higher current ratings are longer.

In the renewable cartridge fuse the fusible metal strip
can be replaced. To replace the fusing element, remove the
ferrules, insert the new fuse strip, and then replace the
ferrules.

Cartridge fuses are intended for higher current ratings
than plug fuses. You can get them in current ratings of 3, 6,
10, 25, 30, 35, 40, 50, and 60 amperes. Up to 30 amperes the
fuses are 2 inches long, and for currents between 30 and 60
amperes the fuses are 3 inches.

Sometimes a power line overload condition is normal. If
the appliance you connect to the outlet is motor operated, the
starting current of the motor can greatly exceed its running
current. Thus, a starting current might be as much as 30
amperes, with normal operating current only 5 amperes.
Ordinary plug fuses used to protect ac lines delivering current to motors may blow regularly. For circuits such as these
you may need a *time lag fuse*, a fuse capable of tolerating an
overload for a longer time than the usual plug fuse.

See Circuit Breakers, *page 45*
Electrical Wire Color Code, *page 102*
Electric Fuses, *page 105*

☐ Garbage Disposal Unit, Inoperative

A *garbage disposal unit* is a motor operated device mounted in the waste pipe line leading from a sink, and is installed in the drainpipe between the sink and its trap. The advantage of a garbage disposal unit is that it grinds all waste into small particles and, since it is always used with water running, has the effect of scouring the waste line and keeping it clear.

Garbage disposal units are equipped with a quick opening fuse and a reset button. Any items which jam the motor of the garbage disposal will cause this fuse to open. When operating the garbage disposal, become accustomed to the kind of sound it makes. If you hear a harsh grinding noise, stop the disposal immediately for it may be working on a large bone, too strong for the garbage disposal to handle, or a knife, fork, or spoon may have fallen into the unit. With the power turned off, reach in and remove the object. Turn on the faucet to let cold water flow into the sink, and then turn on the switch controlling the garbage disposal. If the unit doesn't work, reset the fuse button mounted on the garbage disposal. If this doesn't work, you can unjam it with a special tool supplied with the garbage disposal device when it is first installed. This tool rotates the revolving element. After you have done this, push the fuse reset button, turn on the faucet once again and then the on/off switch for the garbage disposal.

See Appliances Do not Work, *page 23*

☐ Glass, Cutting

A *glass cutter* is a tool used for "cutting" glass, but actually there is no tool that does that. A so-called glass cutter is used for scoring the glass, breaking its surface tension and permitting the glass to break evenly along the score line.

When properly used, a glass cutter makes a distinctive sound. The best way to recognize that sound and to learn how to use a glass cutter correctly is to practice on scrap sections of glass.

Make sure the glass is clean, since dirt will prevent the wheel of the cutter from making a uniform score mark. During the scoring the glass must be supported, preferably on a flat surface covered with some old carpeting or rug. Examine the glass cutter and you will see that it has notches near one end. Hold the cutter so that these notches point down toward the glass. Don't hold the cutter vertically but at an angle.

Before using the cutter, "paint" the area where you intend to make the score mark with kerosene. Use a clean brush, preferably one that has not previously been used in painting. A cheap brush works very well.

Dip the cutter in some light machine oil. Wipe the tool but do not wipe the cutting wheel. Use a ruler or yardstick with the thick edge working as a guide for the cutter. Thus, if you are using a ruler, the beveled edge, if the ruler has one, will be away from the cutter.

Start at the far edge of the glass and bring the cutter toward the near edge using a single, unbroken, continuous stroke at the same time applying a firm, steady pressure on the cutter. Do not stop the scoring stroke once you have started it. Do not go over the score mark. The depth of the score mark isn't important. What is important is that there should be an unbroken score from one end of the glass to the other.

If the piece you have just scored has large areas of glass on both sides, put the yardstick beneath the glass directly along the line of the score mark, with the score on the upper surface of the glass. Press down on both sides of the glass with the palms of your hands, and the glass should break cleanly along the score. While it is easier to work without gloves, it is safer to wear them.

If you want to cut away a narrow strip of glass, score the glass with the cutting tool. Then use the notched edge of the glass cutter to break the strip away. An alternative method is to use a pair of parallel jaw pliers. Cover the jaws of the pliers with cloth to keep the metal away from the glass. Let the large section of glass rest on the flat surface of the scrap carpeting, but so that the narrow strip of glass which is to be removed hangs over the edge. You can then use the cutting tool's notches or the parallel jaw pliers to break away the small glass section. You will find the pliers easier to use. *See* Window Glass, How to Replace Broken, *page 379*

☐ Glazier's Points

See Window Glass, How to Replace Broken, *page 379*

☐ Grease Spots on Wallpaper

To remove grease spots, work on wallpaper as soon as this accident happens. Cover the spot with a sheet of soft white paper. Do not use paper that is glazed or has a shiny finish. Press an electric iron set to its medium hot position against the paper. Hold for just a few seconds, remove and then repeat. If the paper starts to scorch, stop. Set the iron to a lower heat setting and repeat. As the soft white paper becomes discolored by the grease, replace it. Paint stores also sell grease remover compounds, but the trick in getting rid of these spots is to work on them as soon as possible.

☐ Gutters and Downspouts, Maintaining and Repairing

The purpose of a *gutter* is to carry rain away from your roof and deliver it to a *downspout*. Gutters should be at a slight pitch so that water will flow downhill to the spouts. The gutters and downspouts work together as your roof drainage system.

Ideally, the gutter should drain completely. Water remaining in the gutter accelerates rust and is a breeding ground for mosquitos. Examine gutters after a rain to make sure they are draining. To maintain gutters, examine them twice a year and remove all accumulated leaves or other debris. Even if the gutter has a downward slant, leaves can cause water accumulation. You can minimuze this work by covering the gutters with a plastic mesh and putting wire strainers over the opening to the downspout. This doesn't completely eliminate the leaf and debris problem, but it helps minimize it.

The best way to clean a gutter is to get up on a ladder and remove leaves and twigs by hand. After doing so, run scrap cloth along the inside length of the gutter to reveal any possible rust spots.

After the gutter is clean, pour a bucket of water into the gutter and watch its movement. It should flow smoothly and easily toward the downspout. If it does not or tends to form a pool, then the downward slope of the gutter is incorrect. You can also check the slope of the gutter with a bubble glass. Gutters are held in place by hangers or by spikes covered with sleeving. Adjust them if necessary. Generally, just one or two of these gutter supports need to be modified.

The gutter and downspout are at right angles to each other. Since this is a sharp bend, it is quite easy for it to become clogged. Clogging is evident when the gutters fill with water, even though they have a good down slope, with a higher level of water at the area near the downspout.

To clean out a downspout, use a plumber's snake. As you work the snake through the downspout, keep filling the downspout with water. This will help break up accumulated deposits of debris and flush them away. To prevent further problems of this kind, install a leaf strainer at the top of the downspout.

Gutters are made of aluminum, plastic, and galvanized steel. Aluminum and plastic are more desirable since they do not rust. Theoretically, galvanized steel should also be immune, but it can rust where the plating wears off. To remove rust spots, scrape thoroughly with a wire brush. When you are finished, the cleaned area should be shiny with no rust spots showing. Cover the area by painting it with a thin coating of asphalt roof paint (Fig. G-1). If you get the stuff on

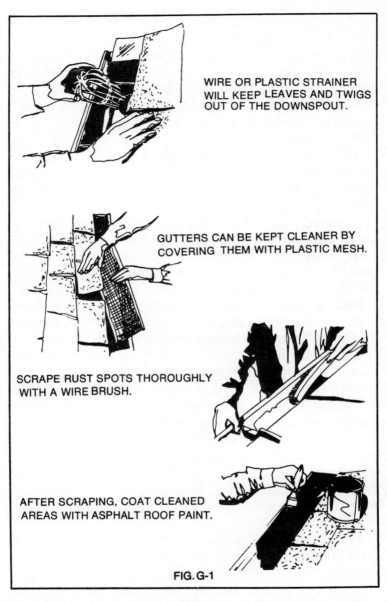

WIRE OR PLASTIC STRAINER WILL KEEP LEAVES AND TWIGS OUT OF THE DOWNSPOUT.

GUTTERS CAN BE KEPT CLEANER BY COVERING THEM WITH PLASTIC MESH.

SCRAPE RUST SPOTS THOROUGHLY WITH A WIRE BRUSH.

AFTER SCRAPING, COAT CLEANED AREAS WITH ASPHALT ROOF PAINT.

FIG. G-1

your hands, remove it with kerosene. Then cover with a coating of plastic cement or roof cement.

If any large section of a gutter or downspout is so severely rusted that there are holes in it, the best thing to do

156

is to replace the entire section. It is also possible to get a leak in a gutter or downspout joint. This can be repaired by using-50-50 solder and a brazing torch. Before soldering, make sure the entire area is not only clean but bright. Remove all rust and paint. If you are working with a galvanized gutter, clean until the zinc coating is removed. You can use a wire brush, a file, or emery cloth.

Apply the flux to the thoroughly cleaned joint, on both sides. Apply the flame of the brazing tool near the joint but not on it. The joint must be hot enough to melt the solder so it runs down into the joint. Work your way along the joint until you have a continuous seam of solder. After you have finished, wipe the joint clean so no flux remains. The reason for this isn't to make the joint look attractive, but to remove the flux whose chemical composition may attack the joint.

If a hole in a gutter isn't too large, you can repair it with roofing cement. Make sure the area around the hole is clean and dry. Apply the roofing cement and then cut a strip of roofing paper, large enough to cover the hole and put it firmly into the roofing cement. Then apply more roofing cement on top of that. Don't build up the repair since it will then act as a block to the free movement of water in the gutter.

If the hole is in a gutter made of aluminum, you can do a repair with liquid aluminum cement. Kits are also available for making gutter repairs. They contain all the required supplies and directions.

Water from the downspout should exit onto a cement *splash block*. The purpose of the splash block is to take the water away from the foundations of the house. The splash block should be on a downward slope away from the house, with a slope of about 1 inch per foot (Fig. G-2). Do not simply lay the splash block on the ground. Instead, dig a shallow trench so that the edges of the splash block are flush with the ground. If you are located in a region where heavy rainfall is common, you can add an extra length of downspout. It is easier, though, to use a rollout plastic spray hose at the bottom of the downspout, so called since it is rolled up when not in use and is unrolled by the force of water entering it from the downspout. The best type to get is the one that has a

157

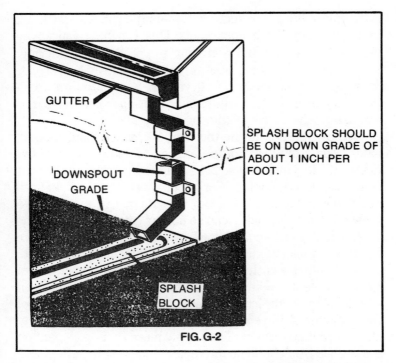

GUTTER

DOWNSPOUT
GRADE

SPLASH BLOCK SHOULD
BE ON DOWN GRADE OF
ABOUT 1 INCH PER
FOOT.

SPLASH
BLOCK

FIG. G-2

number of tiny holes so that the exiting water is distributed over a large surface area instead of one spot, where it can cause a soil washout.

You can also pipe the roof water to a storm water drain, a dry well about 15 feet or more from the house. Make sure the bottom of the dry well is lower than the basement floor of the house. The dry well should be in earth that drains rapidly; otherwise, you will get surface flooding.

In some areas where rain is heavy and persistent, or where the position of the house encourages the movement of water into the basement, a splash block may be inadequate. Roof water can be routed away from the house by using pipe. Fit one end of the pipe over the bottom end of the downspout. Dig a trench to accommodate the pipe and lead it to a storm water drain or dry well, so that the water emerges to the surface at least 15 feet away from the house. To prevent freezing that could lead to bursting of the pipe, make sure the trench holding the drainpipe is below the frost line (Fig.

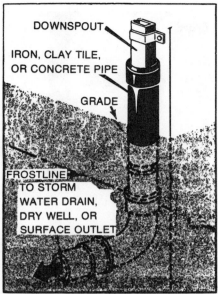

DOWNSPOUT

IRON, CLAY TILE,
OR CONCRETE PIPE

GRADE

FROSTLINE
TO STORM
WATER DRAIN,
DRY WELL, OR
SURFACE OUTLET

PIPE CAN BE USED TO ROUTE WATER FROM THE DOWNSPOUT TO
A WATER DRAIN OR DRY WELL. PIPE SHOULD EXTEND BELOW THE
FROST LINE.

FIG. G-3

G-3). The pipe can be iron, clay tile, concrete or plastic. Of these, plastic is probably the most desirable since it will not rust and is lightweight, easy to handle. Iron pipe is sometimes used in this application, but it is heavy and will rust.

See Aluminum, Joining, *page 21*
Basement, Waterproofing, *page 27*
Brazing, *page 34*
Damp Basements, *page 71*
Exterior Metal Surfaces, Painting, *page 119*
Metals, Joining, *page 208*
Rust, Removing, *page 288*
Soldering, *page 312*

☐ Hacksaws, How to Use

A *hacksaw* is desirable on two counts. It is inexpensive and useful for many in-home repair jobs. You can use it to remove rusted nuts and bolts and for cutting wood, metal, plastic, steel, or copper pipe.

There are two basic types of hacksaw, one with an adjustable frame and the other with a fixed, solid frame. Either type consists of two parts—the frame and the blade. The adjustable type is more suitable for in-home repairs for you can use blades of different lengths (Fig. H-1). You can replace blades when worn, and you can use blades intended for specific jobs.

For the adjustable hacksaw you can get blades ranging from 10 to 12 inches in length. The length of the blade is measured between its two mounting holes, one at either end of the blade. The blades are made of tungsten alloy steel or high-speed steel. You can buy blades in packages of five or 10, but buying a package of blades is more economical than getting one at a time. Since the spare blades can rust, give them a light coating on both sides with machine oil. Wipe the blade with a cloth and then wrap the blades in newspaper held in place with rubber bands. You can then store the blades until you need them.

The adjustable hacksaw has a wing nut at one end—the end adjacent to the handle. To remove the blade, loosen this nut and the blade will come right out. A common error is not putting the blade in correctly. Hold the blade so that the teeth of the blade point away from the handle and so that they face downward. The blade has two holes which mount on pins. Put the blade so the holes fit over the pins and then tighten the wing nut (Fig. H-2). Make the wing nut finger tight; it isn't necessary or desirable to use a tool.

After you mount the blade, examine it before you completely tighten it. It should be straight and not curve or twist anywhere along its length. If it does, you will not be able to cut straight and you may snap the blade.

Since you have a choice of coarse blades, those having fewer teeth per inch, or fine blades, those having the most teeth per inch, it sometimes becomes a problem of selecting a blade. A blade with coarse teeth will cut faster and will not become clogged as quickly with metal burrs. But you may find it very difficult to cut with such a blade, particularly through tempered metal.

Hacksaw blades have 14 to 32 teeth per inch. The larger the number of teeth, the finer cut you can make. When you must cut through a rather thick metal, try a blade having 14 teeth per inch. You could, for example, use such a blade when cutting through iron. Steel is harder, so for large sections try a blade having 18 teeth per inch. For heavy pipe, copper, brass or angle iron, use a blade with 24 teeth per inch. For thin copper tubing, use a blade having 32 teeth per inch (Fig. H-3).

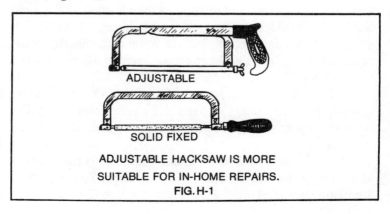

ADJUSTABLE

SOLID FIXED

ADJUSTABLE HACKSAW IS MORE
SUITABLE FOR IN-HOME REPAIRS.
FIG. H-1

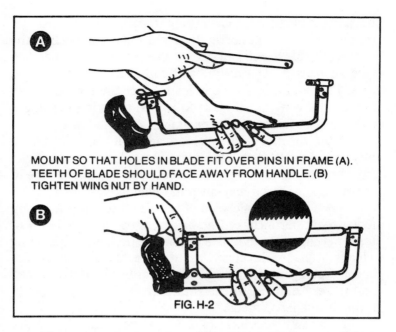

MOUNT SO THAT HOLES IN BLADE FIT OVER PINS IN FRAME (A).
TEETH OF BLADE SHOULD FACE AWAY FROM HANDLE. (B)
TIGHTEN WING NUT BY HAND.

FIG. H-2

The cutting action takes place only on the push stroke. If you can, lift the saw just slightly on the return stroke to make your work easier.

To hold the hacksaw correctly, extend the finger adjacent to the thumb along the frame (Fig. H-4). Hold the pistol grip of the hacksaw tightly with your other fingers. Use your other hand to hold the opposite end of the frame. Of course, since you are using both hands on the frame of the saw, the work will need to be held in place. A vise is ideal. Using both hands on the hacksaw has two advantages. It helps you control and guide the tool, letting you put maximum thrust against the tool. It also keeps your fingers away from the cutting teeth.

With some metals you will find yourself unable to do more than to take short strokes. However, when possible, cut with long strokes and use as much of the blade length as you can.

From time to time you will have hacksaw cutting jobs in which the frame will interfere with the work. You can adjust the blade so it is at right angles to the frame (Fig. H-5). As

14 TEETH PER INCH

18 TEETH PER INCH

FOR LARGE SECTIONS
OF MILD MATERIAL

FOR LARGE SECTIONS
OF TOUGH STEEL

24 TEETH PER INCH

32 TEETH PER INCH

FOR ANGLE IRON. HEAVY
PIPE. BRASS. COPPER

FOR THIN TUBING

HACKSAW USAGE DEPENDS ON THE NUMBER OF TEETH PER INCH
FIG. H-3

you cut through metal, you may find it necessary to readjust the position of the work in the vise.

Cutting thin metal may be easier from a cutting point of view, but it is also possible for the saw to deform the work. To prevent this, mount the metal between two blocks of wood which are then held in a vise. You can also use a single block and one or more C clamps to hold the work (Fig. H-6).

□ Hammers

For general in-home repairs, a claw hammer, 12-13 ounces, is suitable. The best type is one having a metal

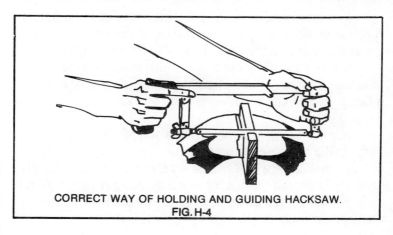
CORRECT WAY OF HOLDING AND GUIDING HACKSAW.
FIG. H-4

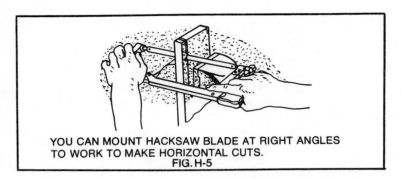

YOU CAN MOUNT HACKSAW BLADE AT RIGHT ANGLES
TO WORK TO MAKE HORIZONTAL CUTS.
FIG. H-5

handle that is integral—that is, one piece, with the head. This eliminates permanently any chance for the head of the hammer coming off. The head of the hammer is useful for driving nails; the claw section is ideal for removing them.

You get maximum hitting power by holding the handle at its end. To start a nail, hold it firmly and then tap it gently with the hammer. All you want to do at the start is to get the nail firmly positioned in the wood. Then remove your fingers from the nail and hit the nail straight. If you are nervous about holding a nail to get it started this way, use a pair of pliers instead.

If you want to avoid hammer marks on wood, use a nail set as a means of driving the nail in. If you don't have a nail set, use another nail as a driver for the final ⅛ of an inch. What you can do this way depends on the kind of nail you are driving.

For removing nails, use the claw end of the hammer. You can avoid getting hammer marks on the wood by putting a small wood block under the head of the hammer (Fig. H-7).

If a nail bends while you are driving it, you have two choices. You can try to straighten the nail, using a pair of pliers. Or you can remove the nail and start all over again with another nail.

If you want to avoid splitting wood while driving a nail, first drill a hole, either partially or completely. If partially, the nail will have a better grip on the wood. If completely, there will be less chance for wood splitting. Make sure the hole you drill has a diameter that is less than that of the nail you are driving.

You can use a hammer for straightening nails. Use the anvil part of a vise or else hammer the nails straight on a concrete surface.

The *curved claw* nail hammer (generally referred to as a claw hammer) is used for driving nails or nail sets. For light work, use a 7-ounce hammer. For heavier work with common nails, try a hammer whose weight is in the 12 ounce to 20 ounce range. You will get greater driving force if you hold the hammer near the end of the handle, but better control as you move your hand closer to the opposite end. The head of the hammer should be parallel with the head of the nail. Glancing blows, blows at an angle, can bend the nail. Always start a nail by tapping lightly until the point of the nail has pierced the wood surface so that the wood grips the nail, holding it firmly in place.

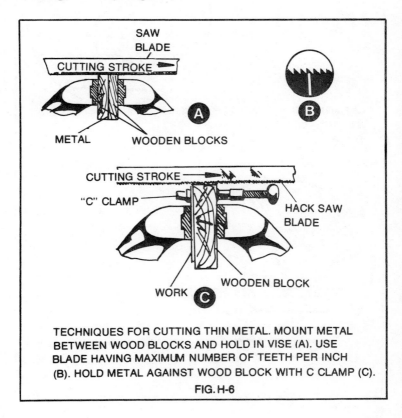

TECHNIQUES FOR CUTTING THIN METAL. MOUNT METAL BETWEEN WOOD BLOCKS AND HOLD IN VISE (A). USE BLADE HAVING MAXIMUM NUMBER OF TEETH PER INCH (B). HOLD METAL AGAINST WOOD BLOCK WITH C CLAMP (C).

FIG. H-6

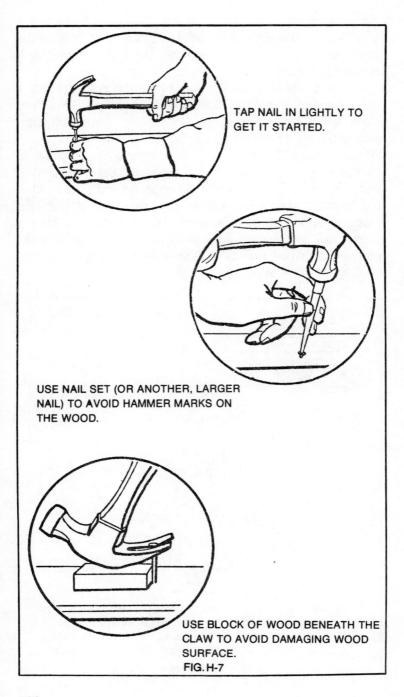

TAP NAIL IN LIGHTLY TO GET IT STARTED.

USE NAIL SET (OR ANOTHER, LARGER NAIL) TO AVOID HAMMER MARKS ON THE WOOD.

USE BLOCK OF WOOD BENEATH THE CLAW TO AVOID DAMAGING WOOD SURFACE.
FIG. H-7

Use a ripping hammer for opening wooden boxes, crates or separating nailed boards. The ripping hammer is almost the same in appearance as the claw hammer, but in the ripping hammer the pronged end is flatter.

For working with metal, such as driving in rivets, use a *ball peen* hammer. Start by driving the rivet with the ball end and then complete the job with the opposite, flat end of the hammer.

Tacks are sometimes difficult to drive because of their small size. Get a *tack hammer* that is a magnetic type. This will help hold the tack so you can drive it easily.

For heavy work such as driving a wedge for splitting logs, use a sledge hammer. These range in weight from 2 pounds to 20 pounds.

For driving cold chisels, large nails, spikes and stakes, use the double faced blacksmith hammer. A mallet is used for driving wood chisels or any other tool having a wood handle.

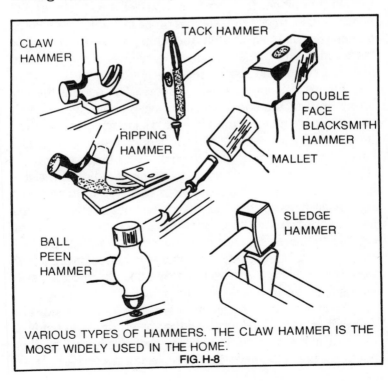

VARIOUS TYPES OF HAMMERS. THE CLAW HAMMER IS THE MOST WIDELY USED IN THE HOME.
FIG. H-8

Mallets are made of plastic, rubber, and wood. The relatively soft face of the mallet will not damage wooden handled tools (Fig. H-8).

To keep metal tools from rusting, wipe them occasionally with machine oil. It is best to store them in areas having low humidity.

☐ Hex (Hexagonal) Wrench

See Wrench, Allen, *page 389*

☐ Hinges, How to Install

Hinges are available in a variety of sizes, styles, shapes, and materials. They may be reversible, non-reversible, left-hand, or right-hand. So the first step in installing a hinge is to make a correct selection. The job is easy if you simply plan to replace a hinge, but not all that simple if you must decide on the hinge to use.

With a hinge, the object is to attach two parts, one of which is fixed in position and the other movable. With some hinges you can mount so that the hinge can be transposed or reversed. Other hinges are made specifically for a left-hand door or a right-hand door. These are non-reversible hinges.

Figure H-9 shows a pair of doors. The door at the left opens inward; the one at the right opens out. Even though both doors are mounted on a left-hand supporting frame, they require different hinges. The first door needs a left-hand hinge the second door needs a right-hand hinge.

Now suppose the door is to be mounted on the right-hand frame (Fig. H-10). The door that opens in requires right-hand hinges; the door that opens out needs left-hand hinges. As you can see, whether a door calls for left or right-hand hinges depends on two factors: whether the door opens in or out and whether the door is mounted on the left or right frame. Note that if you switch a door from suspension on a left frame to a right frame, you also switch hinges.

You may need to define what is meant by the outside of a door. Obviously, if a door faces the street, the street side of the door is the outside. For the interior of a house or other building, the outside is that side facing a corridor. In an

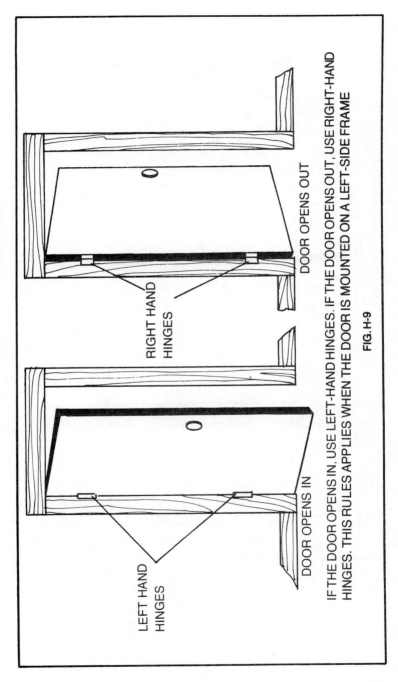

LEFT HAND HINGES

DOOR OPENS IN

RIGHT HAND HINGES

DOOR OPENS OUT

FIG. H-9

IF THE DOOR OPENS IN, USE LEFT-HAND HINGES. IF THE DOOR OPENS OUT, USE RIGHT-HAND HINGES. THIS RULES APPLIES WHEN THE DOOR IS MOUNTED ON A LEFT-SIDE FRAME

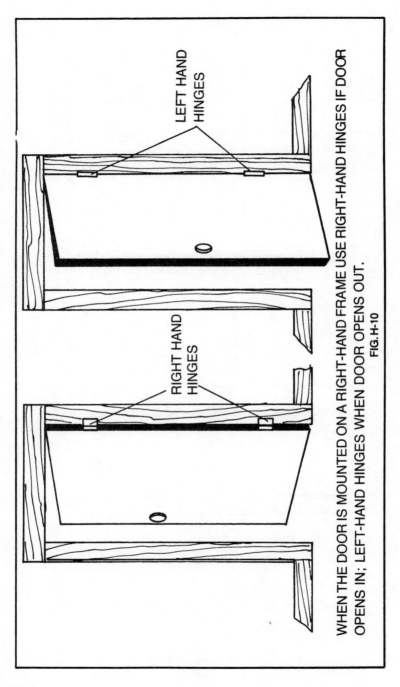

RIGHT HAND HINGES

LEFT HAND HINGES

WHEN THE DOOR IS MOUNTED ON A RIGHT-HAND FRAME USE RIGHT-HAND HINGES IF DOOR OPENS IN; LEFT-HAND HINGES WHEN DOOR OPENS OUT.

FIG. H-10

apartment house, all the doors face a corridor with their outside surfaces. The reason it is important to have this information is that it will help you determine if you need left or right-hand hinges. Stand on the outside of the door. If the door opens away from you and moves to the right, it will require right-hand hinges. If it opens away from you to the left, then you will need left-hand hinges.

The Butt Hinge. The butt hinge is a good example of a reversible hinge (Fig. H-11). You can use it for doors (such as cabinet doors) mounted on either the left or right side frames. The butt hinge is one of the simplest types. Like all other hinges, you can get it in a large variety of sizes, shapes and styles. The holes in the hinge (as in all other hinges) are pre-drilled, with the hinge often held in place by a total of eight flat head machine screws. When properly mounted, the screw head should be flush with the metal surface of the hinge. Screws are often supplied with hinges in the same package. The color of the head of the screw should match that of the hinge itself. However, if you plan to paint over the hinge, the original color is of no consequence.

The Pin Butt Hinge. The pin butt hinge is so-called since the pin joining the two parts of the hinge is removable

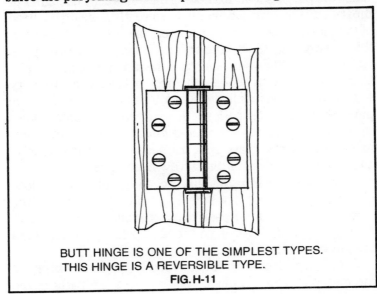

BUTT HINGE IS ONE OF THE SIMPLEST TYPES.
THIS HINGE IS A REVERSIBLE TYPE.
FIG. H-11

USE LOOSE PIN BUTT HINGE IF YOU WANT TO BE
ABLE TO REMOVE DOOR WITHOUT REMOVING HINGE.

FIG. H-12

(Fig. H-12). However, the loose pin butt hinge can be a left-hand or a right-hand type, so here you must select carefully depending on the type of mount you want.

Since the butt hinge and the loose pin butt hinge look so much alike, why use one in preference to the other? The advantage of the loose pin butt hinge is that you can remove the door without unscrewing the hinge. Just force the pin up and out and the job is done. This is desirable if you plan to remove the door for cleaning, painting or polishing; otherwise, the common butt hinge is just as good a choice.

One problem with the loose pin butt hinge is that sometimes the pin gets lost. Removing the pin is easy enough. Put the flat edge of a screwdriver blade directly beneath the head of the pin and then, using a hammer, tap the opposite end of the screwdriver, the handle end, until the pin starts to move up. If the hinge has been painted, the pin may tend to stick. Chip away the paint beneath the head of the pin and then try to push the pin out using the screwdriver and hammer. If the pin is bent, your only option will be to replace it. Sometimes the only way you can get a replacement pin is to buy a new hinge. If the screws have been painted over, you may need to chisel away the paint in the screw head slots.

Loose Joint Hinge. This hinge is similar to the loose pin butt hinge except that the pin is built into one half of the hinge, and there is no possibility of losing it (Fig. H-13). With this type of hinge, all you need do is to lift the door until the pin clears the hinge.

To keep hinges working smoothly, put a few drops of machine oil along the hinge center where the parts of the

172

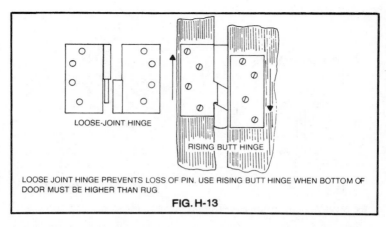

LOOSE-JOINT HINGE

RISING BUTT HINGE

LOOSE JOINT HINGE PREVENTS LOSS OF PIN. USE RISING BUTT HINGE WHEN BOTTOM OF DOOR MUST BE HIGHER THAN RUG

FIG. H-13

hinge make moving contact. After oiling, wipe clean with a cloth.

Rising Butt Hinge. Sometimes, you may want the bottom of the door to clear an obstruction, such as a rug. With the rising butt hinge the door not only swings out, but up at the same time, giving the door a chance to clear a rug. When the door is closed, it swings in and also down. When installing a hinge of this type, put a firm support beneath the door, such as a section of ¼-inch plywood. This will help you make sure the door will clear the rug or other obstruction at the bottom of the door. If you let the door rest on the rug at the

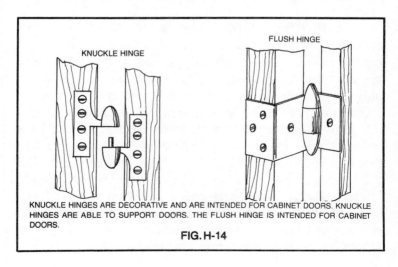

KNUCKLE HINGE

FLUSH HINGE

KNUCKLE HINGES ARE DECORATIVE AND ARE INTENDED FOR CABINET DOORS. KNUCKLE HINGES ARE ABLE TO SUPPORT DOORS. THE FLUSH HINGE IS INTENDED FOR CABINET DOORS.

FIG. H-14

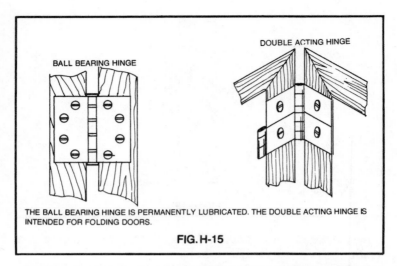

DOUBLE ACTING HINGE

BALL BEARING HINGE

THE BALL BEARING HINGE IS PERMANENTLY LUBRICATED. THE DOUBLE ACTING HINGE IS INTENDED FOR FOLDING DOORS.

FIG. H-15

time you install the hinge, there will always be considerable friction between the bottom of the door and the rug surface.

Knuckle Hinge. There are a number of variations of the loose joint hinge, and the knuckle hinge is one of them. The pin of the knuckle hinge is smaller than that of the loose joint hinge, and it becomes easier to mount and dismount doors. Another advantage is that the knuckle hinge is somewhat more decorative (Fig. H-14). When the door is closed, just the "knuckle," a relatively small part of the hinge, is visible.

Flush Hinge. Door hinges are required to support considerable weight, so you cannot assume all hinges are capable of doing this. Some hinges, such as the flush hinge, are intended for cabinets or for use on lightweight doors only. Flush hinges are made with a variety of decorative sections that are visible when the cabinet doors are closed.

Ball Bearing Hinge. Lubricating a hinge can be a nuisance since the moving parts are mounted in such a way that it is often difficult to get in at them with lubricant. The ball bearing hinge solves this problem since it is permanently lubricated (Fig. H-15). Such hinges are often used on doors that open to a building exterior, and they get much more opening and closing action than other doors. Ball bearing hinges for exterior doors are heavy duty types.

174

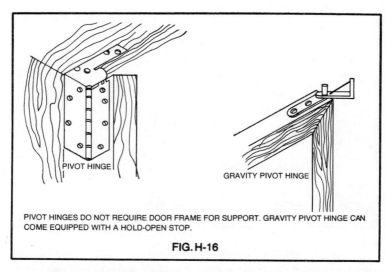

PIVOT HINGE

GRAVITY PIVOT HINGE

PIVOT HINGES DO NOT REQUIRE DOOR FRAME FOR SUPPORT. GRAVITY PIVOT HINGE CAN COME EQUIPPED WITH A HOLD-OPEN STOP.

FIG. H-16

Double Acting Hinge. The double acting hinge is designed for folding doors. The hinge is made so it lets the door open in either direction.

Pivot Hinge. Use this hinge for overlay doors which are recessed or flush doors. Unlike the butt and loose pin butt hinges, the pivot hinge does not need a door frame for mounting. Another type of pivot hinge is the gravity pilot hinge. You can get these with or without a hold-open stop (Fig. H-16).

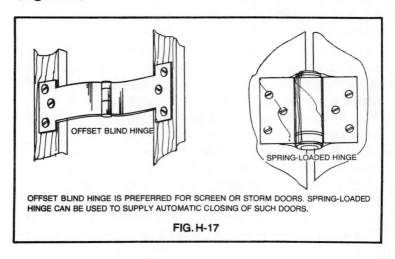

OFFSET BLIND HINGE

SPRING-LOADED HINGE

OFFSET BLIND HINGE IS PREFERRED FOR SCREEN OR STORM DOORS. SPRING-LOADED HINGE CAN BE USED TO SUPPLY AUTOMATIC CLOSING OF SUCH DOORS.

FIG. H-17

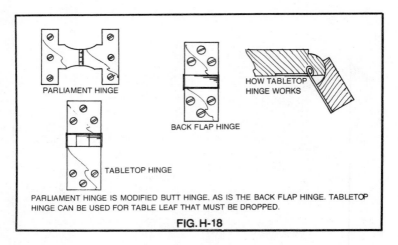

PARLIAMENT HINGE

BACK FLAP HINGE

HOW TABLETOP HINGE WORKS

TABLETOP HINGE

PARLIAMENT HINGE IS MODIFIED BUTT HINGE. AS IS THE BACK FLAP HINGE. TABLETOP HINGE CAN BE USED FOR TABLE LEAF THAT MUST BE DROPPED.

FIG. H-18

Offset Blind Hinge. You will find offset blind hinges used on storm doors or screen doors (Fig. H-17). The hinges are often held in place with self tapping screws if the fastening is for metal to metal. If the screen door is aluminum, use aluminum screws. Contact between different metals produces galvanic action, corroding screw threads and the area around the screw hole. Ultimately the screw loosens and doesn't support the hinge. Offset blind hinges are designed to let doors open fully without being restricted by the hinge.

With hinges of all types, there may be a temptation to use fewer screws than the hinge can accommodate. If the hinge calls for a total of eight screws, for example, use eight and not a lesser number. This will distribute the pulling force of the door on the hinge and will make the hinge/door combination more secure. If a screw becomes loose, tighten it. If the screw can no longer get a grip on the door frame, pack the screw hole with part of a wooden matchstick or toothpick. This will enable the threads of the screw to get more gripping surface.

Spring-Loaded Hinge. Automatic door closers are often used with storm or screen doors. In place of such closers, you can use spring-loaded hinges. These springs have a built-in mechanism that pulls the door closed after it has been opened. They also have the further advantage that they exert pressure against the opening of the door, keeping the door from slamming against an inside wall. You can get spring loaded hinges that have a screw for adjusting the spring tension. Such hinges supply years of service if they get a drop or two of lubricating oil from time to time.

Parliament Hinge. The parliament hinge is a modified form of butt hinge and is reversible. You can use this hinge if, for some reason, you want the pin of the hinge to project out beyond the face of the door. Size for size, the parliament hinge does not have the support strength of a butt hinge. The pin length is smaller than the butt hinge.

Back Flap Hinge. Like the parliament hinge, the back flap hinge is a modified form of butt hinge (Fig. H-18). However, it doesn't have much support strength and generally has fewer screw holes than the butt hinge. You will find it more commonly used in furniture. The back flap hinge is a reversible type.

Tabletop Hinge. This hinge is called tabletop because of its use in tables having a leaf that may be lowered. Unlike most of the hinges described so far, the tabletop hinge isn't made up of two equal hinge parts. One section of the hinge is longer than the other. Tabletop hinges are usually placed so they aren't visible, but you will also find some that are deliberately used as part of furniture decor.

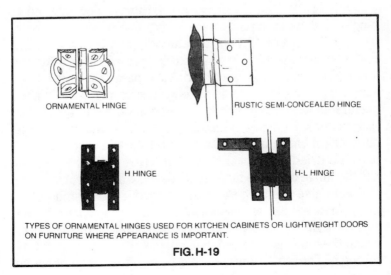

ORNAMENTAL HINGE

RUSTIC SEMI-CONCEALED HINGE

H HINGE

H-L HINGE

TYPES OF ORNAMENTAL HINGES USED FOR KITCHEN CABINETS OR LIGHTWEIGHT DOORS ON FURNITURE WHERE APPEARANCE IS IMPORTANT.

FIG. H-19

Ornamental Hinge. You will often find ornamental hinges used on kitchen cabinets and also on furniture (Fig. H-19). The screws are designed to match the color and finish of the hinge, but it is frequently difficult to find exact screw replacements. Instead of a single screw, you may need to replace a complete set. Where the ornamental hinge is made of solid polished brass, it is a good idea to coat the hinge with clear lacquer or polyurethane to avoid repeated polishing.

Semi-Concealed Hinge. Hinges can be concealed so they do not show when the door is closed, and this can be done either wholly or partially. Semi-concealed hinges can be quite ornate. Some are hammered iron; others are brass. Hinges of this kind are also used to supply a rustic appearance. H and H-L hinges belong to the semi-concealed hinge family. They are so-called because of their fancied resemblance to the letters H and H-L. The H and H-L hinges show more of the hinge than the semi-concealed types and are often used on cabinets, such as kitchen cabinets, where decor is important. When buying such hinges, make sure they match cabinet pulls and are in harmony with the kitchen design in general. For example, rustic type hinges would seem out of place in a modern kitchen with heavy emphasis on chrome.

Strap, T And Continuous Hinges. You may need hinges that must support very heavy doors, such as those used by garages or "lift up" basement types. One such hinge is the strap, made of iron. Strap hinges come in different sizes. The strap hinge is a reversible type with a built-in pin. When used outdoors, it is a good idea to paint the hinge, preferably with a rustproof paint to protect the hinge against the weather. Or apply a suitable primer followed by a coat of outdoor oil-base paint. Be sure to oil the pin area after the paint has dried. Paint cannot reach in to the pin, but water can and the hinge can have inner rust. Oiling will prevent this and will also give the hinge a chance to work more smoothly.

When you use wood screws with the strap hinge, select screws that will make a deep penetration of the wood to which the hinge is fastened, but which will not go completely through. The screw head should fit into the hinge holes so

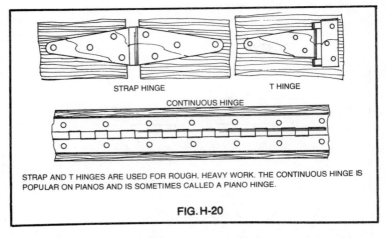

STRAP HINGE   T HINGE

CONTINUOUS HINGE

STRAP AND T HINGES ARE USED FOR ROUGH, HEAVY WORK. THE CONTINUOUS HINGE IS POPULAR ON PIANOS AND IS SOMETIMES CALLED A PIANO HINGE.

FIG. H-20

that the head is slightly below the flat surface of the hinge. Check before you use the screw. Fit the screw through one of the holes in the hinge. The hole edge should be able to support the flat head of the screw—that is, the screw should not fall through the hole. The entire body of the screw must go through the hole without force.

The T-hinge is like the strap hinge, except it isn't a reversible type. The disadvantage of the strap hinge is that it requires a rather wide frame. You can use a much narrower frame with the T-hinge. Like the strap hinge, the T-hinge is intended for heavy duty.

The continuous hinge, also known as a piano hinge, is a reversible type popular for use on pianos, cabinets, and chests (Fig. H-20). Although the cabinet hinge isn't used on doors, its length permits it to sustain a rather heavy load. It has numerous screw holes on both sides of a built-in pin. Continuous hinges are available in a number of finishes and can also be had with chrome plating. Old piano hinges were often made of nickel plate on brass. When restored and polished, they often add beauty and charm. Because of the large number of screws, the finish of the screw heads should match that of the hinge.

Installation. The part of a butt hinge containing the pin is known as the knuckle. When installing butt-type hinges, most require recessing into the frame and door. When

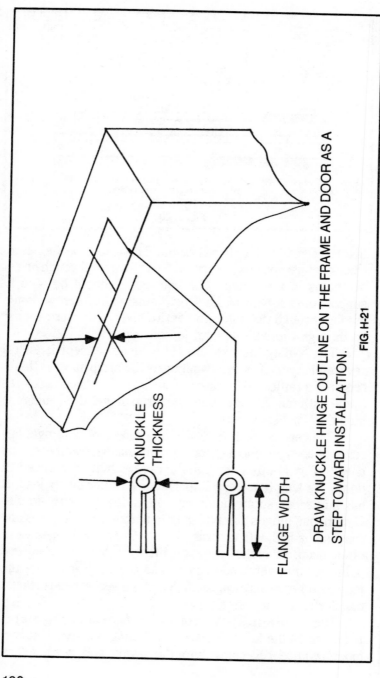

KNUCKLE THICKNESS

FLANGE WIDTH

DRAW KNUCKLE HINGE OUTLINE ON THE FRAME AND DOOR AS A
STEP TOWARD INSTALLATION.

FIG. H-21

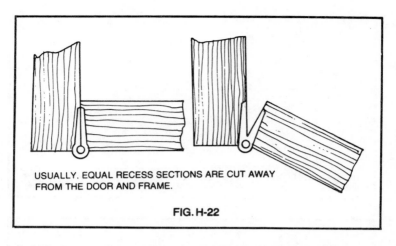

USUALLY. EQUAL RECESS SECTIONS ARE CUT AWAY
FROM THE DOOR AND FRAME.

FIG. H-22

finished, the hinge surface must be flush with the frame and
also with the door. When the door is closed both halves of the
hinge will face each other, with just a slight separation
between them. Only the knuckle of the hinge will be exter-
nally visible.

To install such a hinge, lay it against the door and use
the hinge as a guide in drawing an outline (Fig. H-21). Do the
same with the wood frame. Mark the thickness of the knuckle
on the side of the door.

Most commonly, the hinge is recessed into both frame
and door. Make the recessing equal on both (Fig. H-22).
However, if you prefer, you can cut the recess entirely into

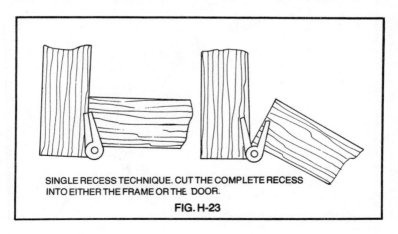

SINGLE RECESS TECHNIQUE. CUT THE COMPLETE RECESS
INTO EITHER THE FRAME OR THE DOOR.

FIG. H-23

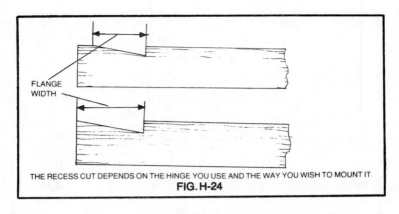

FLANGE WIDTH

THE RECESS CUT DEPENDS ON THE HINGE YOU USE AND THE WAY YOU WISH TO MOUNT IT.

FIG. H-24

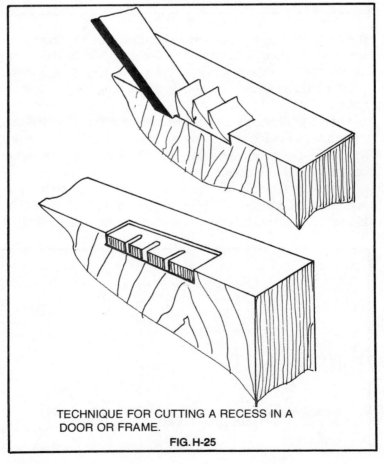

TECHNIQUE FOR CUTTING A RECESS IN A
DOOR OR FRAME.

FIG. H-25

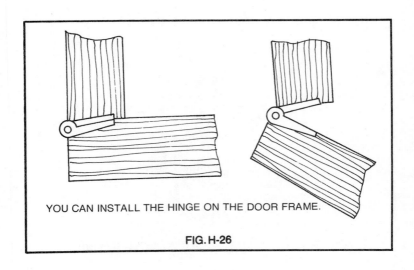

YOU CAN INSTALL THE HINGE ON THE DOOR FRAME.

FIG. H-26

the door or entirely into the frame. This method has the advantage of requiring less work. If you recess both door and frame, then you must make sure they are both in perfect alignment. This problem is eliminated when you use a single recess (Fig. H-23). However, you must still align the door with the frame so that when you finally have the door

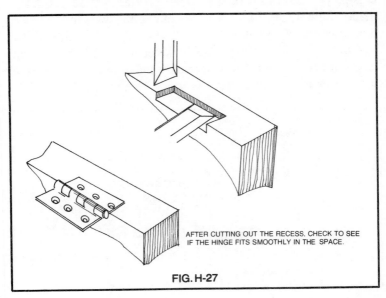

AFTER CUTTING OUT THE RECESS, CHECK TO SEE IF THE HINGE FITS SMOOTHLY IN THE SPACE.

FIG. H-27

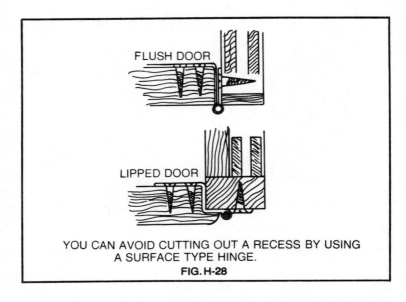

FLUSH DOOR

LIPPED DOOR

YOU CAN AVOID CUTTING OUT A RECESS BY USING
A SURFACE TYPE HINGE.

FIG. H-28

mounted, it is centered between the floor and the top frame of the doorway.

To make the recess or cutout for the hinge, make a series of notches with a saw (Fig. H-24). Using a wood chisel, put the blade of the chisel on the outline you have made of the hinge. Make a series of indentations in the wood with the help of a mallet. Don't try working with a chisel that is dull or whose cutting edge is severely knicked. You can chisel a recess with the previously made saw cuts, letting you remove a small section of wood at a time (Fig. H-25).

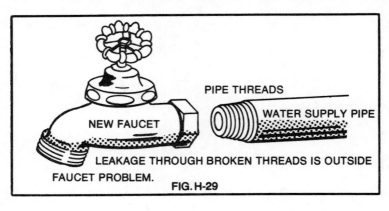

PIPE THREADS

NEW FAUCET

WATER SUPPLY PIPE

LEAKAGE THROUGH BROKEN THREADS IS OUTSIDE
FAUCET PROBLEM.

FIG. H-29

The cuts you made along the outline of the hinge will not only establish the boundaries of work for the chisel, but should keep the wood from splitting too far.

After you have chiseled out the recess for the hinge, fit the hinge into it to see if the surface of the hinge is completely below the surface of the frame or door. You may have a few rough spots which prevent this. If so, you can remove them by sanding or by using the chisel.

When mounting a door, and you need to cut out two or more recesses, do just one. Mount the hinge, using the least number of screws possible and then, supporting the door, see if it will open and close properly. You may need to move the hinge, so you may be required to alter the recess in one direction or the other. If the door opens and closes properly, mount the first hinge securely by putting in the remainder of the screws (Fig. H-26). With the door correctly in position, you will now find it much easier to install the remaining hinges.

It is easily possible to put a hole in the wrong place for a hinge. A good method of avoiding this, after you have cut out the recessed area, is to fit the hinge in place and use it as a template (Fig. H-27). Insert a pencil in each hole and draw the outline of the hole. Then use a nail and position it as close to the center of the hole as possible. Drive the nail in a very short distance. The nail impression in the wood will give you your starting point for the screws.

If, however, you do put a hole in the wrong spot, fill the hole with wood dough or pound in some matchsticks. You will need to do this if the new hole you want to have is very close to the one that was incorrectly located. Otherwise, you need not bother, since the hinge will cover up the unneeded hole.

Not all hinges require recessing. You can buy surface mount hinges and use these for flush and lipped doors (Fig. H-28).

See Nails, Types of, *page 214*
   Screwdrivers, *page 292*
   Screw Holes, Repair of, *page 297*
   Screws, *page 297*

185

☐ Hose Faucet, Replacing

Outside faucets are used for making connections to garden hoses. Sometimes the threads on the faucet used for connecting the garden hose become stripped possibly due to forced cross threading of the hose, or become corroded (Fig. H-29). Other problems include leakage due to a worn washer or valve seat, or because the faucet no longer makes a waterproof connection with the water supply pipe.

To replace the outside faucet, shut off the water supply, and then open the faucet handle to let any water drip out. You will need two wrenches for this job. Put one wrench on the water supply pipe to keep it from turning. Use the other wrench to turn the faucet in a counterclockwise direction.

After the faucet is off, wipe the water supply pipe threads clean and dry with a cloth. Coat the threads with pipe joint compound and then mount the new faucet. If the threads of the water supply pipe and those of the new faucet do not engage easily and smoothly, don't force the faucet on. Turn the faucet gently by hand until you feel the threads engaging, and then make one or two turns in a clockwise direction. You can then use your wrench to make sure the faucet is on securely, and while doing so keep a good grip on the wrench holding the water supply pipe to keep it from turning.

Turn on the water supply valve and then the faucet itself. If you spot any leakage from the faucet, wait for a few minutes to see if it continues. If it does, shut off the water supply, remove the faucet and wrap the threads with some lightweight string. Add more pipe joint compound and then replace the faucet. Make sure the faucet fits tightly. Turn on the water supply and then the faucet handle.

See Aerator, How to Install, *page 16*
    Bathroom Faucets, Installing, *page 29*
    Faucet Handles, Replacing, *page 129*
    Faucet Seat, Dressing a, *page 131*
    Faucets, Compression Type, Leaking, *page 121*
    Faucets, Repairing Non-Compression or Single Lever Types, *page 122*

☐ Incandescent Bulbs, Three-Way

Unlike an ordinary electric light bulb, the three-way type has two filaments and uses a special socket called a three-way. The filaments can be operated separately and, since they are different types, can supply different amounts of light. Thus, one of the filaments could be a 50 watt type, and the other a 100 type, capable of supplying the same amount of light as an ordinary 50 watt or 100 watt bulb. When the two filaments are combined, the light output is equivalent to their sum, or 150 watts. Three-way lamps use either medium or large (*mogul*) bases. The mogul size is used when large amounts of light are needed.

If one of the filaments burns out, you can still use the bulb. In a 50/100/150 watt bulb, if the 50 watt filament burns out, you can still use the bulb as a 100 watt unit. Similarly, if the 100 watt filament burns out, you can still use it as a 50 watt type. In either case you can no longer use the bulb as a 150 watt unit. Three-way bulbs are generally more expensive than ordinary single filament types. See Table I-1.

See Dimmer Switches, *page 72*
Electric Bills, How to Save Money on, *page 103*
Electric Shock, How to Avoid, *page 107*
Extension Cords, *page 118*
Fluorescent Light Bulbs, *page 140*

☐ Iron Pipes, Repairing

You can repair iron pipes by *brazing* (Fig. I-1). Quite often the repair must be made at a coupling that cannot be replaced, because the coupling threads have rusted and the coupling cannot be removed. The rust permits the flow of water through the threads.

Thoroughly clean the area to be brazed. Use a wire brush and remove all rust and scale. Although the leakage

TABLE I-1 Sizes and Uses for Three-Way Bulbs		
Socket and wattage	Description	Where to use
Medium:		
30 70 100	Inside frost or white	Dressing table or dresser lamps, decorative lamps, small pin up lamps
50 100/150	Inside frost or white	End table or small floor and swing-arm lamps
50,100/150	White or indirect bulb with "built-in" diffusing bowl (R-40)	End table lamps and floor lamps with large, wide harps
50/200/250	White or frosted bulb	End table or small floor and swing-arm lamps, study lamps with diffusing bowls
Mogul (large):		
50/100/150	Inside frost	Small floor and swing-arm lamps and torcheres
100/200/300	White or frosted bulb	Table and floor lamps, torcheres

BRAZING IRON PIPE.

FIG. I-1

may come from a particular spot, do not just braze at that one point since the rusting action will continue. The water will eventually find its way out through some other section. Braze all around the edge of the coupling.

If the pipe is close to a wall and the wire brush will not fit into the available space, use emery cloth. If the pipe is near a combustible surface, protect that surface with a heat shield made of metal, or wet the surface and then cover it with wet rags. After the repair has cooled, wipe it thoroughly with a clean rag.

See Pipe, Cutting, *page 274*
 Pipe Joints, Loosening, *page 276*
 Pipe or Tank, Burst, *page 277*
 Pipes, Protecting, *page 279*
 Rust, Removing, *page 288*
 Water Pipes, Leaky, *page 364*

☐Joining Metals

See Metals, Joining, *page 208*

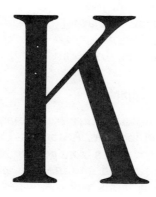

☐ Kitchen Sink, Protecting

Kitchen sinks can get stains which can be difficult to remove. Do not allow dishes to remain in the sink overnight, but clean the sink immediately after you are finished using it. Do not use steel wool for cleaning or an abrasive scouring powder. The best cleaner is soap and hot water.

Fruit and vegetable juices and fruit peelings will stain sinks if allowed to remain, often for not more than a few hours. Tea bags and coffee grounds will also produce stains.

Do not use the kitchen sink for disposing of chemicals used in hobbies such as photography. If you use the sink for washing pots and pans, do not put all of these into the sink. Instead, wash them one at a time, keeping the pot or pan above the surface of the sink. If you prefer to wash them all at one time by immersing them in a sink full of water, protect the surface of the sink with a thick pad made of plastic or rubber.

If your sink has a drain board that is uncovered, do not use it as a cutting board. Don't chop ice on it, and don't push or drag pots and pans across it.

See Aerator, How to Install, *page 16*

☐ Kitchen Trap, Replacing

Although known as *kitchen traps,* these are used for all sinks regardless of location. A trap is a U-shaped pipe that keeps waste and any gases from getting back into the sink. Wastes from the sink fall into the trap and sometimes accumulate there. When this happens, water backs up into the sink. Older style traps have a nut at the bottom of the trap. You can remove this nut by turning it counterclockwise with a wrench. Before you do, remove as much accumulated water from the sink as you can. After you have removed the nut, use a stiff wire to poke into the hole to pull out the accumulated blockage. A good homemade tool for this can be made from a wire coat hanger. Cut, a small *straight* section of the hanger, about 8 inches long. Bend one end of the wire into the shape of a U. Use this for cleaning out the trap.

Sometimes the nut "freezes" into position and cannot be removed. The nut threads may have rusted or the edges of the nut do not offer adequate gripping surface to a tool. You may find it better to replace the entire trap. New traps do not have a bottom nut. Instead, when they are to be cleaned out, the entire U section is removed.

To remove the old trap, start by putting a pan or a pot under it. This is to catch any water remaining in the trap. There are two nuts, marked A and C in Fig. K-1, which must be turned to free the trap. Using a wrench, rotate them counterclockwise. As you do, hold the trap with one hand to keep it from dropping in the pan below it.

To install a new trap, slide a new nut, marked A in the upper section of Fig. K-1, over the pipe, and a nut C over the vertical tube. Also, make sure there is a washer right below nut C. Adjust the trap so it fits snugly at both ends. One of these ends will connect to a vertical tube coming down from

194

the sink. The other end will connect to a section of horizontal tubing going into the drain.

Tighten nuts A and C by hand until you feel them engaging the threads on the trap. Then tighten with the help of a wrench.

The horizontal section of pipe leading from the trap to the drain is known as a *wall bend*. If you want to replace this pipe, start by moving back a circular bit of metal called a *flange*. The flange is decorative only and has no working function. It isn't fastened and simply hides the hole made in the wall for the wall bend.

With the flange out of the way, loosen nuts A and B, shown in the upper part of Fig. K-1. Note that in removing the wall bend it isn't necessary to remove the trap. After you have loosened nuts A and B, using a wrench, move them both back along the bend. The wall bend will then be free.

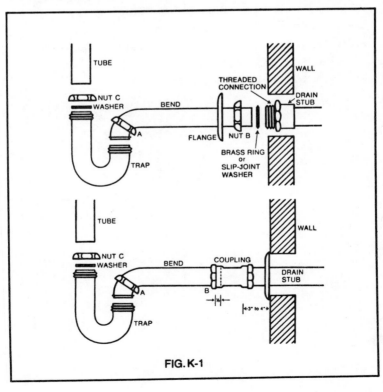

FIG. K-1

195

To replace the wall bend, just reverse the removal steps. Put in the new bend. Make sure there is a washer (sometimes a brass ring is used instead) between nut B and the drain stub. Tighten both washers, at first by hand, and then by using a wrench. Before making nuts A and B tight, make sure both fit on their threads. Adjust each nut a little at a time—that is, don't make one nut absolutely tight and then work on the other.

If the wall bend is too short to connect the trap to the drain stub, you can extend it by using a coupling as shown in the lower part of Fig. K-1. The drain stub should extend about ½ inch into the coupling. Tighten nut B (lower part of Fig. K-1) to hold the coupling firmly in place. Couplings come in various lengths. You can determine the size by measuring the distance between the end of the wall bend and the drain stub. Be sure to allow for ½ inch penetration of the coupling by the wall bend and the drain stub.

See Bathtub Drain, Clogged, *page 32*
    Clogging of Kitchen Sink, Preventing, *page 47*
    Drains, Clogged, *page 81*
    Sink Drain, Sluggish, *page 307*

□ Lamps, How to Fix

There are three problems associated with lamps. The lamp won't light, the light is intermittent, or the light varies in intensity—that is, it flickers. If the lamp doesn't light, try replacing the bulb. If this doesn't produce results, try a different outlet. To make sure the outlet is "live," plug a different appliance, such as a radio, into it. Try moving the plug while it is in the outlet. If the light turns on and off, the fault is due to poor contact between the plug and the outlet. With the lamp plug put into an outlet you are sure is "live," with a new bulb in the lamp and the lamp switch turned on, flex the lamp cord throughout its length. If this results in light, the lamp cord is defective and should be replaced.

If none of these tests produce results, take the plug out of the wall receptacle, remove the lamp and look into the socket. You will see a spring contact near the center of the base. Using a finger, reach in and pull this contact out slightly. Replace the bulb, put the plug back into its outlet, turn on the lamp switch, and the bulb should light.

A lamp assembly consists of a male plug, a length of lamp cord, and the lamp socket housing. The socket housing can be disassembled into an outer shell, an insulating sleeve, the socket and a cap (Fig. L-1). The socket fits into the cap, and the insulating sleeve fits over the socket. The metal

197

outer shell slides over the insulating sleeve and force fits into the cap.

To disassemble a lamp, first remove its plug from the power outlet. The lamp will have some kind of base, usually covered with a soft material such as felt. After you remove the base covering, you will see a hexagonal nut (Fig. L-2). This nut is screwed onto a long metal tube to which all the lamp parts are fastened. Remove the hex nut using pliers. This will permit the base to come off.

The lamp assembly is attached to the other end of the metal tube. Pull this assembly out about an inch or two and unscrew the socket assembly. Remove the outer shell and the insulating sleeve, thus exposing the socket. To remove the socket assembly, unscrew the two wires which come from the base through the metal tube. You can now replace the switch-socket assembly.

To assemble the lamp with its new switch-socket, just reverse the disassembly steps. Connect the two wires to the socket. Push the insulating sleeve over the socket, and then force the outer shell into position. Pull the wires taut through the metal tube, and fasten it to the base with the hex nut.

☐ **Leaky Packing Nut**

The nut that holds a faucet handle and its associated stem to the faucet body is called a *packing nut*. While most faucet leaks are due to faulty washers, sometimes water will also drip from the packing nut. The problem is due to faulty packing underneath the nut.

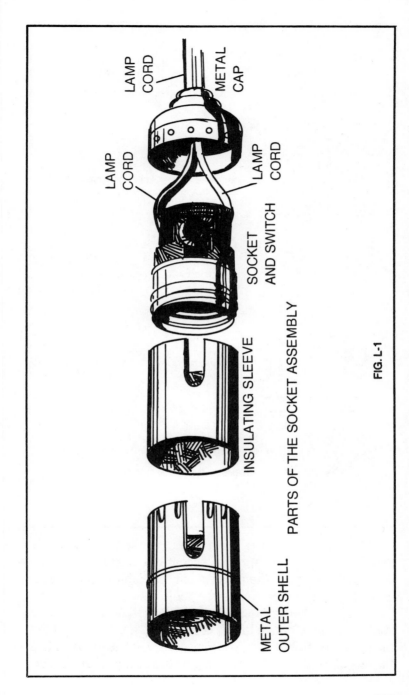

LAMP CORD

METAL CAP

LAMP CORD

LAMP CORD

SOCKET AND SWITCH

INSULATING SLEEVE

METAL OUTER SHELL

PARTS OF THE SOCKET ASSEMBLY

FIG. L-1

REMOVE CLOTH COVERING FROM BASE.

LOOSEN HEX NUT HOLDING CENTRAL METAL TUBE IN PLACE.

PULL SOCKET AND LAMP CORD SEVERAL INCHES OUT OF METAL TUBE.

DISCONNECT TWO WIRES. REPLACE SOCKET ASSEMBLY.

SCREW WIRES INTO PLACE. COVER WITH INSULATING SLEEVE AND OUTER SHELL. PUSH ASSEMBLY INTO METAL CAP. SCREW ENTIRE ASSEMBLY BACK ONTO THREADED END OF METAL TUBE.

FIG. L-2

Remove the nut using a monkey wrench, a suitable sized open end wrench, or a crescent wrench (Fig. L-3). To protect the finish of the packing nut, put a bit of scrap cloth around the nut before using the tool.

Turn off the water supply to the faucet. You may have a "below the sink" valve that is convenient. If not, shut off the main water supply valve. You may or may not need to remove the faucet handle first, depending on the design of the faucet.

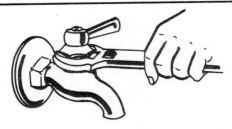

LOOSEN PACKING NUT WITH TOOL SUCH AS
OPEN END WRENCH, CRESCENT WRENCH, OR
MONKEY WRENCH. TURN TOOL COUNTERCLOCKWISE.

FIG. L-3

Don't remove the handle unless you find it necessary to do so.

The packing beneath the nut may be a washer or it may be *Teflon* coated faucet packing. The advantage of a washer is that it makes an exact fit, but you must be sure to get the right size. The advantage of the packing material is that you can use it on any faucet, regardless of size. You can also use *composition packing* (Fig. L-4). This is self forming, self lubricating and self sealing, forming a shape like a washer when under compression by the packing nut.

When using packing material, insert it into the open end of the packing nut (Fig. L-5). Replace the packing nut and turn it clockwise with your fingers until you feel the nut beginning to engage the threads which will hold it in place. Then tighten the nut with a tool.

See Aerator,How to Install, *page 16*

Bathroom Faucets,Installing, *page 29*

Faucet Handles,Replacing, *page 129*

COMPOSITION PACKING FOR PACKING NUTS IS
AVAILABLE IN TWO FOOT ROLLS.

FIG. L-4

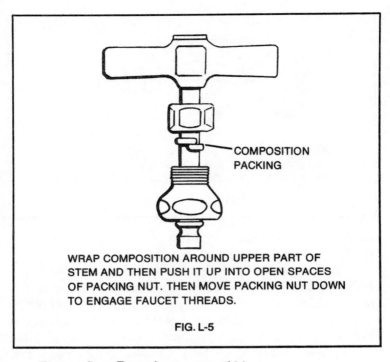

COMPOSITION PACKING

WRAP COMPOSITION AROUND UPPER PART OF STEM AND THEN PUSH IT UP INTO OPEN SPACES OF PACKING NUT. THEN MOVE PACKING NUT DOWN TO ENGAGE FAUCET THREADS.

FIG. L-5

☐ Light Bulbs, Maintenance of

Set up a bulb maintenance schedule to wash bulbs. Dirt on the outside of the bulbs reduces the amount of available light. Do not wash the bulbs until they have had a chance to become cool and reach room temperature. Don't depend on water alone; a small amount of any dishwashing liquid will work wonders. After cleaning, rinse with clear water, and then wipe dry. Make sure the bulbs are absolutely dry before replacing them in light sockets. If the bulbs are mounted in a light diffusing fixture, clean that as well.

Light bulbs used in outdoor locations such as patios and garages may sometimes "freeze" into position due to corrosion. To prevent this, remove the bulbs regularly and clean the threads. After cleaning, coat the threads with a thin layer of petroleum jelly. Put the petroleum jelly on the threads, and then use a clean cloth to cover all the threads. Remove any excess. You should not be able to see a layer of petroleum jelly when you finish.

Light bulbs sometimes work their way loose in sockets, a condition caused by vibration. Loose light bulbs can cause a crackling sound in AM radio receivers. Simply let the bulb become cool and then turn it in a clockwise direction until it is tight.

See Ceiling Light, Defective, *page 42*
    Electric Bills, How to Save Money on, *page 103*
    Electric Shock, How to Avoid, *page 107*
    Floodlights, *page 134*
    Fluorescent Light Bulbs, *page 140*
    Incandescent Bulbs, Three-Way, *page 188*

☐ Listening Room, Modifying

The *bass, midrange* and *treble* controls on a high-fidelity sound system are intended to let you make up for acoustic deficiencies in your listening room. However, even with these electronic aids it is often not possible to get the kind of sound you enjoy most. Even though you have a room that's shaped like a wind tunnel, you can change the listening and recording quality of the room. If you have an average-sized living or bedroom and want to make it a better listening environment, you can do it yourself with ordinary tools and readily accessible supplies.

Generally speaking, an ordinary room has three sets of parallel surfaces: the floor/ceiling and two opposing walls. You can alter the acoustic qualities of such a room, using a wide variety of material limited only by your imagination.

Basically, the materials you use should be soft and multi-surfaced. The softness will help "soak up" the sound; the exposed surfaces will "break up" the reverberation. The

FOAM CUPS FROM 3M COMPANY.

FIG. L-6

efficiency of this process, then, is dependent on the degree of softness and number of exposed surfaces.

In the case of the ordinary room where three sets of parallel surfaces exist, try to break up these surfaces by covering all or parts of one of the opposing surfaces.

For obvious reasons, most people treat the floor instead of the ceiling. However, you could carpet the ceiling and get the same acoustical effect as carpeting the floor. Acoustical tile is also commonly used. Sound experts recommend rugs and carpet rather than tile. The quality of the tile is a major consideration and, once the tile is painted, it loses much of its sound absorption properties.

Drapes on two of the opposing walls are effective. Burlap "wallpaper" works well. Some rooms feature strips of carpeting on the walls with good results.

You can make an effective acoustical wall treatment using foam cups adhered to plywood shapes (Fig. L-6). Cut the shapes from a 4 × 7 plywood panel and then affix to one wall.

Another treatment along the same lines is to affix painted egg cartons on a panel or wall. In both cases, foam cups or egg cartons, the idea is to break up the wall surface to soften the sound.

The extent of the surface treatment doesn't need to be 100%; 75% to 80% coverage should provide adequate acoustical control. You can use scatter rugs in place of wall-to-wall carpeting. You can cover the walls in strips of material, soft velvetized wallpaper, drapes or even a polar bear hide.

Again, generally, a highly fibrous material is better than a smooth, slick one. *Tweed* is better than *vinyl,* for example. The end result should be a room with "controlled" reverberation. A completely "dead" room is undesirable because the sound would be unnatural. When a recording is made in a professional studio, a slight echo is added to give the sound a natural tone.

One of the big problems with "listening rooms," such as those in an apartment building, is the unwanted noise entering from the doors. Treat these with sound absorbing materials to keep unwanted noise out and contain the music within the room, so it doesn't distract your neighbors. Seal doors as tightly as possible around the edges. Insulating material of the kind used to seal doors against wind drafts is excellent for this purpose.

☐ Locks, Frozen

A lock used on a door which faces the outside, possibly a garage door lock or house door lock, can freeze if water can seep into it and temperatures drop below 32°F (0°C). To "unfreeze" such a lock, insert a key as far into the lock as it will go. Then apply a hot soldering iron tip to the key. After the key has been heated, use a pair of pliers and see if the key can be pushed completely into the lock and turned.

You can also try a brazing torch. Play the flame of the torch intermittently over the face of the lock, but be careful so as not to scorch the wood frame of the door. Wear a pair of gloves when you hold the key and see if you can insert it in the lock. It may take a little time for the ice to melt. If you do not have a soldering iron or brazing torch, insert the key as far in the lock as it will go. Then heat the key with matches or a candle.

To prevent further lock freezing, squirt some lubricant into the keyhole. You can use regular lubricating oil, but a better method is to use special lubricants made for this purpose, available in hardware and auto supply stores.

☐ Marble, Removing Stains from

Marble is generally stained by glasses containing some liquid such as liquor or coffee which has spilled over the side of the glass. No single stain remover is suitable for all liquid stains. You can get marble cleaning compounds in department and hardware stores, giving preference to a kit which contains a number of different cleaning compounds. Try rubbing the stain with a small section of rough, hard cloth. Marble stains can also be caused by cigarettes, spills from bottles of medicine, or water that drops on the marble and is allowed to evaporate instead of being wiped away.

If none of the commercial products for removing stains does the job, the marble may need to be repolished. If the marble is part of a table, take the table to a dealer who specializes in marble topped furniture and have the marble restored by machine. Then keep the marble in top condition by applying a top quality paste wax twice a year. If the marble is part of a household fixture, such as a fireplace, you may need the services of a professional marble restorer.

☐ Masonry Surfaces, Painting

Masonry surfaces should be properly primed before painting. If the surface is new, prime it with an exterior latex paint made for masonry. If the surface is common brick, you can use a penetrating type of clear exterior varnish to control efflorescence, flaking, and chipping. Use this varnish if you want to get the natural look of the brick; it will withstand weather.

If the surface is coarse, rough, and porous, first cover it with block filler using a brush so as to penetrate and fill pores. If the masonry has previously been painted and has become somewhat chalky, use an exterior oil primer to rebind the chalk. If there seems to be quite a quantity of chalk, remove it with a stiff bristle brush or by washing the surface with household washing soda or a mixture of trisodium phosphate (TSP) in hot water.

☐ Metals, Joining

Joining two metals, whether they are the same or different types, is known as *sweating*. The strength of the joint, when completed, depends on the kinds of metals used and also on the design of the joint. Thus, you will get a stronger joint if you permit one of the metals to make good surface to surface contact with the other, known as a *lap joint*. A *butt joint*, in which the two metals make contact only with their ends, is structurally weak and should be avoided. If the two metals to be joined must use a butt joint, put a strip of metal across the two, in effect making a lap joint out of a butt joint (Fig. M-1).

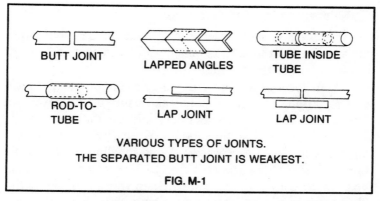

BUTT JOINT

LAPPED ANGLES

TUBE INSIDE TUBE

ROD-TO-TUBE

LAP JOINT

LAP JOINT

VARIOUS TYPES OF JOINTS.
THE SEPARATED BUTT JOINT IS WEAKEST.

FIG. M-1

A butt joint implies that the ends of the two metals are in direct contact. If this isn't so and the gap is greater than 0.002 of an inch, the strength of the finished joint will be greatly reduced.

Before joining two metal parts, whether by soldering or brazing, make sure they are thoroughly clean. If not, rub with emery cloth and remove all particles with a clean cloth. Even if the surface appears to be clean, it may have a coating of oxide. Thus, when copper is really clean, it is bright and shiny; when oxidized, the surface has a dull gloss. Copper exposed to the outside air may develop a greenish tinge. Remove this before soldering or brazing.

Parts to be soldered or brazed must be independently supported (Fig. M-2). This is no problem in the case of metal pipe which has been installed. But if the metal is free standing, clamp the metals to be joined in a vise or force them together with a C-clamp.

The parts to be joined must be heated to a point where the solder or brazing rod material being used will flow into the joint. The two parts should be heated evenly. If one of the metal parts is heavier than the other, apply more heat to that part.

See Aluminum, Joining, *page 21*
   Brazing, *page 34*
   Copper Pipe, Soldering, *page 60*
   Soldering, *page 312*
   Welding, *page 376*

☐ Mildew (on Painted Surfaces)

Mildew is caused by insufficient sunlight and ventilation in damp areas. It looks like bunches of black spots scattered at random over the painted surface.

Your local paint store may carry a commercial preparation for killing mildew. If not, make a mixture of trisodium phosphate (TSP) mixed with household ammonia and water. Use about three large tablespoons of the TSP and a cupful of ammonia in a gallon of water. Avoid inhaling the ammonia fumes. Some skins are sensitive to TSP powder, so wash your hands with soap and water. Keep your hands out of the TSP, ammonia, and water mix. Stir with a clean stick and apply to the painted surface with a clean brush. Make sure you cover the entire area. Give it a chance to dry and repeat. After it has dried, wash it down again with clear water.

An alternative method is to wash the mildewed surface with a mixture of one pint of household laundry bleach in one gallon of water. Bleach is corrosive, so keep it away from your eyes and skin. If you get splashed, wash immediately with clear water and do so repeatedly. After treating the mildewed surface with the bleach water mixture, repeat after the surface has dried. Allow the mixture to remain on the mildewed surface until it dries again, then wash with a clean water rinse. Apply the bleach/water solution with a brush. Whether using TSP or bleach, always wash brushes thoroughly with clean, running water when finished to keep the anti-mildew mixture from affecting future painting jobs.

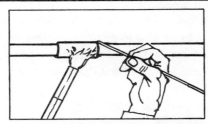

TO MEND A PIPE BREAK, SLIP A SMALL SECTION OF TUBING OVER THE BREAK AND BRAZE EACH END OF THE TUBING.

FIG. M-2

If mildew is a persistent problem, consult your paint store dealer about supplying a mildew resistant paint.

Mildew is also caused by lack of adequate ventilation in rooms which have a high level of moisture, such as bathrooms. An open window is helpful. If the bathroom is not equipped with a window, it may be necessary to keep the ventilating fan turned on even when the bathroom isn't being used.

See Aluminum Siding, Streaking, *page 22*
Fungus Stains on Wood Trim, *page 143*

☐ Mold

See Aluminum Siding, Streaking, *page 22*
Fungus Stains on Wood Trim, *page 143*
Mildew (on Painted Surfaces), *page 210*

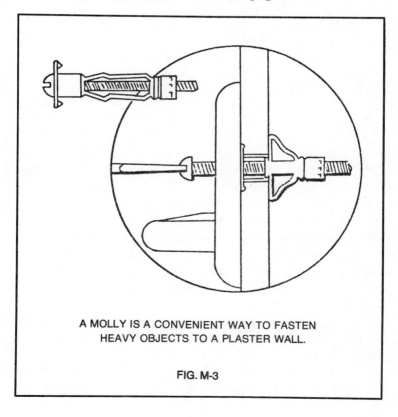

A MOLLY IS A CONVENIENT WAY TO FASTEN
HEAVY OBJECTS TO A PLASTER WALL.

FIG. M-3

☐ Molly Screws

Molly screws are helpful when you want to fasten heavy objects such as mirrors, towel bars, or ornamental objects to a plaster wall (Fig. M-3).

Drill a hole through the plaster that will accommodate the molly. Do not make the hole too large; it should be just big enough to let you force the screw through. If your drill bit isn't large enough, you can ream out the hole with a flat blade screwdriver.

Put in the screw until it is flat with the wall surface. Turn the screw a bit. This will spread the casing of the screw behind the wall, and the screw will then be held firmly in place.

Remove the screw using a flat blade screwdriver. Put the screw through the object to be supported and then back into the molly. Tighten the screw.

See Anchor Screws, Plastic, *page 22*

Toggle Bolts, *page 332*

☐ Musty Odor

A *musty odor* is generally associated with basements, although rooms and closets can sometimes have this problem. A musty odor is always due to dampness. The cure is ventilation. If possible, open basement windows and the door to create a movement of air. If there is water in the basement caused by seepage through the walls and floor, you will have a constant source of mustiness. The cure is to paint the walls and floor with a waterproofing paint or cement. If the basement is dry but still musty, use a dehumidifier.

The problem with basements is that their location generally doesn't permit the free movement of air. Install a fan, but give the circulating air a chance to exit through a window or door.

For closets that are musty, there are various chemical compounds which absorb water vapor. You can get such chemicals in paint or department stores.

Sometimes an entire house will develop a musty odor if the house is completely closed, with doors and windows shut, while the occupants are away on vacation. Open windows, fans, and air conditioning will correct this problem.

Concrete floors in closed rooms, possibly an enclosed porch or, more likely, in a basement, can sometimes be the cause of a musty odor particularly if the air is humid or if the concrete is over moist ground. The problem is caused by fungus growth in the cement. Apply a mildewcide to the floor, following the instructions on the container. Be sure to cover the surface completely and let the mildewcide remain for at least 24 hours. Wash the floor. When the floor has dried, coat it with concrete floor sealer, available in paint stores. If you plan to cover the floor with carpeting, it would be advisable to wait to see if the musty odor has been permanently eliminated.

See Basement, Waterproofing, *page 27*
    Damp Basements, *page 71*
    Gutters and Downspouts, Maintaining and Repairing, *page 154*
    Mildew (on Painted Surfaces), *page 210*

☐ **Nails, Removing**

For in-home repairs, the best tool to use for removing nails is the curved claw hammer. But while this hammer is specifically designed for this job, it does present two problems. The first is that it tends to curve or bend the nail being pulled. The other is that the head of the hammer will mar the finish of the wood. Of course, if the wood is rough lumber and there is no concern about the nails being pulled, then there is no problem.

However, if you want to salvage the nails and you do not want to mar the wood finish, put a block of wood beneath the head of the hammer. And, as further protection, put a bit of scrap cloth beneath the wood block (Fig. N-1). If you have some scrap rug material, cut a square about 2 inches and use this instead of the cloth. Place the rug scrap so that its back is against the wood block, and the carpeting is against the wood containing the nail. This placement will keep the rug square firmly against the block, and the rug against the wood will keep it from being marred.

Whether or not the nail will be curved or bent after you remove it depends on the length of the nail and the height of the wood block. The higher the wood block, the less the curvature of the nail. However, it isn't generally advisable to use blocks that are more than 1 inch high. If you want to recover the nails after removing them, put them on a cement block and use the head of the claw hammer to straighten them.

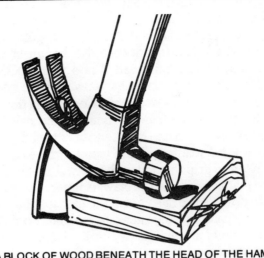

PUT A BLOCK OF WOOD BENEATH THE HEAD OF THE HAMMER.
CLOTH OR SCRAP RUG MATERIAL BENEATH THE BLOCK WILL
PROTECT THE WOOD FINISH.
FIG. N-1

Removing a nail assumes you can put the claw of the hammer beneath the head of the nail. This may not be immediately possible if the head of the nail has been hammered in deeply. In that case you have two options. If the bottom end of the nail has penetrated the wood and you are able to reach it, tap it with the hammer until the opposite end of the nail, the head end, is pushed above the surface of the wood. If this isn't possible your other choice is to cut the

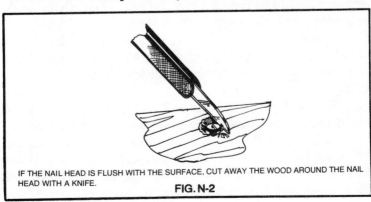

IF THE NAIL HEAD IS FLUSH WITH THE SURFACE, CUT AWAY THE WOOD AROUND THE NAIL
HEAD WITH A KNIFE. **FIG. N-2**

wood around the head of the nail until you can get the claw of the hammer beneath it (Fig. N-2). You may have some difficulty in doing this, since the head of the nail will be flush with the wood surface. In that case, take a pair of pliers and put them beneath the nail head. Put a thin block of wood beneath the pliers and then press down on the ends of the tool, just enough to lift the nail a bit. Keep doing this until you can get the claw of the hammer beneath the nail head.

Nail heads are soft and may bend or come off during your efforts to get the head above the wood surface. In that case you may need to grip the nail with pliers. Pull enough of the nail out so that you can use the claw hammer. You can use the hammer to remove the nail even if the nail head has come off, since the nail has grip rings near its top end. Force the claw end of the hammer around the nail until it is tight and then try to remove the nail.

See Hammers, *page 163*
    Nails, Types of, *page 214*
    Pliers, *page 280*
    Staples, Removing, *page 327*

□ Nails, Types of

There are four basic types of nails: *common, casing, finishing* and *brads,* although there are variations. The common nail has a flat head with small serrations for a short distance below the head along the shank of the nail (Fig. N-3). The purpose of the serrations is to provide a better gripping area. The remainder of the nail is smooth and ends in a point, with the opposite end having a round head.

The letter d for—common, casing, and finishing nails indicates the length of the nail and its size. Nails range from 2d to 7d, with 2d the shortest. Brads are identified by length in inches.

To select the proper size nail, measure the thickness of the wood through which it is to be driven and multiply by three (Fig. N-4). If the wood thickness is ½ inch, then the nail should be 1-½ inches long. This means that 1 inch of the nail length will be used for holding. Figure N-5 shows nail sizes to use for woods of different thicknesses.

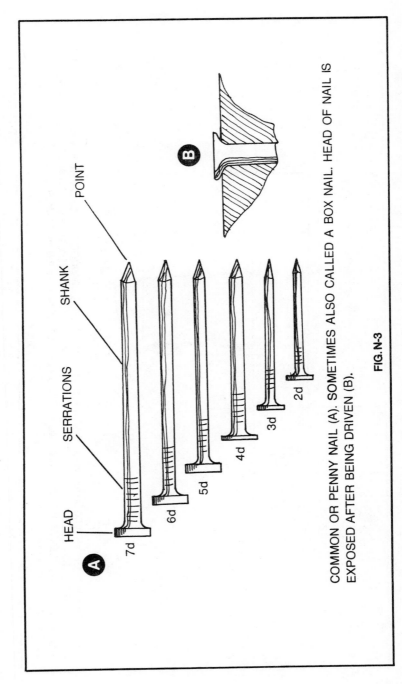

COMMON OR PENNY NAIL (A). SOMETIMES ALSO CALLED A BOX NAIL. HEAD OF NAIL IS EXPOSED AFTER BEING DRIVEN (B).

FIG. N-3

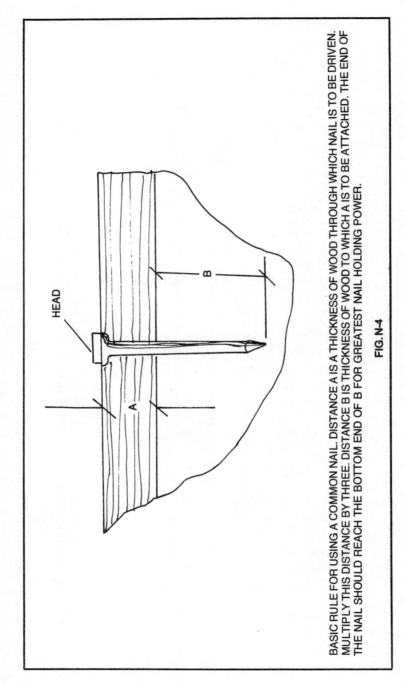

BASIC RULE FOR USING A COMMON NAIL. DISTANCE A IS A THICKNESS OF WOOD THROUGH WHICH NAIL IS TO BE DRIVEN. MULTIPLY THIS DISTANCE BY THREE. DISTANCE B IS THICKNESS OF WOOD TO WHICH A IS TO BE ATTACHED. THE END OF THE NAIL SHOULD REACH THE BOTTOM END OF B FOR GREATEST NAIL HOLDING POWER.

FIG. N-4

218

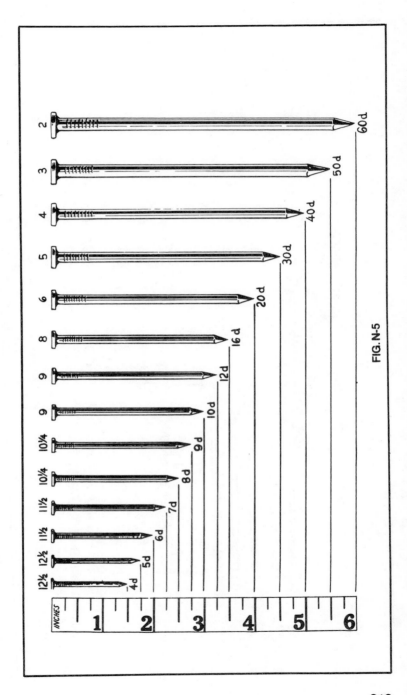

FIG. N-5

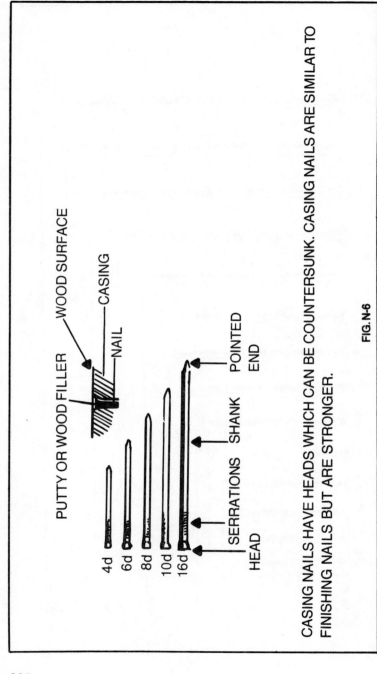

PUTTY OR WOOD FILLER

WOOD SURFACE

CASING

NAIL

POINTED END

SHANK

SERRATIONS

HEAD

4d
6d
8d
10d
16d

CASING NAILS HAVE HEADS WHICH CAN BE COUNTERSUNK. CASING NAILS ARE SIMILAR TO FINISHING NAILS BUT ARE STRONGER.

FIG. N-6

LIKE CASING NAILS. FINISHING NAILS HAVE ROUND HEADS WHICH CAN BE HAMMERED FLUSH WITH A WOOD SURFACE OR COUNTERSUNK.

FIG. N-7

Casing and finishing nails are quite similar, but casing nails are slightly stronger (Fig. N-6). These nails have small heads which can be driven flush with or countersunk to be below the surface of the wood (Fig. N-7). Finishing nails are available in different colors and can often be made to match wood colors. In this case the nail isn't driven below the level of the wood, with the head of the nail remaining flush with the wood surface. When a nail is to be countersunk, the space above the head of the nail can be filled in with wood putty or wood filler (Fig. N-8). Let the putty or filler harden for a day, then make the surface smooth with fine sandpaper prior to painting.

Use brads when nailing wood that is ¼ inch thick or less (Fig. N-9 and Table N-1). Brads are lightweight, thin, and short with heads that can be countersunk. They bend rather easily.

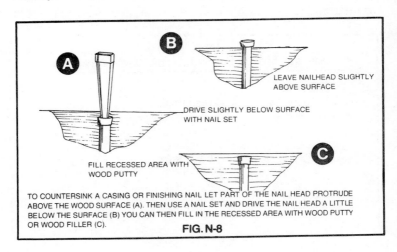

LEAVE NAILHEAD SLIGHTLY ABOVE SURFACE

DRIVE SLIGHTLY BELOW SURFACE WITH NAIL SET

FILL RECESSED AREA WITH WOOD PUTTY

TO COUNTERSINK A CASING OR FINISHING NAIL LET PART OF THE NAIL HEAD PROTRUDE ABOVE THE WOOD SURFACE (A). THEN USE A NAIL SET AND DRIVE THE NAIL HEAD A LITTLE BELOW THE SURFACE (B) YOU CAN THEN FILL IN THE RECESSED AREA WITH WOOD PUTTY OR WOOD FILLER (C).

FIG. N-8

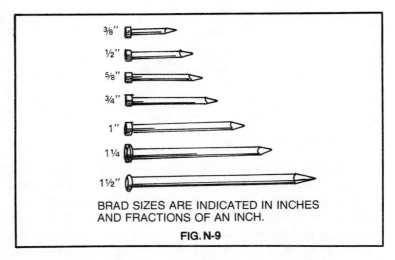

3/8"

1/2"

5/8"

3/4"

1"

1 1/4

1 1/2"

BRAD SIZES ARE INDICATED IN INCHES
AND FRACTIONS OF AN INCH.

FIG. N-9

The possibility of wood splitting when driving a nail can be minimized by drilling a partial or through hole using a fine drill whose diameter is much less than that of the nail. You can also avoid wood splitting by dulling the point of the nail. To dull the point, rest the head of the nail on a wood surface. With the nail held vertically, tap the point of the nail with a hammer, just enough to dull the sharp point. Make a small starting hole in the wood with a sharp nail or drill, and then use the nail whose point has been flattened a bit.

Stagger nails so you do not drive them through the same wood grain. To strengthen a nail's holding power, drive it in

TABLE N-1
Nail and Brad Sizes to Use for Different Thicknesses of Wood.

Thickness of wood to be nailed	Type of Nail	Size
3/4"	casing	6d
	finishing	6d
5/8"	finishing	6d-8d
1/2"	finishing	4d-6d
3/8"	finishing	3d-4d
1/4"	brads	3/4"-1"
	finishing	3d
	lath	1"

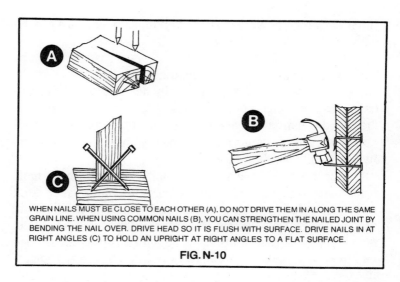

WHEN NAILS MUST BE CLOSE TO EACH OTHER (A), DO NOT DRIVE THEM IN ALONG THE SAME GRAIN LINE. WHEN USING COMMON NAILS (B), YOU CAN STRENGTHEN THE NAILED JOINT BY BENDING THE NAIL OVER. DRIVE HEAD SO IT IS FLUSH WITH SURFACE. DRIVE NAILS IN AT RIGHT ANGLES (C) TO HOLD AN UPRIGHT AT RIGHT ANGLES TO A FLAT SURFACE.

FIG. N-10

three-fourths of the way and then bend the remainder of the nail, driving the head of the nail into the wood surface. To fasten an upright to a surface that is at right angles to it, drive the nails in at an angle, using nails on both sides of the upright (Fig. N-10).

Special nails are available for fastening wood to concrete (Fig. N-11). Drill a pilot hole through the wood to avoid splitting and to permit the nail to go through the wood, holding the nail firmly in place.

Use a *ring nail* for maximum holding power when several boards are to be joined (Fig. N-12). Drive the nail so its top portion is flat with the surface of the top board. The ring nail has annular rings along its entire length, supplying op-

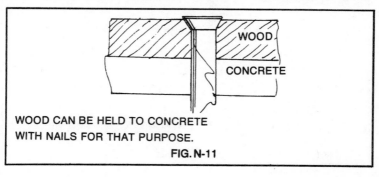

WOOD

CONCRETE

WOOD CAN BE HELD TO CONCRETE WITH NAILS FOR THAT PURPOSE.

FIG. N-11

timum gripping power. Once driven in, ring nails are practically impossible to remove.

To fasten fabric or leather to a wood surface, use upholstery nails (Fig. N-13). These are available in different colors and head designs. It is usually necessary to drive the nails close to each other with a possible separation of about 1 inch. If the nail shank bends when driven, remove the nail and discard it. Trying to straighten the shank to salvage the nail will only weaken it.

Use rustproof nails for outdoor work. Ordinary nails have heads which will rust, particularly if a water based latex paint is used. To prevent rust, countersink nails and fill in with putty before painting. Rust stain killers are available in paint stores. If rust spots have begun to show, cover each nail head with the rust stain killer before doing any repainting.

If you have redwood outdoors, such as a redwood porch, use only aluminum alloy, stainless steel, or hot dipped galvanized nails. Such nails last longer and don't produce rust stains. The problem with rusting is that not only does the head of the nail look unsightly, but rust stains can dribble down vertical members of the redwood assembly. Rusting nails, of course, eventually lose their holding power.

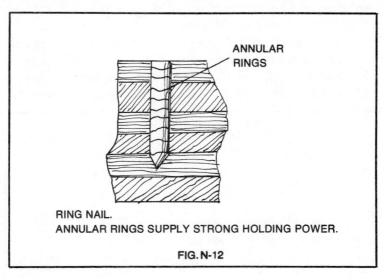

ANNULAR RINGS

RING NAIL.
ANNULAR RINGS SUPPLY STRONG HOLDING POWER.

FIG. N-12

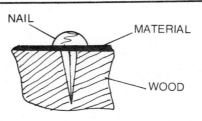

NAIL

MATERIAL

WOOD

UPHOLSTERY NAILS HAVE LARGE HEADS AND THIN SHANKS. HEADS COME IN A VARIETY OF DESIGNS. USE LIGHTWEIGHT HAMMER.

FIG. N-13

See Anchor Screws, Plastic, *page 22*
        Floors, Squeaky, *page 137*
        Hammers, *page 163*
        Molly Screws, *page 212*
        Screws, *page 297*
        Toggle Bolts, *page 332*
        Wallboard, Nailing, *page 356*

□ Nuts, Removing

A nut can sometimes become "permanently" attached to its bolt. There are three main reasons for this. The nut has been painted, and now the paint has hardened into the threads of the bolt, possibly covering the nut as well. The nut and bolt have remained unpainted, but the threads of the bolt have rusted. Finally, the thread and bolt may be attached because the nut was never put on the bolt properly in the first place. The nut has been "cross threaded" and the threads of the nut and bolt, instead of meshing properly, now ride across each other.

If the bolt and nut have been painted, apply paint remover and allow it to "soak" the bolt and nut. After the paint has softened, remove as much of it as you can, but avoid damaging the threads of the bolt. Scrap the paint away from the flats of the nut to give the wrench a chance to get a good grip on them. If you aren't working in a crowded space, put a 1 foot length of iron pipe over the handle of the wrench to get more turning force. Try tapping the sides of the nut with a hammer to see if you can loosen the nut.

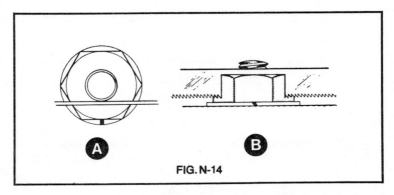

FIG. N-14

If the nut and bolt have rusted together, use various "rust remover" liquids available in paint and hardware stores. Keep applying the rust remover over a period of several hours.

No matter what you may do, it may be necessary to cut the nut and head apart. Use a fine hacksaw blade, preferably one with 32 teeth to the inch. Cut vertically through the nut with the blade as close to the bolt as possible (Fig. N-14). If there is a lock washer beneath the nut, don't try to cut through it but stop at this point. Lock washers are sometimes made of hardened steel, and you may wear out or dull the teeth of the hacksaw blade.

Remove the hacksaw and, using a cold chisel, insert its end into the cut portion of the nut. A few taps with a hammer should separate the cut portions of the nut.

If there is room beneath the nut to let you insert a hacksaw blade, try doing so and cut through the bolt. If, using either of the approaches just described, you find it very difficult to make a cut or to continue cutting, apply a few drops of cutting oil to the hacksaw blade.

You can also use a brazing torch to separate nuts and bolts. Apply the flame of the torch to the nut, trying as much as possible to keep the flame away from the bolt. The heat of the flame will cause the nut to expand. Sometimes you will hear a crack as the nut separates from the bolt. Don't wait for the nut to cool. Instead, put a wrench on the nut and turn it. It's a good idea to have a wrench on hand that will fit the nut immediately, such as an open end or box wrench.

☐ **Open End Wrench**

See Wrench, Open End, *page 395*

☐ Paint Brushes and Rollers, Cleaning

After using a paint brush for some time, paint tends to collect in the area where the hair of the brush is joined to the handle. This paint deposit has a tendency to dry even while the brush is in use, making the brush less flexible. It also makes the brush more difficult to clean when the job is finished.

To counteract this, remove as much of the paint from the brush as you can (Fig. P-1). If the paint you are using is water based, fill a can or jar with warm, soapy water and work the brush up and down. Or hold the brush under a faucet, using warm water. The idea is to get rid of as much of the accumulated paint as you can. If you are using an oil or *alkyd* paint, work out as much of the paint as possible using newspapers or a cloth, and then apply *turpentine*. Put some of the turpentine in a small can or jar and then work the brush around in it. See Figs. P-2 through P-4.

The idea here is to soften the paint and keep it from forming a hard deposit. This hardening takes place much more quickly with rapid dry paints, such as the water base types.

Another technique is to use two brushes for the same job. While one is soaking in water or turpentine, you can continue working with the other. The soaking will keep the

REMOVE AS MUCH OF THE PAINT AS YOU CAN AND THEN SOAK THE BRUSH IN THINNER OR PAINT REMOVER. KEEP WORKING THE BRUSH BACK AND FORTH ALONG THE BOTTOM OF THE CAN. THINNER ISN'T NECESSARY FOR WATER BASED PAINTS

FIG. P-1

paint at the bottom of the brush hairs from becoming dry and will help dissolve the accumulated paint.

You can also use a steel tooth comb for cleaning and maintaining a paint brush (Fig. P-5). The comb will straighten brush hairs that have become crisscrossed. If these retain some paint and are allowed to dry, they may make it impossible to use the brush again. When combing the

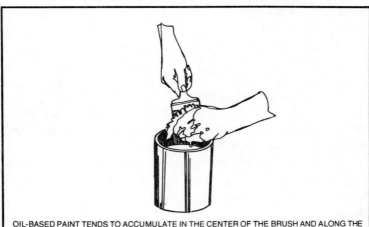

OIL-BASED PAINT TENDS TO ACCUMULATE IN THE CENTER OF THE BRUSH AND ALONG THE FERRULE. SQUEEZE THE BRISTLES WHILE APPLYING THINNER. AFTER REMOVING THE PAINT, WASH THE BRUSH IN SOAPY WATER, AND THEN RINSE IN CLEAR WATER.

FIG. P-2

AFTER WASHING THE BRUSH, USE A FLAT STICK TO REMOVE AS MUCH OF THE WASH WATER AS POSSIBLE.

FIG. P-3

brush, put it in a flat position on some old newspapers and then work the comb outward from the heel of the brush to its end. You will need to clean the comb when you are finished. You can do this with a rag, but do make sure all traces of paint are removed. If the brush you cleaned was used with a water based latex paint, put the comb in a pail of clean water, agitate it and then remove, wiping the comb thoroughly with a rag. If you combed a brush used with oil paint, soak a rag with turpentine and then use it to wipe all remnants of paint away from the comb.

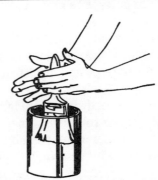

YOU CAN ALSO TWIRL THE BRUSH IN AN EMPTY CAN TO CLEAR THE BRUSH OF THE WASH WATER. THE PURPOSE OF THE CAN IS TO KEEP YOU FROM GETTING SPLASHED.

FIG. P-4

COMB THE BRISTLES USING A WIRE BRUSH. WRAP THE BRUSH IN HEAVY PAPER TO KEEP THE BRISTLES STRAIGHT. SUSPEND THE BRUSH BY ITS HANDLE.

FIG. P-5

Always store brushes properly. After cleaning a brush, wrap it in brown wrapping paper. The bags you get in your supermarket are ideal. Cut the bags apart into flat sheets and wrap the paper around the brush so the brush portion is completely covered. Then add another layer of wrapping material. Hold this in place with a rubber band. Store brushes flat, never on end. Another method is to drill a small hole in the end of the wooden handle. The paper wrapped brush (or brushes) can then be supported in a vertical position by a nail driven into a shelf.

It is just as important to clean paint rollers. Put some newspapers on the floor and then work the roller back and forth until the papers absorb as much of the paint as possible. If the papers become soaked, replace them and keep moving the rollers until no more paint is transferred to the newspapers.

The roller is now ready for washing. Be sure to remove it from its handle. If the roller was used with a latex based water paint, hold the roller under running water. Keep working the roller material with your fingers until the water from the roller runs clear. If running water isn't available, use successive pails of water. After you can squeeze no more .water out of the roller, dry the roller by running it over some newspapers or wipe dry with a cloth.

For rollers used with oil based paints, you can use a tray. An extra tray, just for this purpose and not for painting, is extremely helpful. Put about an inch of turpentine or cleaner recommended by the paint manufacturer in the tray, and then move the roller back and forth in the solvent. Work the roller back and forth on some newspapers. Replace with fresh newspapers as those you are working on become saturated with paint. Dispose of the paint cleaner from the tray, wipe the tray as clean as you can with a rag, and then put in about an inch of cleaning liquid. Work the roller back and forth in this fresh supply of solvent. Take the wooden paddle you received when you bought your paint or a small length of board. Work it across the roller to remove any paint that may have remained near the bottom of the roller pile.

Remove the roller from the fluid and move the roller back and forth on newspapers. You can now wash the roller in warm water to which you have added detergent.

Wrap the roller in paper or put it in a plastic storage bag. Store the roller vertically or else remount it on its handle and suspend the handle from a hook mounted in its end. Or you can drill a hole near the end of the handle and support it by a nail. Do not let the roller rest on its surface; otherwise, the roller may tend to deform making it difficult to use again.

□ Paint Brushes, Care and Maintenance

Brushes for water based and oil based paints are different, so it's necessary to get the right brush for the paint to be used. A set of brushes is like a set of tools, so don't expect a single brush to be suitable for every painting job. Three brushes, 2-inch, 4-inch and 6-inch sizes, would represent a minimum, but bigger or smaller brushes might be necessary.

One of the nuisances in painting is that hairs may be pulled out of the brush. If these are allowed to remain in the paint, they can spoil the appearance of the finish; if they are removed, it may be necessary to stroke over the surface again. When buying a new brush or prior to using an old brush, rub the brush energetically back and forth across the palm of your hand. Any loose hairs will be pulled forward and can then be removed. Since the action will tangle the brush hairs, comb them with a brush comb available in paint stores.

If the brush is to be used with an oil base paint, suspend it in linseed oil overnight. Do not let the brush rest on its bristles in the oil. Instead, suspend the brush so the bristles do not touch the bottom of the container. The linseed oil treatment will make the brush easier to clean. After the oil treatment, squeeze the oil out of the brush by putting it flat on some newspapers, and then run a strip of wood from the ferrule out to the ends of the brush. As a final step, comb the brush, again working outward from the ferrule.

When painting, it is customary to load the brush with paint and then to rub the brush against the inside of the lip of the paint can. This isn't a good practice for two reasons. The first is that some paint will flow into the rim. Even if it is removed (as it should be) when the can cover is replaced, enough of the paint will remain. This paint will dry and make it difficult to open the cover when the paint is to be used again. Another reason is that using the rim as a paint remover bends the bristles at the corners of the ferrule, putting them under strain at these points.

A better method is to run a wire across the center diameter of the top of the can (Fig. P-6). This wire can be held in place by running another wire around the can near the top edge. This means you will now have one loop of wire

DON'T CLEAR PAINT FROM BRUSH BY RUBBING IT AGAINST INSIDE RIM OF PAINT CAN. PUT A WIRE ACROSS OPEN TOP OF CAN FOR THIS PURPOSE.

FIG. P-6

going around the can and a straight wire going across the top. You can join the straight and looped wires where they cross. When painting, use the straight wire for getting excess paint off the brush. A wire hanger is excellent for this purpose. Naturally, the wires will need to be removed when replacing the can's cover.

Brushes should be cleaned immediately after painting is completed. The longer paint remains on the bristles, the more difficult it will be to remove. Cleaning brushes used with water based paints is quite easy. Remove as much of the paint as you can first by working the brush back and forth on some newspapers until no more paint can be obtained from the brush. Put the brush under a faucet. Using a lukewarm water and soap, work the soapy mixture with your fingers into the hairs of the brush. Pay particular attention to those brush hairs near the ferrule for paint tends to accumulate here. Use a brush comb to make sure all traces of paint have been removed. If you don't have a brush comb, use an old kitchen fork.

Wipe the brush thoroughly with a rag, and put paper around the brush. Make sure the paper wrapping permits the bristles of the brush to extend fully and that they are not bent by the wrapping. Hold the wrapping in place with a rubber band. If necessary, drill a hole near the top of the brush handle so the brush can be supported by a nail. Do not permit the brush to stand on its bristles. At regular intervals, possibly once every three months, remove the wrapping, wash the brush, comb it, and then wrap and store it again.

You can follow the same procedure with a brush used for oil based paint, except that the solvent will be turpentine or a commercial paint brush cleaner. After all traces of paint have been removed, wash the bristles thoroughly in soapy water. Remove the brush and dry it thoroughly with a cloth. When you are sure the bristles are dry, dip the brush in linseed oil and then wrap the brush in paper, held in place with a rubber band. Make sure you allow enough room so the bristles aren't bent in by the wrapping. About once every three months repeat the linseed oil treatment.

If a brush has been stored with some paint on it, the brush can be reconditioned by removing the dried paint. If the brush is a cheap one, it may not be worth the time, effort, and money to do the cleaning. It is generally desirable to salvage a good brush. As a first step, soak the brush, assuming it was used with an oil base paint, in turpentine or a commercial brush cleaner. It may take two or three days before the bristles become soft enough to permit you to work with them. At the end of a two or three day period, use a scraper to see if you can remove as much of the softened paint as possible. This will expose some of the lower paint layers, so you may need to repeat the brush soaking process.

You will also find it helpful to remove the brush from the solvent and to try to separate the bristles with your fingers. This will also give the solvent a chance to get in at some of the bristles.

Put the brush in a pail of hot water and soap to remove as much of the solvent as you can. With the help of a small scrubbing board, available in toy or department stores, give the brush a rubdown. First, soak the brush in hot water and then sprinkle the scrubbing board surface with soap powder. Wash the bristles of the brush just as though you were washing clothes on a scrubbing board. Rinse the brush in clear water, comb the brush, let it dry, and then soak it in linseed oil. The brush will then be ready for use or storage.

☐ Paint, Cracks in

Paint, whether oil based or latex, will show cracks if the surface to be painted isn't properly prepared so the paint can bond to the surface. Paint will also crack when put over a previous coat that is flaking, peeling, or cracking.

Painting over cracked paint is no solution. The only method is to remove the paint.

☐ Paint, Removing

You can remove paint or varnish by scraping, using an electric scraping iron, a chemical remover, which burns it off or by sanding. Scraping is suitable where the area is small and the paint hasn't made a strong bond with the wood. Removing paint by using a liquid paint remover is possibly the best method.

Liquid paint remover evaporates rapidly and is difficult to use on outdoor surfaces. You can use a paste remover instead.

You can use a brazing torch for removing paint (Fig. P-7). It is quite useful if the paint consists of several layers which have hardened. With a torch, paint softens quickly. You will also need a scraper with a long handle to scrape off the paint as it is loosened by the torch. If you are right-handed, hold the torch with your left hand and the scraper in your right. Always work from right to left, with the torch playing on the paint ahead of the scraper. Hold the torch at an oblique angle to the work, never at right angles. Pry up the paint and peel it off with the scraper following behind the torch.

Because some of the scrapings will tend to burn or smolder, have thoroughly wet rags and a bucket of water on hand. A fire extinguisher is better. Don't remove paint outdoors on windy days. If you are using a torch to remove paint from clapboard or overlapping siding boards, hold the torch so the flame points down. Be careful. It is possible for the flame to get into cracks, starting a fire that cannot be seen. To make sure, wet the surface down thoroughly after you have scraped the paint away. Touch the area with the palm of your hand to feel if heat is being produced.

Electric heaters are sometimes used for removing paint. These are very slow and do not work as well as chemical removers. Be careful when using an electric heater

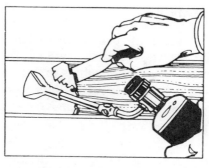

PAINT CAN BE REMOVED BY USING A BRAZING TORCH.

FIG. P-7

so as not to burn your fingers on the hot metal surface of the unit. The problem with metal heaters is that they do not permit the control you can have with a torch, and there is always the possibility of burning the wood surface.

Chemical removers may raise the grain of the wood and so, after the wood has dried thoroughly, it may be necessary to sandpaper it, something that should be done anyway if the surface is to be repainted. With a raised grain more extensive sandpapering may be needed, though.

Paint removers are available either as semi-paste or liquid. There are considerable differences among them. The kind you select will dictate the amount of work you will need to do, and the kind of wood surface you will have when you are finished. The least expensive paint remover uses a heavy base of paraffin. It will remove the paint, but it also means you must remove the paraffin after you have scraped the paint away. This involves using paint thinner. If you add the cost of the paint thinner to that of the paint remover, plus the extra work involved, then this type is no bargain.

Another type of paint remover is the no-cleanup type, so-called because it eliminates the need for using paint thinner after paint removal. However, "no cleanup" paint removers simply substitute one chore for another, for the wood surface must be sanded to eliminate chemicals deposited by the remover.

The washaway or water wash removers are best. These terms mean that after the paint remover has done its job, the surface of the wood can be washed with water to get rid of all traces of the remover. Although its initial cost may be higher, the washaway remover means less work and, since no thinner is needed, it is less expensive overall.

Some paint and varnish removers, especially those in the so-called bargain, low price class, are highly flammable and are often made with *methylene chloride*. Avoid inhaling the fumes, work in a well ventilated area, and do not smoke or allow the use of matches.

If the painted or varnished surface is horizontal, you can pour the paint remover directly on the wood (Fig. P-8). Try to put the wood surface into a horizontal position if you can do so, since it will make the removal work much easier. Apply enough remover so the entire surface is covered. Use a clean paint brush to spread the remover to cover all parts of the wood (Fig. P-9). Wear rubber gloves to protect your skin.

POUR REMOVER ON HORIZONTAL SURFACE. FOR INCLINED OR VERTICAL SURFACES, USE SEMI-PASTE REMOVER.

FIG. P-8

SPREAD REMOVER WITH A BRUSH. BRUSH CAN BE INEXPENSIVE TYPE, WITH SOFT BRISTLES. USE BRUSH WITH NATURAL WOOD HANDLE IF POSSIBLE.

FIG. P-9

It takes time for the remover to work on the paint, possibly a minimum of 30 minutes. Once you have put on the remover, let it alone and give it a chance to do its job. Don't stir it, brush it, or move it in any way. Don't walk away and forget about it, for you will want to get rid of the remover before it has a chance to dry.

Once the paint or varnish has been softened by the solvent, you can remove it with some rags, medium steel wool, or a scouring pad. If you use a scraper, watch that you do not gouge the wood.

If you have used a water wash remover, you can wash away the old paint and any remaining solvent by using a sponge and a pail of water. You may need to use several rinses. The final rinse should not show any evidence of paint. If the paint removal was done on furniture that can be taken outdoors, you will find it convenient to use a garden hose.

Sometimes it may be necessary to use a second application of remover, especially if you are working with wood that has had several coats of paint which have become hard with the passage of time. Enamels may be particularly difficult to work with and may also require several brushings with remover.

A second application doesn't necessarily mean the entire wood surface must be covered completely. Put the remover only on those areas where the paint has resisted removal.

Under certain circumstances, you can use a handheld power sander for removing paint. Use coarse sandpaper, but do not hold the tool in any one spot too long to avoid gouging the wood. Fine sandpaper will clog too quickly. Do not use a power sander on quality furniture if you want to keep the original wood surface (Fig. P-10).

Removing paint from curved and carved surfaces or from irregular areas can be much more difficult than from a flat surface. If you are working on furniture, remove all the old hardware. If this hardware has been painted and you want to clean it, put some of the paint remover in a small glass jar and let the hardware soak in it. After removing the hardware, wash it thoroughly. When it is completely dry, you can lacquer it to preserve the finish and to make it look bright.

See Alligatoring (Paint), *page 20*

Chalking (Paint), *page 44*

DO NOT USE POWER SANDER ON FINE FURNITURE. POWER SANDER IS SATISFACTORY WHEN WOOD SURFACE NEED NOT BE PROTECTED.
FIG. P-10

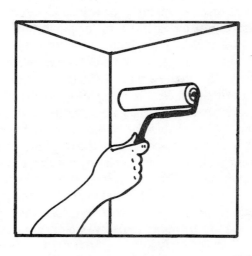

WITH ROLLER LOADED WITH PAINT, START BY MOVING UPWARD.
WORK TOWARD AREA THAT HAS PREVIOUSLY BEEN PAINTED BY
BRUSH.

FIG. P-11

☐ Paint Rollers, How to Use

Paint rollers are highly suitable for covering large areas, but using a roller doesn't eliminate brushes. Often the two must be available on the same job. Rollers are used with sloping trays made of metal or plastic. These can be purchased separately or as part of a roller painting kit.

To use a roller, pour paint into the tray until about two-thirds of the corrugated sloping bottom is covered. Dip the roller into the shallow part of the tray and move it back and forth until the roller is completely covered. Lift the roller. If it drips paint back into the tray, the roller is carrying too much paint. Squeeze some of the paint out by rolling and pressing it against the upper part of the tray above the paint.

To paint with the roller, start by moving upward, then back and forth, up and down, in long even strokes and then across (Figs. P-11 and P-12). Load the roller with paint again as required. A common error is to overload the roller. The correct way is for the roller to carry enough paint, but not so much that it drips on the way from the tray to the wall. Do not use excessive pressure on the handle of the roller.

When painting a wall or ceiling, you may find it easier to use a roller having a long handle. This will enable you to avoid using a ladder and will help you finish the job much

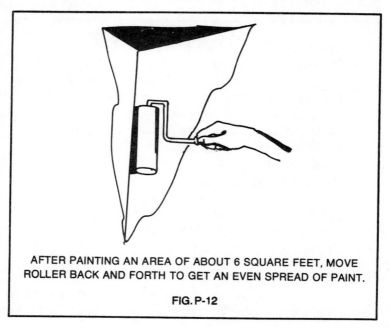

AFTER PAINTING AN AREA OF ABOUT 6 SQUARE FEET, MOVE ROLLER BACK AND FORTH TO GET AN EVEN SPREAD OF PAINT.

FIG. P-12

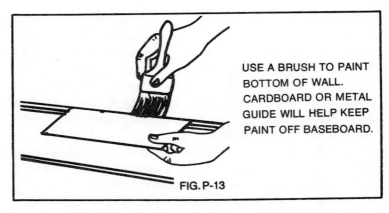

USE A BRUSH TO PAINT
BOTTOM OF WALL.
CARDBOARD OR METAL
GUIDE WILL HELP KEEP
PAINT OFF BASEBOARD.

FIG. P-13

faster. When painting a room, use a brush to cover areas of
the walls and ceiling where they meet. When working near
the baseboard, use a guide made of cardboard or aluminum to
keep the paint from going on to the wood trim (Fig. P-13).

If you plan to paint the walls but not the ceiling, you will
have the problem of getting a sharp paint line across the walls
where they touch the ceiling. At the same time you must not
get any paint on the ceiling. Pads with roller edges are
available for this, letting you paint close to the ceiling (Fig.
P-14).

☐ Paint, Splattered

You will find it almost impossible to avoid dropping
paint onto floors or to keep it off your hands. If you use a

water base latex paint, you will find it relatively easy to wash it off your hands, or face, by using warm water and soap. However, for either latex or oil based paints, you will find it still easier to maintain personal cleanliness by covering your hands and arms with a protective cream. Ordinary facial cosmetic cream will do. You might try a thin coating of petroleum jelly or *Vaseline*. Inexpensive plastic gloves or an old pair are also helpful.

Don't wait until you are finished painting to clean up dropped or splattered paint. Do it as you go along. It is much easier to remove wet paint than paint that has had a chance to dry. If you are working with an oil base paint, saturate a scrap cloth with turpentine and keep it handy when you paint. When working with a water base paint, saturate a cloth with water for cleanup purposes.

If you drop paint on an asphalt tile floor, don't try to remove it with turpentine or mineral spirits since you may damage the tile permanently. Wipe away as much of the paint as you can with a scrap cloth. Then let the remainder of the paint dry and scrape it off.

You can avoid painting adjacent surfaces that are to remain unpainted by using adhesive paper tape. Such "self stick" paper is easy to remove after the painted surface has dried. If you get paint on glass, remove as much of the paint as you can while it is still wet. If some of the paint remains, let it dry and then scrape it off, using a razor blade, preferably a single-edge type.

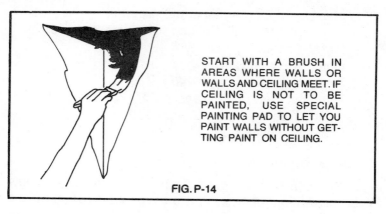

START WITH A BRUSH IN AREAS WHERE WALLS OR WALLS AND CEILING MEET. IF CEILING IS NOT TO BE PAINTED, USE SPECIAL PAINTING PAD TO LET YOU PAINT WALLS WITHOUT GETTING PAINT ON CEILING.

FIG. P-14

Wear a hat while painting. You can get special hats in any paint store, but an old hat will do just as well. Getting paint out of your hair, particularly an oil base paint that has dried, can be difficult.

☐ Paint Sprayers, Using

Whether you use a brush or roller is often determined by the area of the surface to be painted. For small jobs, such as wood trim, a brush is often the fastest and easiest method. For larger areas, such as ceilings, a roller is not only faster but often eliminates the need for a ladder.

The fastest painting method, however, is through the use of a paint sprayer. It also has the added advantages of producing a uniform coating with no brush or roller marks. Its disadvantage is that it is somewhat wasteful of paint.

Prior preparation of the paint is extremely important with a sprayer. It is necessary to stir the paint thoroughly to make sure it has no lumps and that the pigment is completely distributed throughout the paint. The paint must be thinned so it can be used with the sprayer, but if it is made too thin the paint coating will run. Paint manufacturers supply explicit instructions on how much to thin paints. It is always helpful to locate a paint store having a knowledgeable salesman to get full information on how much to thin a particular paint.

If you have never used a paint sprayer, get your paint dealer to show you exactly how. You will find the unit has a fan that will let you adjust the spray to accommodate the width of the surface to be painted. For narrow surfaces, adjust the sprayer to its narrow setting. If you plan to spray a wide surface, such as a wall, adjust for a wide spray.

You will find it helpful to use the spray on some test material first. This will give you some idea of the thickness of the paint and whether the sprayer fan is set correctly. The idea in spraying is not to lay down a heavy, thick coat but to cover the surface uniformly and adequately. A coat of paint that is too thick may blister or form surface ripples.

When spraying, hold the nozzle so it is about 8 inches from the surface being painted. Don't aim the sprayer directly at the surface when you start, but at some point slightly beyond. The beginning stroke tends to accumulate some paint. You will have a smooth, even flow when you reach the area to be painted. Hold the sprayer so it is parallel to the surface and move it with a steady, even stroke back and forth. If the surface you are painting has corners and edges, paint these first.

When you paint with a brush, you may not need to use a drop cloth to cover nearby furniture, particularly if you are working on a very small area. With a roller, a drop cloth is necessary, and it is also essential when paint spraying. Not all the paint from the spray will adhere to the surface being painted; some of it will bounce back and may then be carried by air movement to different parts of the room. The ideal method is to remove all furniture, paintings, bric-a-brac and ornaments, making the room as bare as possible. If the room has a light fixture, cover it with newspapers held in place with *cellophane* or masking tape.

An advantage of a sprayer is that there are no brushes to be cleaned, but the paint sprayer does need maintenance. Clean the sprayer as soon as possible after painting is completed. If you used a water base paint, clean the sprayer with a mixture of detergent and water. Clean the spraying tank thoroughly, fill it with detergent and water, and then use the spray. If you used an oil base or alkyd paint, follow the same procedure but use thinner—the same material that was originally used to thin the paint.

With the sprayer, you may have received a short length of metal to be used for cleaning the fluid tip if it should become clogged. Do not use nails or wire to unclog air holes in the tip.

If you use the spray outdoors, select a day in which there is no wind. Whether indoors or outdoors, wear a respirator to avoid inhaling paint vapors (Fig. P-15). All surfaces, whether indoors or out, must be dry and completely free of any dust or dirt.

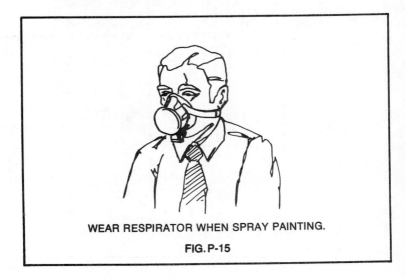

WEAR RESPIRATOR WHEN SPRAY PAINTING.

FIG. P-15

What to Use And Where

(Interior Surfaces)

MASONRY																
Asphalt Tile							X									
Concrete Floors						X.	X.	X			X				X	
Kitchen & Bathroom Walls		X.	X.										X			X.
Linoleum							X									
New Masonry	X.	X.											X		X	X.
Old Masonry	X	X										X	X		X	X.
Plaster Walls & Ceiling	X.	X.											X		X	X.
Vinyl & Rubber Tile Floors						X	X									
Wall Board	X.	X.											X		X	X.
METAL																
Aluminum Windows	X.	X.										X		X	X.	X.
Heating Ducts	X.	X.										X		X	X.	X.
Radiators & Heating Pipes	X.	X.										X		X	X.	X.
Steel Cabinets	X.	X.												X		X.
Steel Windows	X.	X.										X		X	X.	X.

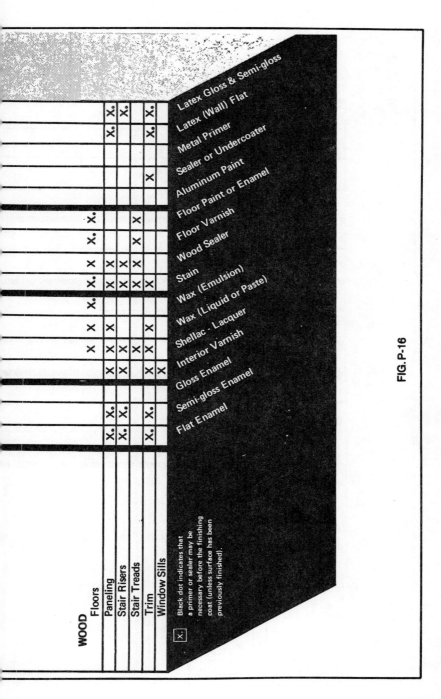

FIG. P-16

X. Black dot indicates that a primer or sealer may be necessary before the finishing coat (unless surface has been previously finished).

What To Use And Where
(Exterior Surfaces)

Surface								
MASONRY								
Asbestos Cement	X°						X	
Brick	X°	X			X		X	X
Cement & Cinder Block	X°	X			X		X	X
Concrete/Masonry Porches And Floors						X		
Coal Tar Felt Roof			X	X				
Stucco	X°	X			X		X	X
METAL								
Aluminum Windows	X°		X°		X°		X°	X°
Steel Windows	X°		X°		X°		X°	X°
Metal Roof	X°						X°	X°
Metal Siding	X°		X°		X°		X°	X°
Copper Surfaces		X						
Galvanized Surfaces	X°		X°				X°	X°
Iron Surfaces	X°		X°		X°		X°	X°

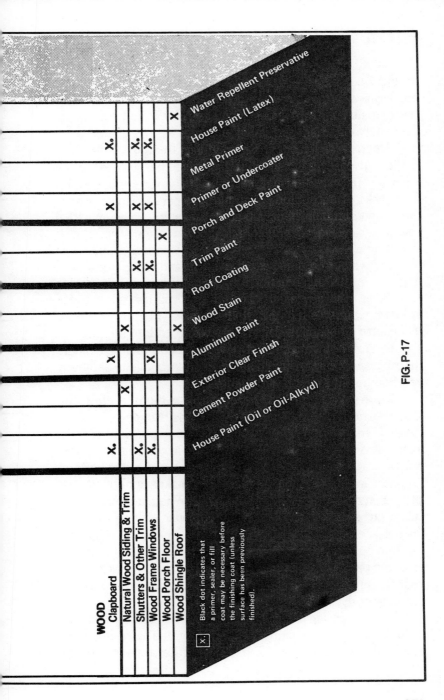

FIG. P-17

253

Of all in-home repairs, painting is one of the easiest to do and, because the result is usually an improvement in home appearance, it is enjoyed and appreciated. Still, you can do better painting and get better results by following certain procedures. See Figs. P-16 and P-17.

Preparing The Surface. One of the most commonly neglected techniques is preparation of the surface before painting. If you are painting an outside wood surface and it has cracks or seams, or there are open spaces in joints where two wood surfaces join, you can make a quick repair with a *caulking gun* loaded with a caulking cartridge (Fig. P-18). Caulking also makes your home more weatherproof, helps prevent windy drafts from blowing in, and helps keep your home at a more even temperature.

After you have applied the caulk, you can use a putty knife to get a smoother, firmer finish. Use the putty knife to make sure the caulking compound is forced into all holes or seams. Wait until the caulk has dried before starting to paint. Instructions supplied with the caulking cartridge usually tell you how long this will be.

If you plan to paint windows, examine them carefully for loose putty or areas where the putty has dropped out (Fig. P-19). If you have old putty remaining from a previous repair, make sure the putty is soft and malleable. Unless it is, you will be wasting your time. A special V-shaped putty knife is available in paint stores (Fig. P-20). It makes applying putty and getting a professional finish easier. When you finish with putty, put some linseed oil in the can, just enough to cover the surface, and close the can tightly. If air can leak into the can, the putty will become dry and useless. When you complete the putty repair on your window, smooth the putty with your finger or a putty knife. Do not paint until the putty is thoroughly dry.

When painting outside, make sure the surface is clean. If there is any loose paint, remove it with a wire brush or sand it by hand or machine (Fig. P-21). If there are any cracks

CAULK ALL SEAMS, JOINTS AND CRACKS BEFORE PAINTING OUTDOOR SURFACES.

FIG. P-18

or holes in the wood surface, fill them with wood putty (Fig. P-22).

If you want to get down to the bare wood surface, use a *propane torch*. Keep moving the flame and do not let it remain too long in any area. As the paint softens, scrape it away. Use a scraper with a long handle to protect your fingers against the heat (Fig. P-23). Don't expect to get off every last bit of paint with the torch. You may have spots of paint buildup that will resist the heat. However, you can use a scraper later to take care of them.

Try to avoid hand sanding large painted surfaces. Instead, use your power drill. You can get a sanding wheel that will do the work faster and easier. If you plan to paint metal, you can remove rust, scale, and any blistered paint by using a wire brush attachment for your drill (Fig. P-24).

Whenever you paint, whether indoors or out, use a drop cloth (Fig. P-25). You can also get these in plastic. Cloth is preferable because it is easier to handle. If you must move a ladder across a drop cloth, you'll find that the ladder will sometimes tear plastic but will not hurt cloth. Be sure to cover furniture and floors indoors, and shrubs and walks outdoors. It is a lot easier to practice prevention than to engage in cleanup. In some cases paint can cause permanent damage to rugs and furniture. The fact that a paint is a water base type does not always mean water can remove a stain. Water base means the paint is soluble in water, not that it can be completely removed by it.

Get into the habit of using *masking tape* to avoid painting surfaces which are not to be painted (Fig. P-26). Masking tape will also let you get a straight line. If you want to paint two adjoining surfaces using two different colors, masking tape is practically a must. And, if you are painting two different colors on surfaces next to each other, wait for one paint to dry before starting on the other.

Mixing Paint. Always mix paint thoroughly. When buying paint, ask the supplier to mix it for you. Paint stores have mixing machines which do an excellent job of shaking the paint can. But don't depend on this alone. If paint was mixed in the store for you, get a mixing paddle to continue the job when you get home. There are two types of paddles. One is just flat wood; the other is made of aluminum and has holes in it. You'll get a better mixing job with the metal mixer. Stir thoroughly and make sure the paddle reaches all the way in and scrapes the bottom of the paint can. Hold the mixer vertically and move it in all directions. Lift the paddle and let the paint drip back into the can. There should be no solid lumps, and you should be able to feel no lumps when

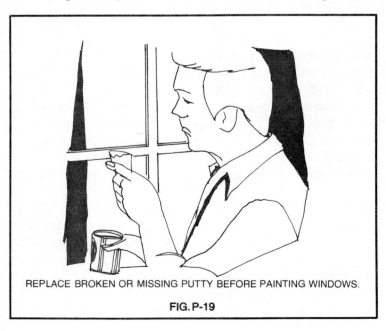

REPLACE BROKEN OR MISSING PUTTY BEFORE PAINTING WINDOWS.

FIG. P-19

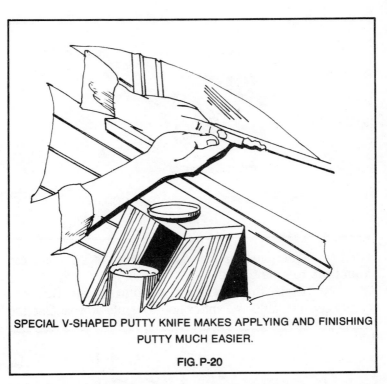

SPECIAL V-SHAPED PUTTY KNIFE MAKES APPLYING AND FINISHING
PUTTY MUCH EASIER.

FIG. P-20

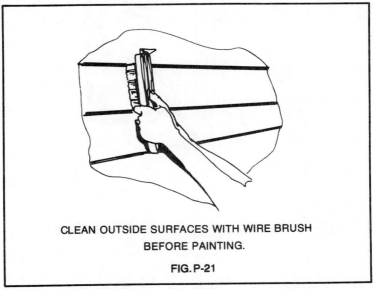

CLEAN OUTSIDE SURFACES WITH WIRE BRUSH
BEFORE PAINTING.

FIG. P-21

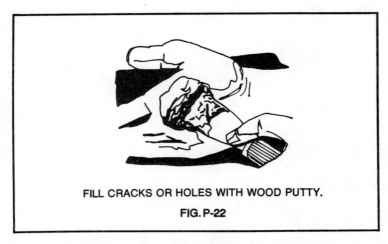

FILL CRACKS OR HOLES WITH WOOD PUTTY.

FIG. P-22

stirring. When painting, stir the contents of the paint can from time to time.

You will also find it helpful to get a mixing can. This is an empty can available in paint or home supply stores. Use the

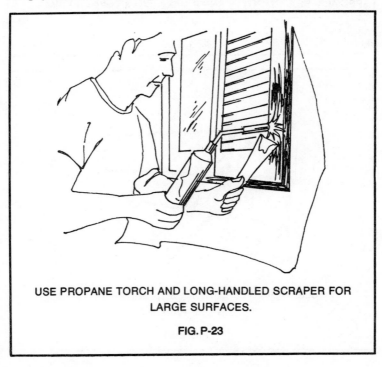

USE PROPANE TORCH AND LONG-HANDLED SCRAPER FOR LARGE SURFACES.

FIG. P-23

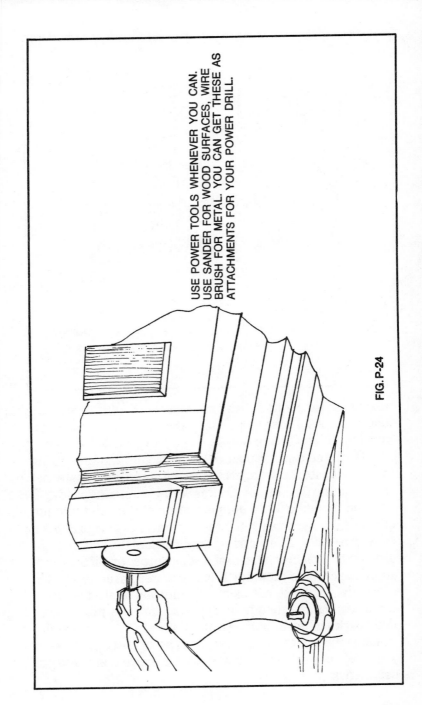

USE POWER TOOLS WHENEVER YOU CAN. USE SANDER FOR WOOD SURFACES, WIRE BRUSH FOR METAL. YOU CAN GET THESE AS ATTACHMENTS FOR YOUR POWER DRILL.

FIG. P-24

USE DROP CLOTH INDOORS AND OUT TO PROTECT FURNITURE, RUGS, AND SHRUBS.

FIG. P-25

mixing can for paints which have been allowed to stand for a long time. As a first step, shake the can of paint for a few minutes. Turn the can upside down and then back again.

Open the can and pour a small amount into the mixing can. Reach into the original can of paint and stir the paste that has settled on the bottom. Do this with your mixing paddle. If you find this difficult to do, pour more of the paint into the mixing can so you can get at the bottom of the original paint can more easily. Keep stirring until you feel the settled paint dissolving. You may need to add some turpentine if the can is an oil based type or water if it is a water based type. Add sparingly, for these are paint solvents and dilute the paint. Keep mixing and then pour the paint into the mixing can. Pour back and forth between the two cans and, as you do, examine the paint to make sure it has no lumps (Fig. P-27). If you notice any dried sections of paint, remove them. You can use a stick.

USE MASKING TAPE TO KEEP FROM SMEARING SURFACES
ADJACENT TO AREA BEING PAINTED.

FIG. P-26

If you have an old can of paint and no amount of mixing will dissolve all the lumps in it, there are a few techniques you can use to get rid of them. Cut a section of screen wire slightly smaller than the diameter of the can of paint. Insert the screen so it rests flat on the surface of the paint (Fig. P-28). As you paint, your brush will gradually push the screen down. The paint lumps, larger than the holes in the screen, will gradually be pushed down to the bottom of the can.

Another method, possibly better, is to cover an empty mixer can with a screen. The screen must be larger than the opening of the can. Slowly pour the paint into the screen area and it will drip down into the mixer can. By filtering the contents of the old can of paint in this way, you will avoid contaminating your brush with long strips of paint that have dried in the can.

Always read the instructions on the can of paint. Some manufacturers do not recommend mixing as this may introduce air bubbles into the paint. If the can of paint is old or has been previously used, you may find a layer on the bottom that

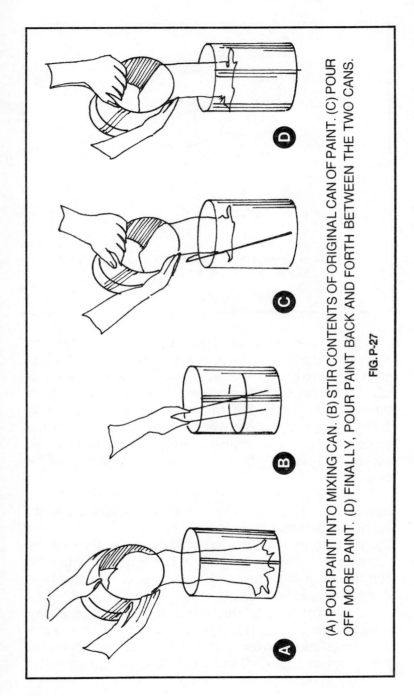

(A) POUR PAINT INTO MIXING CAN. (B) STIR CONTENTS OF ORIGINAL CAN OF PAINT. (C) POUR OFF MORE PAINT. (D) FINALLY, POUR PAINT BACK AND FORTH BETWEEN THE TWO CANS.

FIG. P-27

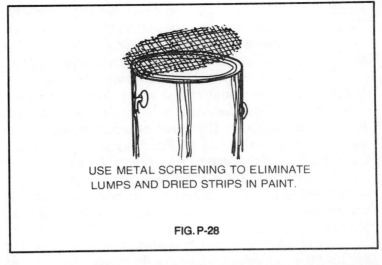

USE METAL SCREENING TO ELIMINATE
LUMPS AND DRIED STRIPS IN PAINT.

FIG. P-28

is hard and resists mixing. In that case the paint is too old and should be discarded.

Helpful Hints. One of the advantages of water base paint is that cleanup is much easier than with oil base types. But you can make your job easier. If you work with a roller tray, line it with aluminum foil before putting in the paint (Fig. P-29). Press the foil firmly against the bottom and sides of the tray. The foil should be large enough to cover all of the bottom and the three sides, plus some overhang. Bend the overhang firmly against the tray. There should also be some overhang in the front of the tray.

This foil idea is very helpful if you want to use two or more water base colors. When you finish with one color, remove the foil, rinse the tray to get rid of any paint, and then put in a new foil lining for the next color. If you use rollers, keep one roller for one color, and another roller for the second color. When you are finished with the first color, let the roller soak in a pail of water while you work with the second color. Then, at cleanup time, you can do all your cleaning at once. You can follow the same procedure if you use brushes.

When buying paint brushes, be sure to get the brush most suitable for the kind of paint you are going to use.

Brushes for oil base paints and for water base types are different. Also, do not expect one brush to do all the work. For large surface areas use a 4-inch or 5-inch brush. For smaller areas you can use either a 1-inch or 2-inch brush.

Never dip the brush completely into a can of paint. Instead, put the brush in so only about one-third to one-half of it is covered. Touch the brush to the surface being painted lightly at several spots. Then use long brush strokes, covering the paint spots as you do. Finish by painting back and forth and then in a zigzag manner (Fig. P-30).

When you must paint in a corner, always use the flat side of the brush (Fig. P-31). Because of the narrower area, it is almost natural to use the side of the brush, but this is an incorrect technique.

Don't try to use a wide brush when painting in corners or any hard to reach places. When you do so, you force the end bristles of the brush to separate and curl away from the brush. Always use a small brush for such applications.

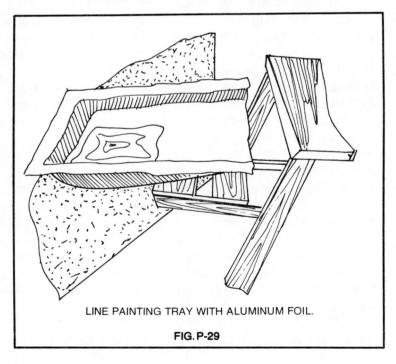

LINE PAINTING TRAY WITH ALUMINUM FOIL.

FIG. P-29

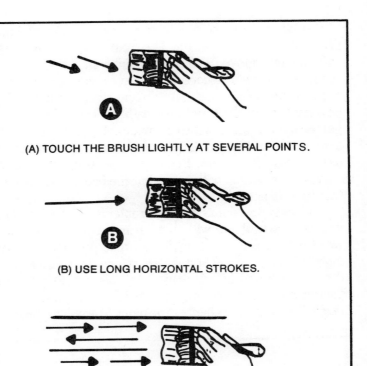

(A) TOUCH THE BRUSH LIGHTLY AT SEVERAL POINTS.

(B) USE LONG HORIZONTAL STROKES.

(C) FINISH WITH BACK AND FORTH STROKES.

FIG. P-30

One of the biggest problems in painting is to avoid ridges and lap marks when working on a flat surface. Always send your brush stroke into the wet paint area, not away from it (Fig. P-32).

No matter how careful you may be, there will always be some paint dripping down the side of the can. There is a ridge around the top of the can. While it is supposed to work as a recess for the cover, enabling the cover to make an airtight fit, it also collects paint. When it overflows, paint will come running down the side of the can. To avoid this, or at least to minimize it, punch several holes in the ridge. This will let accumulated paint flow back into the can.

Always put some newspaper beneath a can of paint to protect the surface beneath. The trouble with newspapers is that you must move them as you paint some other part of the room. Since the newspapers may have collected some paint, there is always the possibility of smearing. Instead of papers, try a paper plate right beneath the can (Fig. P-33). To get the plate to stick to the can, put a dab of paint in its center before you set the can down on it. Do this even though you use a drop cloth. The drop cloth will ultimately become somewhat smeared with paint, but the paper plate will keep this from happening too quickly.

Working outdoors has its problems. The advantage is you have no problem with ventilation. Always check on the weather. If there is a possibility of rain, postpone the painting job. Also postpone if it is very windy, for there is always the chance that dust or leaves will blow onto the freshly painted surface. If you are bothered by insects, add a small amount of insect repellent to the paint. It won't be necessary

USE FLAT SIDE OF BRUSH WHEN PAINTING INTO CORNERS.

FIG. P-31

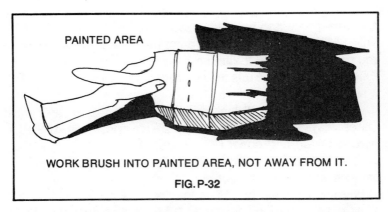

PAINTED AREA

WORK BRUSH INTO PAINTED AREA, NOT AWAY FROM IT.

FIG. P-32

to use much, and it will not affect the color or the consistency of the paint. Further, it will help keep insects away from the painted surface. You will also find it helpful to spray the area near the object being painted with insect repellent (Fig. P-34).

Rollers. Painting wire fences can be a nuisance because of the nature of the surface to be painted. To do this type of painting job, get a long nape roller (Fig. P-35). If you use a brush, you will find yourself spending hours at it. When you use the roller, you will find that it will paint the front of

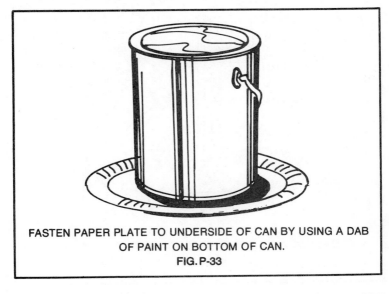

FASTEN PAPER PLATE TO UNDERSIDE OF CAN BY USING A DAB OF PAINT ON BOTTOM OF CAN.

FIG. P-33

the wire fence and will also cover most of the sides of the wire. After painting the front, paint the back. This will cover the rest of the sides. Examine the entire fence when you are finished. If you have missed any spots, you can touch up with a small brush.

Working with a paint roller is one of the easiest and fastest ways to cover large surfaces. Use crisscross strokes, then paint up and down (Fig. P-36). If you are to paint a ceiling, get an extension handle for your roller. Some roller handles are made in sections which can screw together, giving you a handle that is as long or as short as you want. You can paint a ceiling by using a ladder and a shorter handled roller, but working from floor level with a long handled roller is faster. Climbing up and down a ladder and moving it constantly is a nuisance.

Just as there are paint brushes for every job, there are various kinds of rollers (Fig. P-37). You can get a roller to do the trim, although trim can also be painted just as easily with

ADD SMALL AMOUNT OF INSECT REPELLENT TO PAINT.

FIG. P-34

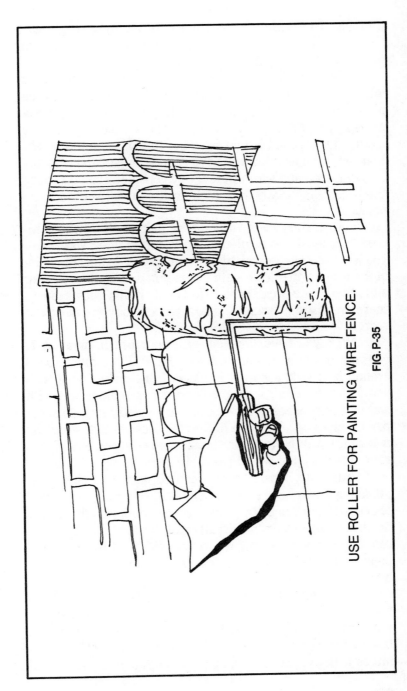

USE ROLLER FOR PAINTING WIRE FENCE.

FIG. P-35

269

a brush. There are special rollers for painting rough surfaces. You can also get an extra wide roller if you want to paint large surface areas.

Cleanup Work. There are three "areas" where you will need to do cleanup work after painting. The first is the place where you did the painting. This includes getting rid of newspapers and paper painting plates and picking up drop cloths. The second is getting rid of the paint on the brush. You can clean brushes you have used with latex base paints by using soap and warm water. Use repeated rinsings. Soap the brush thoroughly and wash until you can see no more paint.

For brushes used with oil base paints, clean with commercially available paint cleaner or turpentine. Make sure you have removed every bit of paint. If you do not, the hairs of the brush will stick together, making it difficult or impossible to use the brush again. However, if this does happen, there are various brush cleaners you can buy in your paint store.

After you have finished with your brush, wrap it in brown paper or aluminum foil (Fig. P-38). Put a rubber band around it to hold securely in place. For brushes used with water based paints, wrap the brush when soaking wet with water. For brushes used with oil base paints, include some paint thinner or turpentine in with the brush before wrapping it with the foil. Never store brushes standing on end. Clean rollers just as you would paint brushes.

Ordinarily, if you cover a can of paint very tightly by pounding down on the cover, you will be able to use your excess paint at some other time. Before replacing the cover, however, wipe clean the circular ridge around the top of the can. If you don't, putting the cover back on will cause this paint to splatter all over you. Tap the cover into position with a hammer.

You have a problem, however, When a can of paint is fresh, it is full of paint. There is very little air between the top surface of the paint and the cover. As you use the paint, the volume of air above the paint becomes greater. This air mixes with the paint, forming a film on top of the surface of

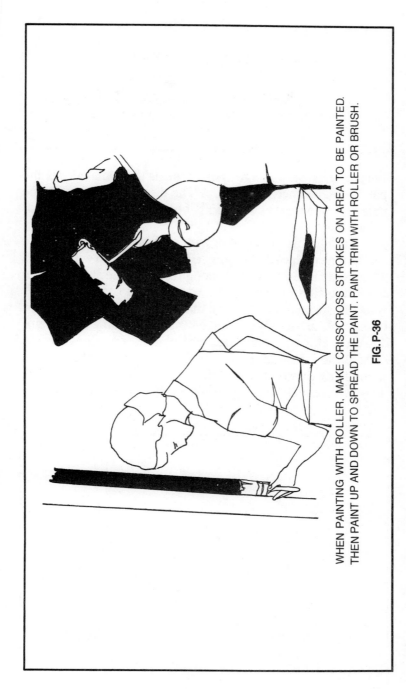

WHEN PAINTING WITH ROLLER, MAKE CRISSCROSS STROKES ON AREA TO BE PAINTED. THEN PAINT UP AND DOWN TO SPREAD THE PAINT. PAINT TRIM WITH ROLLER OR BRUSH.

FIG. P-36

ROLLER BRUSHES ARE AVAILABLE FOR JUST ABOUT EVERY
TYPE OF SURFACE: BEVELED, ROUGH AND CARVED.

FIG. P-37

the paint. The advantage is that it seals the remainder of the paint from contact with the air. The disadvantage is that you must remove this "skin of paint" before you can use the paint again.

To minimize paint skin with oil base paints, cover the top surface of the excess paint left over in the can with a small amount of turpentine—just enough to cover the area. You can try a thin film of water with water based paints, but with water the problem is that two things will happen to it. Water base paints are highly soluble in water, and some of the paint and the water will mix. The remaining water will evaporate and fill the inside of the can with water vapor. One way of minimizing this is to pour leftover paint into a smaller can. This will reduce the amount of air over the surface of the paint.

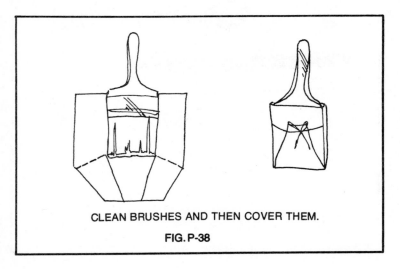

CLEAN BRUSHES AND THEN COVER THEM.

FIG. P-38

When working with varnish, always stir the contents, but never shake the can. When you cover a can of varnish, you not only cover the varnish but the layer of air above it. Shaking the can traps some of the air in the varnish, producing bubbles in it. These bubbles become trapped. When you apply the varnish and it dries, the bubbles will form very tiny bubbles on the surface.

You'll find it easier and better, when painting outdoors, to use a pad applicator. Try the pad on fences, concrete block, gables, siding, shingles, and shakes. When the pad shows signs of wear, remove it from its holder and turn it over for further use. You can also replace the pad. Like brushes, pads are available in different widths. Where you have a large surface area to cover, use a wide pad as a time saver. Clean the pads just as you would brushes.

☐ **Peeling (Paint)**

Peeling paint consists of small strips of paint pulling away from the painted surface, often dropping off and exposing it. Peeling happens if the surface to be painted isn't adequately prepared. Do not paint over dirty surfaces, over surfaces which give evidence of peeling, or over greasy or oily surfaces.

If the surface to be painted has peeled previously, you will need to get down to the bare wood. Sand, scrape, or use paint remover. Make sure the surface is clean and dry and then use a quality paint.

See Alligatoring (Paint), *page 20*
Chalking (Paint), *page 44*
Checking (Paint), *page 45*
Doors, Painting, *page 79*
Exterior Metal Surfaces, Painting, *page 119*
Masonry Surfaces, Painting, *page 207*
Paint Brushes and Rollers, Cleaning, *page 229*
Paint Brushes, Care and Maintenance, *page 234*
Paint, Cracks in, *page 237*
Paint, Removing, *page 238*
Paint Rollers, How to Use, *page 243*
Paint, Splattered, *page 245*
Paint Sprayers, Using, *page 247*
Paint, Tips on How to, *page 250*
Plywood, Painting, *page 280*

□ Pipe, Cutting

The best way to buy *pipe* is to get it cut to the exact length you need, with the correct diameter and, if necessary, threaded at one or both ends.

Pipe is made of various materials including copper, wrought iron, lead, steel, brass, copper, and plastic. Piping is sometimes incorrectly referred to as *tubing*. Tubing has much thinner walls.

Pipe can be cut with a tool known as a pipe cutter, identified as No. 1 or No. 2. A No. 1 pipe cutter is used for pipes having diameters from as little as ⅛ inch to 2 inches. The No. 2 pipe cutter is for large diameter pipe, from 2 inches to 4 inches. However, there are some variations, so if you buy a pipe cutter make sure its minimum and maximum diameter cutting capabilities are what you want (Fig. P-39).

Pipe can be cut with a hacksaw but using the tool for this purpose has several disadvantages. It is difficult to produce a cut that is exactly straight, it is tough to make the cut a precise right angle with the pipe, and the edges of the cut can be rough. Use the correct hacksaw blade (one with the right number of teeth) and file the end of the pipe when the cutting is finished. Hacksaws are suitable when the end of the pipe need not be threaded.

A pipe cutter can produce a clean, sharp, right angle cut. Before cutting, mark the pipe precisely where the cut is to be done. If the pipe is dirty, clean the area where you are going to make the mark, using steel wool or sandpaper. If, for some reason, it is difficult to make a mark or line with a pencil or ballpoint pen, use a fine blade hacksaw.

To use the pipe cutter, put the cutter around the pipe. Advance the cutter blade control until the blade rests directly on the mark you have made.

Don't try to work holding the pipe in one hand and the cutting tool in the other. If the pipe is quite long, you can rest it on a pair of sawhorses, but a better arrangement is to clamp the free end of the pipe in a vise. If the pipe has a finish which must be protected, such as chrome, put a section of heavy cloth, rubber, or a wood block in the jaws of the vise so as not to damage the pipe's finish. However, if you plan to cut at or near the center of the pipe, or a foot or more away from an end, it will be much easier to use two vises, one for each end of the pipe.

With the cutter wheel firmly against the pipe, give the cutter one full turn. If you will examine this cut, you will see it has made a complete circle. If the tool has been properly mounted, the circle will end on itself.

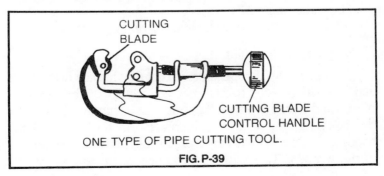

CUTTING BLADE

CUTTING BLADE CONTROL HANDLE

ONE TYPE OF PIPE CUTTING TOOL.

FIG. P-39

Before continuing with the cutting, apply some pipe cutting oil around the first cut. This will make the cutting job easier. You can now continue rotating the cutting tool and, with each complete turn, advance the cutting head knob a bit so that the blade bites deeper into the pipe. Continue turning slowly until the pipe is cut completely through.

When you have finished, wipe the end of the pipe with a thick cloth to remove any metal burrs. If the cutting tool you used is sharp, you will find the cut end of the pipe ready to use. If not, you may need to dress the cut end by filing to remove burrs or roughness.

☐ Pipe, Electrical

☐ Pipe Joints, Loosening

A problem with pipe joints is that the threads of the pipe and its coupling tend to rust, particularly if the pipe is made of iron and works in a high humidity environment. To loosen the coupling, tap it with a hammer and then use a long handled wrench with a section of pipe slipped over the handle of the wrench. This will give you greater leverage.

Various liquid chemicals are available for application to rusty couplings. Apply the liquid, and let it soak in for at least 10 minutes.

If none of these tactics work, wipe the joint completely clean of any anti-rust liquid you have applied. Wet some rags and tie them tightly around the two sections of pipe leading into the coupling. Using a brazing torch, apply the flame around the coupling. This will force the coupling to expand and break away from the pipe. The purpose of the wet rags is to keep the pipe cool and to keep it from expanding. You will then be able to use your wrench to remove the coupling.

See Pipes, Frozen, *page 278*
    Pipes, Protecting, *page 279*
    Rust, Removing, *page 288*
    Water Pipes, How to Protect from Freezing, *page 362*
    Wrench, How to Use Adjustable, *page 391*

☐ Pipe or Tank, Burst

Don't try to repair the pipe or tank while water is coming out of it. Instead, go to the water valve that controls the pipe or tank and turn it off. If you can't find the valve or don't know immediately where it is, find the main water shutoff valve and close it. That will shut off the flow of water throughout the house, but it will give you time to find the supplementary valve for the pipe or tank and close it.

A burst pipe can be due to water that has frozen in a pipe. If the burst is a large one, then the pipe or tank will need to be replaced, a job for a plumber.

See Brazing, *page 34*
    Copper Pipe, How to Repair, *page 56*
    Copper Pipe, Soldering, *page 60*
    Hacksaws, How to Use, *page 160*
    Iron Pipes, Repairing, *page 189*
    Metals, Joining, *page 208*
    Pipe, Cutting, *page 274*
    Pipe Joints, Loosening, *page 276*
    Pipes, Frozen, *page 278*
    Pipes, Protecting, *page 279*
    Rumbling Noise in Hot Water Tank, *page 288*

☐ Pipes, Frozen

The pressure of ice in a pipe can cause the pipe to burst. If you have a pipe with trapped water that has frozen, open the valve or faucet nearest to the frozen section of the pipe, preferably both. Using a brazing torch, gradually heat the pipe. Start at the open valve or faucet end of the pipe and work your way back gradually along the length of the pipe. Don't start at the middle of the pipe for the heat may generate steam and, since this will be blocked by ice on both sides, could cause the pipe to burst. In any event, the idea isn't to generate steam, but simply to melt the ice. All you want to do is to warm the pipe enough to start melting the ice.

Piping is often mounted near studs or other wood framing. Be careful not to set any of these on fire. You may want to wet down any areas that are wood and near the flame to prevent this possibility. Keep the flame away from any joints which may be soldered.

An alternative method for thawing water pipes is to use an infrared bulb. Follow the same precautions as with a brazing torch. Be careful not to touch the bulb when hot. An infrared bulb may take longer than a torch to unfreeze a pipe, but the danger of fire due to an open flame is eliminated.

See Brazing, *page 35*

Copper Pipe, How to Repair, *page 56*
Copper Pipe, Soldering, *page 60*
Hacksaws, How to Use, *page 160*
Iron Pipe, Repairing, *page 189*
Metals, Joining, *page 208*
Pipe Joints, Loosening, *page 276*
Pipes, Protecting, *page 279*
Rumbling Noise in Hot Water Tank, *page 288*
Rust, Removing, *page 288*
Water Pipes, How to Protect from Freezing, *page 362*

☐ Pipes, Protecting

If you plan to leave your home during the winter months, and you live in an area in which temperatures fall below the freezing point (32°F or 0°C), you should do something about protecting the pipes. When water freezes, it expands. This expansion can cause pipes to burst. Not only does this ruin the pipe, but there can be extensive water damage.

There are various ways of preventing damage. Set the thermostats in your home to their minimum setting, but not less than 40°F. This will keep your home above the freezing temperature. As an alternative, drain your water pipes. You can do this by locating the water valve, generally located at the low point of the water supply piping.

After you have done this, drain all toilet tanks by closing their associated valves, located near the floor and to the left as you face the toilet. Then flush the toilets. Shut off the switch that controls electricity to the hot water tank. Wait a day to let the hot water in the tank become cool, and then drain the water by letting it empty into a succession of pails.

Check that the water system is closed by opening all the faucets in the house, one by one, and then close them. Pour some antifreeze into the different sinks in the house and into any bathtub and/or shower drains. Also put some antifreeze into all toilets. If your home is heated by steam or hot water, make sure to drain these systems as well.

When you turn your home water system on again, do so slowly and carefully. First, turn on the main water pipe. Give the water a chance to flow through the various pipes and to fill them. When you first turn the faucets on, you will find them acting erratically with water coming out in short bursts. Open all faucets slowly to give the water a chance to expel the air from the pipes. If you have an electrically heated water supply, fill the tank with water first before you turn on the electrical power to the tank. When you turn on the valves to the toilets, do so slowly. You may hear some knocking in the pipes, but this will stop as soon as the water piping is filled.

☐ Pliers

There are a number of different types of pliers, but one of the most useful for in-home repairs is the *slip joint* type. It is so-called since the plier jaws can be made larger or smaller because of the slip joint construction.

Pliers have a tremendous number of uses. You can use them for holding a nut while tightening a bolt with a screwdriver (Fig. P-40). You can bend wire or flat metal, or straighten bent nails (P-41). Use the slip joint pliers for turning nuts. If you want to hammer a nail without risking finger damage, use the pliers to hold the nail. Use the pliers as a temporary rest for a hot soldering iron tip.

☐ Plywood, Painting

The most common type of plywood is fir, possibly because it is the least expensive. Such wood is sometimes said to have a "wild" grain that becomes particularly noticeable if the plywood is stained. The reason for dark and light areas after staining is because parts of the surface are softer than others. The softer portions soak in more of the stain and look darker. To keep this from happening, first cover the surface of the plywood with a clear sealer made especially for this purpose.

If you plan to paint the plywood instead of using stain, you may still run into some difficulties with parts of the wood looking darker. Use the clear sealer to get a more uniform painted surface.

See Alligatoring (Paint), *page 20*
Chalking (Paint), *page 44*
Checking (Paint), *page 45*
Doors, Painting, *page 79*

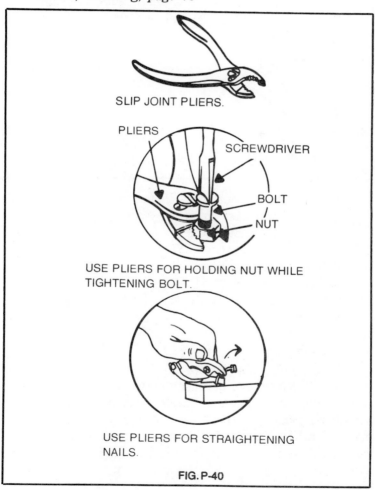

SLIP JOINT PLIERS.

PLIERS

SCREWDRIVER

BOLT

NUT

USE PLIERS FOR HOLDING NUT WHILE TIGHTENING BOLT.

USE PLIERS FOR STRAIGHTENING NAILS.

FIG. P-40

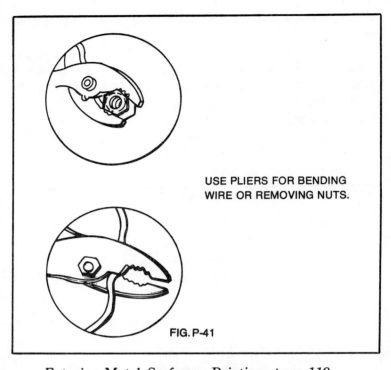

USE PLIERS FOR BENDING
WIRE OR REMOVING NUTS.

FIG. P-41

☐ Putty Knife

A *putty knife*, also known as a *spackling knife*, is often confused with a scraper because the two look so much alike. A putty knife, as its name indicates, is used for applying and smoothing plaster or spackling compound, or for patching with putty. The blade end of the tool is much wider than the part of the blade connected to the handle. Made of spring steel, a putty knife is very flexible, thin, and has a sharp blade.

A scraper has a much stiffer blade than a putty knife, is thicker, and has a chisel-like blade. It is designed for removing paint. Intermixing the two tools, the putty knife and scraper, not only makes the work more difficult but contributes to unsatisfactory results.

When you are finished using either a putty knife or scraper, remove all traces of paint, spackle, or plaster. Then wipe the blade with an oily rag. If possible, store these tools in non-humid areas.

☐ **Quick Check of Television Set**

See Television Set—Quick Check, *page 330*

□ Radiators, Painting

To get the maximum amount of heat from a radiator, the best thing to do is not to paint it. Unfortunately, radiators are unsightly, have a tendency to rust, and are dirt collectors. Radiation of heat is also hindered by dirt which can accumulate near the bottom of the radiator. To get more heat or as a prior step to painting, clean this area with a paint brush that is long (to let you reach hard to get at spots) and has soft bristles.

If the radiator has been painted previously, it is best to remove the old paint before repainting. The radiator may have several coats of paint so the job will be quite difficult, particularly since some of the painted areas will be hard to reach. Work in a well ventilated room, keeping all windows open. To do a good job, it would be best to remove the radiator. The radiator is held on to its steam valve by a large nut, and you will need a large size wrench to turn it. If you cannot do this, let the radiator remain in position, but fasten some papers to the wall behind the radiator to protect the wall against paint remover or paint.

The best time to paint the radiator is in the spring or summer when you don't need the services of the radiator. This will also give the paint ample time to dry. However, if you must paint during cold days, be sure to turn the radiator off and keep it turned off until the radiator is cold.

A single application of paint remover may not be enough. After putting on a first coating of paint remover, wait about 15 minutes to give the remover a chance to work. Then use a scraper to remove as much of the paint as you can. If any paint spots remain or there are rust spots, work on these with a wire brush. You may find it necessary to put on another coat of paint remover.

After you have removed all paint and rust spots, wash the radiator with mineral spirits or carbon tetrachloride. Mineral spirits are preferable. The fumes of carbon tetrachloride are toxic. Wear a face mask, make sure all windows are open, and use an electric fan to get adequate air circulation.

Do not use the paint as it is supplied in the can. Make a mixture of paint and paint thinner with a ratio of three-fourths paint to one-fourth thinner. Brush on one coat of paint, making sure you reach all parts of the radiator. Paint only those parts of the radiator that are visible. It isn't necessary to paint any part of the radiator that is hidden by an adjacent wall.

After the first coat is completely dry, put on a second coat. Be sure to let the paint dry thoroughly before turning the steam valve on again.

The heating efficiency of the radiator will be reduced by painting it, and this also applies to metallic paints. You might also want to try a heat resistant enamel since it will not darken as much as ordinary paints. You can use any wall type paint, oil paint or enamel, but do not use a water base paint as it can cause rusting.

There may be some odor from the radiator after it has been painted and turned on. This odor is temporary and will disappear after the radiator has been in use for some time.

You can avoid painting by using a radiator cover or putting it in a metal radiator enclosure. Even though the enclosure has open grills, it also restricts the free flow of heat and contributes to radiator inefficiency.

See Alligatoring, (Paint), *page 20*
   Blistering (Paint), *page 33*
   Chalking (Paint), *page 44*

☐ Rawl Plugs

☐ Romex Cable, Cutting and Installing

The choice of *BX* or *Romex* cable for electrical house wiring depends on local electrical codes. For the past few years, Romex has gradually replaced BX since electrical wiring with Romex is much easier and faster. Romex is nonmetallic cable and, unlike BX, is not covered with an outside metallic shield.

Allow at least 6 inches of wire for connections inside the electrical box in which the Romex is to be connected (Fig. R-1). Remove the outside insulation of the Romex by using a razor blade or sharp knife, making sure you do not cut into the wires. Remove any insulating paper covering the wires.

Attach a connector to the cable. Install the connector in the electrical box, holding the connector to the electrical box with a locknut supplied with the connector. Strip back about ¾ inch of insulation from each of the wires, and you can then make your connections.

☐ Rumbling Noise in Hot Water Tank

This can be caused by overheating and can also be due to hot water backing up into the cold water supply line. Another symptom is hot water coming out of the cold water faucet. Shut off the source of heat to boiler immediately and call a plumber.

See Water Pipes, Noisy, *page 365*

☐ Rust, Removing

Rust is a form of oxidation in which a material combines with the oxygen in the air. In the case of iron, for example, the rust that forms is iron oxide.

You can remove rust in several ways. You can use a wire brush or emery paper, various liquid chemicals or *Naval Jelly*. Brush the Naval Jelly on any metal surface and then just wash it off.

To prevent tools from rusting, always store them in a dry place. Put some machine oil on a rag and wipe the tools with it. Always lubricate the moving parts of any hand tool with a drop or two of a good lubricating oil. Don't leave tools outdoors overnight. If tools become wet during use, dry them carefully, and then wipe them with an oil soaked rag. Rust spreads. If you see a rust spot developing, remove it immediately by sanding and then wipe with an oiled rag.

For small areas of steel, remove the rust and then coat with colorless nail polish. A thick coating isn't necessary. The nail polish prevents air from reaching the metal, so oxidation doesn't take place. When using the nail polish,

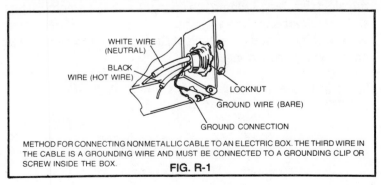

WHITE WIRE (NEUTRAL)

BLACK WIRE (HOT WIRE)

LOCKNUT

GROUND WIRE (BARE)

GROUND CONNECTION

METHOD FOR CONNECTING NONMETALLIC CABLE TO AN ELECTRIC BOX. THE THIRD WIRE IN THE CABLE IS A GROUNDING WIRE AND MUST BE CONNECTED TO A GROUNDING CLIP OR SCREW INSIDE THE BOX. **FIG. R-1**

brush slightly beyond the rusted area. The surface being coated must be clean and dry.

See Iron Pipes, Repairing, *page 189*
  Metals, Joining, *page 208*
  Pipes, Protecting, *page 279*
  Water Pipes, Leaky, *page 364*

☐ Scraper

See Putty Knife, *page 282*

☐ Screens, How to Fix Damaged

The purpose of a screen is to let fresh air in and keep insects out. It doesn't take much of a hole in the screen to act as a passageway for both. Further, once a screen has a hole, it is inevitable that the hole will become larger. The sharp edges of loose screen wires around the hole can also cut fingers.

Buy screening or patches to match the existing screen. For this job, you will need, in addition to the patches, shears, and a small block of wood. You can use fine wire or nylon thread for very small holes.

As a first step, square off the hole in the screen using shears. Cut a rectangular patch of screen material so it is about 1 inch larger in length and width than the hole. If you will examine the patch, you will see it is made of horizontal and vertical wires that are intermeshed. Remove one wire from each of the four sides of the patch and, using a block of wood, bend the edges of the patch wire over a block of wood (Fig. S-1).

Working from the outside of the screen, insert the patch

290

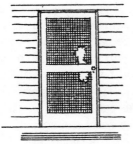

DAMAGED SCREEN LETS INSECTS ENTER HOME

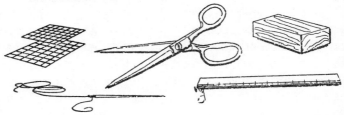

TOOLS YOU WILL NEED INCLUDE PATCHING MATERIAL, SHEARS, AND A BLOCK OF WOOD. FOR SMALL HOLES A NEEDLE AND NYLON THREAD OR FINE WIRE WILL DO. USE RULER FOR MEASURING PATCH SIZE.

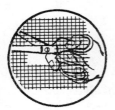

TRIM HOLE SO IT FORMS SQUARE OR RECTANGLE.

REMOVE OUTER WIRE ON ALL FOUR SIDES OF PATCH.

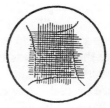

PUT PATCH ON BLOCK OF WOOD AND BEND END OF PATCH OVER.

FIG. S-1.

into the screen so that the patch covers the hole. Working from the inside, bend the wires of the patch inward toward the center of the hole. You may need some help—someone to hold the patch firmly from the outside while you work from the inside. While you can bend the wires of the patch with your fingers, you will find it easier and faster to use a block of wood for this purpose. It will also keep your fingers from being jabbed by the wire ends of the patch.

If, after you finish the patch, you paint the screen with screen paint, the patch will be scarcely noticeable.

If part of your window or door screen has become rusty, cut out the rusty section with a pair of shears or diagonal cutters. Make a rectangular hole and then put in a patch. Paint the screen to prevent further rusting. Aluminum screens do not have a rust problem, but they can get holes, just as any other screen. For such screens, use aluminum patches.

You do not need screen patching material if the hole is very small, possibly about the size of a dime or less. You can use fine wire having the same color as the screen or a nylon thread having a matching color (Fig. S-2). If you plan to repaint the screen, the fine wire for patching can be of any color.

☐ Screwdrivers

There are two types of screwdrivers you'll need for in-home repairs. One is the *straight* or *flat blade;* the other is the *Phillips* (Fig. S-3). The advantage of the Phillips is that it gets a better grip on the screw head. However, you can only use the Phillips with screws that have Phillips heads. Similarly, the straight or flat blade driver can be used only with screws that have straight, slotted heads. Screwdrivers are extremely useful tools and are absolutely essential for in-home repairs. It is helpful to have a set of each type.

Screwdrivers are made in three parts: a head or handle, a metal shank, and a blade to fit the slot head of a screw. The blade and shank, made of tool steel in better screwdrivers, make up one piece. The blade is usually round, but larger screwdrivers sometimes have square shanks. The purpose

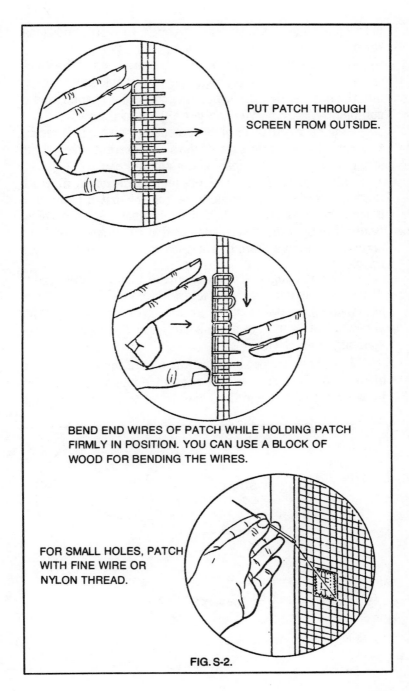

PUT PATCH THROUGH
SCREEN FROM OUTSIDE.

BEND END WIRES OF PATCH WHILE HOLDING PATCH
FIRMLY IN POSITION. YOU CAN USE A BLOCK OF
WOOD FOR BENDING THE WIRES.

FOR SMALL HOLES, PATCH
WITH FINE WIRE OR
NYLON THREAD.

FIG. S-2.

is to let you use a tool, such as a wrench, to supply additional turning force.

The shank of the screwdriver is embedded in the handle. When you buy a driver, make sure the shank extends deep into the handle, that the handle is grooved or shaped, and is sufficiently large so you can get a good grip on it.

Some screwdrivers have detachable heads. This means you can have a variety of drivers of different sizes, both straight edge and Phillips, with a single head.

Other types of screwdrivers include the *offset,* in which the blade forms a right angle to permit the driver to get into places that cannot be reached by ordinary screwdrivers. Another is the *ratchet* screwdriver that can be used to drive screws or remove them by rotating or pushing down on the handle.

When driving a screw, keep the blade of the screwdriver as nearly in a straight line with the head of the screw as possible. Try not to tilt the screwdriver when using it, for you will not be taking full advantage of the force you are applying (Fig. S-4).

The screwdriver should fit the slot of the screw. If the blade is too small, you will not get enough contact area between the screw and the blade to let you turn the screw

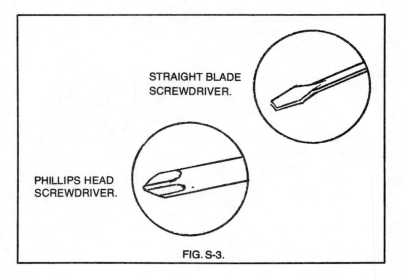

STRAIGHT BLADE SCREWDRIVER.

PHILLIPS HEAD SCREWDRIVER.

FIG. S-3.

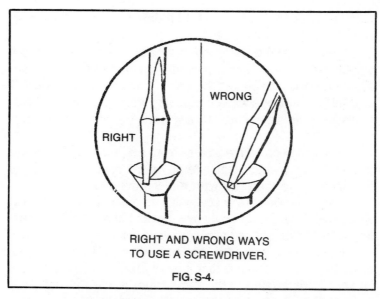

RIGHT AND WRONG WAYS
TO USE A SCREWDRIVER.

FIG. S-4.

correctly. If the blade is too large, it may not fit in the screw slot.

You can exert more force on the driver by using two hands, one for turning the handle and the other for pushing against the top of the screwdriver (Fig. S-5). If, even with a

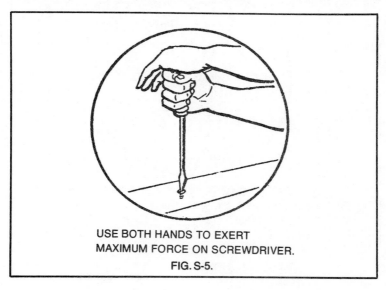

USE BOTH HANDS TO EXERT
MAXIMUM FORCE ON SCREWDRIVER.

FIG. S-5.

previously drilled hole, you find it difficult to drive a screw, coat the screw threads with wax or soap.

You will find it easier to drive a screw through wood if you first drill a hole, either partially or completely (Fig. S-6). This will also let you get the screw started much easier. It will help hold the screw in place by engaging the first few threads of the screw, and it may keep the wood from splitting.

You can keep screwdrivers from rusting by oiling them. Put some lightweight machine oil on the shank and blade of the driver, and then rub with a clean dry cloth.

Never work with a screwdriver on a "live" electrical appliance—that is, an appliance that is plugged into an outlet, whether or not the appliance is turned on.

Keep your screwdrivers, and other tools, in an open tote box. Its advantage is that it has a handle so you can carry all your tools around at the same time. Because it is open, you can find the tool you want rather quickly.

Don't use a screwdriver whose blade has become worn or rounded. If you know how to dress the blade of a driver, do

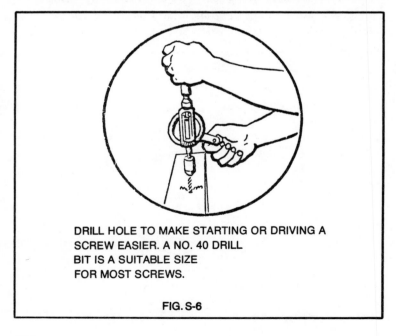

DRILL HOLE TO MAKE STARTING OR DRIVING A
SCREW EASIER. A NO. 40 DRILL
BIT IS A SUITABLE SIZE
FOR MOST SCREWS.

FIG. S-6

so. If not, replace the screwdriver. Don't throw the old screwdriver away, though. Keep it for odd jobs around the house, such as opening cans of paint, punching holes into cans, or for some scraping purposes.

See Screw Holes, Repair of , *page 297*

Screws , *page 297*

□ Screw Holes, Repair of

Sometimes the hole made by a screw will become enlarged, and the screw will no longer grip the inside surfaces of the hole. This can happen if the screw has been worked back and forth a number of times, or if the original screw has been replaced with one that is smaller.

To avoid starting a new screw hole, plug the hole with one or two wooden matchsticks. Be sure to remove the striking head first. Tap the matchstick in with a hammer so it forms a force fit. You can also use any scrap bits of soft wood or even toothpicks. Also, consider using a slightly larger screw.

You can use wood dough or plastic wood as a screw hole filler but these take time to dry before you can put in the new screw. They do have the advantage of supplying a smoother working surface, so it is easier to drive the screw in more accurately than using the matchstick method.

See Screwdrivers , *page 292*

Screws , *page 297*

□ Screws

Like nails, screws are used to join various materials. They are stronger than nails, but their strength depends on their size, shape, material, weather, and the substances into which they are driven. A new screw, made of iron, is strong but it can rust. Screws, however, require more time and more effort to work with than nails.

Screws are made of various metals, and the most common is iron. Brass screws are sometimes used where a decorative head is needed, but they are more expensive. Screws are available in various finishes, including nickel, chrome or chromium plating, stainless steel, and black.

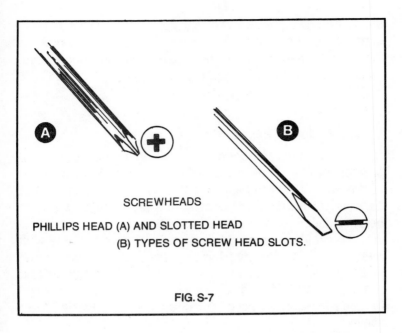

SCREWHEADS

PHILLIPS HEAD (A) AND SLOTTED HEAD
(B) TYPES OF SCREW HEAD SLOTS.

FIG. S-7

The main parts of a screw are its *head, shank,* and *threaded section.* Basically, there are two head types—*slotted* and *Phillips* (Fig. S-7). The advantage of the Phillips head is that there is greater contact between the screwdriver and the screw head, enabling the user to supply greater driving force with less chance of the screwdriver slipping away from the head of the screw.

The most common types of heads for screws for either Phillips or slot head, are the *flat, round* and *oval* (Figs. S-8 and S-9). Flat head screws are used where the head of the screw is to be flat with the surface of the wood, or countersunk.

Screw sizes are determined by length and by gauge (Fig. S-10 and Table S-1). For a flat head screw, the length is the distance from the flat portion of the head to the tip. For a round head, length is measured from directly beneath the head to the tip. For an oval, it is from the outermost edge of the head to the tip. The gauge of a screw is the maximum thickness of its shank. This is measured directly beneath the screw head. When ordering screws, do so by head type,

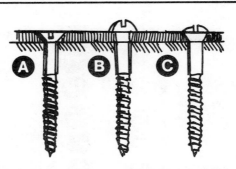

SCREW HEADS CAN BE FLAT (A) ROUND (B) OR OVAL
(C) THE FLAT HEAD TYPE CAN BE RECESSED.

FIG. S-8

length, and gauge number. Iron is assumed as the metal for a screw, unless otherwise specified—thus, No. 8, round head, Phillips, 1-¼ inches. This would be an iron screw with a Phillips head. It would be 1-¼ inches long, and its shank diameter would be gauge No. 8. Gauge sizes range from the smallest or No. 0, to the largest, No. 24.

To make it easier to drive a screw into wood, drill a through hole whose diameter is smaller than the diameter of the screw. Take a cake of dry soap and rub it over the threads of the screw. You will find it takes less energy to drive the

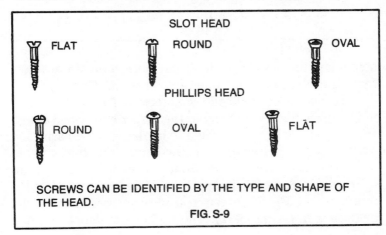

SCREWS CAN BE IDENTIFIED BY THE TYPE AND SHAPE OF THE HEAD.

FIG. S-9

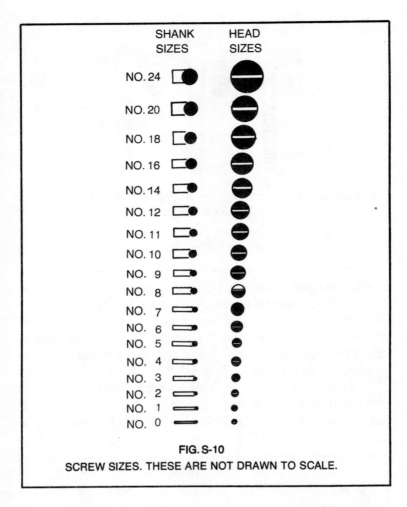

screw into the wood. The hole and lubrication of the screw threads are very helpful when working with hard woods.

To conceal screw heads, countersink the screws and fill in the space above the head of the screw with wood dough (Fig. S-11). Wait for the dough to harden and then sand and paint to suit. An alternative method is to drive the screw in so its head is well below the surface. Then force fit a section of a dowel, a plug, into the space above the screw and tamp in with a mallet. The dowel can protrude from the surface or can be flush with it (Fig. S-12). The surface can then be sanded and painted. If the force fit will not hold the dowel, put a drop or two of glue on the bottom surface of the dowel plug and also on the head of the screw.

In the case of flat head screws whose heads are covered, there is a disadvantage in that the screw is no longer visible. It isn't readily available for removal should that become necessary.

While screws are used for wood, some are also made for metal. Wood screws have threads which do not reach the head of the screw. There is a length of about one-third of the screw beneath the head which has no threads. Screws for sheet metal work have threads which go right up to the underside of the head.

See Screwdrivers, *page 292*

Screw Holes, Repair of, *page 297*

□ Shellac, Applying Liquid

Liquid shellac is available is clear and orange. Both supply a durable finish for floors that have been sanded down to the bare wood.

Apply a coat of shellac to the floor using a brush or roller, which these should either be new or else absolutely clear of any paint from previous use. After applying the first coat of shellac, let it dry for at least four hours.

You can then apply the second coat of shellac, allowing this coat to dry overnight for a minimum of 12 hours. Sand the

TABLE S-1			
Sizes of Screws to Use for Different Thicknesses of Wood.			
Wood Thickness	Screw	Length	Pilot Hole
3/4"	#8	1 1/2"	5/32"
5/8"	#8	1 1/4"	5/32"
1/2"	#6	1 1/4"	1/8"
3/8"	#6	1"	1/8"
1/4"	#4	3/4"	7/64"

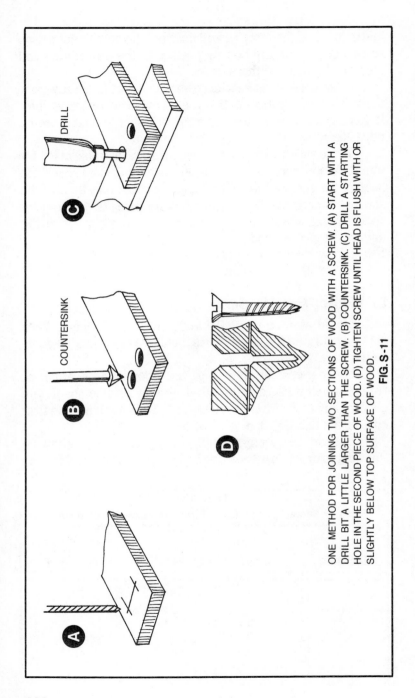

ONE METHOD FOR JOINING TWO SECTIONS OF WOOD WITH A SCREW. (A) START WITH A DRILL BIT A LITTLE LARGER THAN THE SCREW. (B) COUNTERSINK. (C) DRILL A STARTING HOLE IN THE SECOND PIECE OF WOOD. (D) TIGHTEN SCREW UNTIL HEAD IS FLUSH WITH OR SLIGHTLY BELOW TOP SURFACE OF WOOD.

FIG. S-11

entire floor surface, by hand, using medium grade sandpaper. Vacuum the floor thoroughly. After vacuuming, go over the floor with a clean cloth to pick up any dust that may have remained. You can then apply the third and final coat of shellac, but let it dry for a minimum of 24 hours before walking on it.

You can protect this final coating of shellac by waxing and buffing. To protect the finish, always pick up furniture; don't drag it across the floor. If any water drops onto the floor, wipe it away as soon as possible, using any clean, absorbent cloth. Use scatter rugs on floor areas that have heavy traffic. Clean, wax, and buff regularly.

See Floors, Sanding, *page 135*

☐ Shower Head, Faulty

Shower heads should be able to supply a uniform spray of water. If the water seems to come from only part of the head or if the water doesn't come out with adequate force, the head may need to be cleaned (Fig. S-13).

To clean the head, you will need *channel lock pliers* and adhesive tape. The purpose of the tape is to protect the finish of the nut holding the shower head in place, often chrome plated or, in older fixtures, nickel plated. As a first step, put two layers of adhesive tape around the nut. Wipe the nut thoroughly before putting on the tape, since the tape will adhere better if the nut is clean and dry. If you don't have tape and you don't have channel lock pliers, wrap the nut tightly with any scrap piece of cloth. In place of the channel locks,

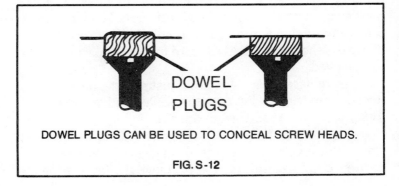

DOWEL
PLUGS

DOWEL PLUGS CAN BE USED TO CONCEAL SCREW HEADS.

FIG. S-12

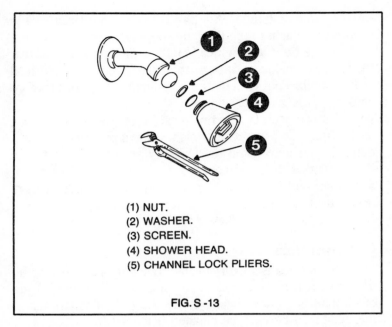

(1) NUT.
(2) WASHER.
(3) SCREEN.
(4) SHOWER HEAD.
(5) CHANNEL LOCK PLIERS.

FIG. S -13

use a monkey wrench. You should have one or the other, preferably both, of these tools in your repair kit.

Using the tool, turn the nut in a counterclockwise direction until it is completely loosened. You will then be able to push it back and to remove the shower head. When you do, you will see a washer and a screen. Examine the washer. If it has cut edges or seems worn, replace it. Washers are inexpensive, and it is a good idea to replace them anyway. With the help of an old toothbrush, clean the screen. Do this under running water so the force of the water pulls away any particles. Clean the shower head with the help of a toothpick. Poke the toothpick through each hole in the head and then rinse the shower head. Make sure that every particle of dirt is removed.

To replace the shower head, just reverse the steps you took in removing it. Put back the washer and the screen and then, using the tool, tighten the nut.

Don't try to force the nut. Turn it at first with your fingers until you feel the threads engaging. After you have tightened the nut with the tool, remove the tape. Wipe the nut with a cloth to restore the shine. Now you can test the results of your work. If you find water leaking from the nut after reassembly, disengage the nut and put some pipe joint compound on the threads at the top end of the shower head.

This cleaning procedure is useful only if the shower head is in good working condition. If it is corroded and possibly clogged with rust, you may need to replace the screen or the entire shower head assembly. Separate shower head assemblies are available in hardware stores and in home maintenance supply stores.

☐ Sink, Bath and Shower Faucets, How to Replace

Do not assume that all faucets are alike and interchangeable. They are not. You can use a different style if you wish, but what is important is to make sure that your new faucet will fit right in place of the old one. The best procedure is to remove the old faucet and to take it along with you when buying a new one. Get a return guarantee—that is, if the new faucet will not fit, you have the option of returning it.

To put in a new faucet, you will first need to remove the old one. Try removing the old one first, for getting a faucet out can sometimes be extremely difficult, tough enough to make you change your mind. The faucet is held in place by one or more nuts, located beneath the sink. The work area is very restricted, making it very awkward to remove the nuts. The best tool is a *basin cock wrench,* but if you do not have one you could try a monkey wrench, an adjustable wrench, or an open end wrench.

Some faucets are single types. Others are double with one faucet for hot water, the other for cold. Other faucets have a single spout with separate controls for hot and cold water. If you have a single faucet, you do not have a measurement problem. With a double faucet, make an exact measurement of the separation of the two holes, in inches, from the center of one hole to the center of the other.

Faucets may or may not come equipped with a pop-up drain. The pop-up drain is used to control the flow of water out of the sink. One of the most common types of faucet is the 4-inch lavatory faucet without a pop-up drain. The shanks of such faucets are ordinarily 4 inches center to center (Fig. S-14).

Your first step is to shut off the water and remove the old faucet. As you do, note the position of washers and nuts. If you have never done this before, make a rough sketch, or else notes. Putting in a new faucet is simply the reverse procedure to taking out the old one.

If you will examine the two shanks of your new faucet, you will see that each has a locknut and a washer. Remove these. Put some plumber's putty in the groove beneath the metal frame of the fixture (Fig. S-15). The purpose of the putty is to make a tight seal between the fixture and the top of the sink.

You will now need to work beneath the sink. There you will see the two pipes that supply water to the faucet. First, put a locknut over each of these pipes and then the washer that was supplied with the new faucet. Put the new faucet in place so that each shank slides over the pipes beneath the sink. Move the locknuts up, one at a time, so they engage the male threads of the faucet shanks. At this time turn the locknuts by hand until you feel the threads engaging. Don't use force since the locknuts should turn easily. Turn the nuts several times and, if they do so smoothly, you can use a tool for further turning. As you rotate the nuts, the washer will rise with the upward movement of the nuts. Make the nuts as tight as you can. Remove any excess putty that squeezes out from the base of the fixture. Turn on the water and try your new faucet.

See Aerator, How to Install, *page 16*

Bathroom Faucets, Installing, *page 29*

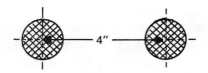

FAUCETS ARE COMMONLY MOUNTED ON 4-INCH CENTERS.

FIG. S-14

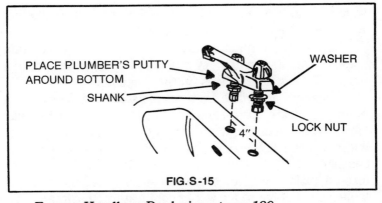

PLACE PLUMBER'S PUTTY AROUND BOTTOM

SHANK

WASHER

LOCK NUT

4"

FIG. S-15

☐ **Sink Drain, Sluggish**

If water drains very slowly out of your sink, you are well on your way to having a clogged drain. If the sink has a strainer, remove it. Some strainers are held in place by a single center screw; others just fit into place. If it is the screw type, put the screw aside after removing it so it has no opportunity of falling into the sink. Take out the strainer. If its holes are clogged, clean it with a dry cloth. Make sure all holes are free and clear.

If the sink is still sluggish, let all the water drain out of it and then turn on the hot water tap. Let the water come out of the tap slowly. The object is not to fill the sink, but to let the hot water get into the drain where it may have a chance to dissolve accumulated grease or soap. Let the hot water run for about 10 to 15 minutes. Do not turn on the cold water tap. You want the water to be as hot as possible. If, for some reason, your hot water supply isn't working, heat some water in a kettle, preferably one with a spout. Pour the hot water into the drain, but do so slowly.

If the drain remains sluggish, try a chemical drain opener, available in grocery stores or supermarkets. Use a funnel. Follow instructions on the container.

Cleaners are made from *caustic soda* with *bauxite* and other chemicals. Be careful not to get the cleaner on your hands. Wash your hands thoroughly if you do make contact with the cleaner. If you use lye, do not pour in crystals since undissolved crystals can form a hard block inside the pipe. Instead, make a solution of lye and water. Use about two full tablespoons of lye to a quart of cool water. Be careful. The mixture gets very hot. Put a small amount of the lye in water at a time and stir thoroughly. Allow to cool, then add more lye.

It is much better to buy a prepared solution of commercial drain cleaner than to make your own. In either case, give the drain cleaner an ample opportunity to work. It takes time, generally several hours or more, for the drain cleaner to be fully effective. When the drain is cleared, let hot water run through it for about 10 minutes. Once again, it isn't necessary to turn the hot water faucet on full force. The purpose of the hot water is to remove all traces of drain cleaner, plus any dissolved grease that may still be adhering to the inner walls of the drainpipe.

You will find it helpful to have a funnel around the house for just such emergencies. All drains clog, sooner or later. Use the funnel for pouring drain cleaner into the drain. This will keep the drain cleaner away from the porcelain finish of your sink. Do not use the funnel for any other purpose. A good storage place for the funnel is in the cabinet beneath the sink. After using the funnel, wash it thoroughly.

You can avoid future sink clogging by a little preventive maintenance. Don't allow food or peelings of any kind to get into the drain. Always use a strainer. These are available in various sizes, styles and shapes (Fig. S-16). You can get a stainless steel basket strainer, a strainer cut, a strainer with a center post that lets you control opening size, or a flat strainer.

Let hot water run down the drain once a day. You need not use the water full force, just enough to prevent grease and food from collecting on the inner wall of the drainpipe. Also, use a triangular sink garbage container for parings and peelings. Keep it in a corner of the sink so you can put parings and other garbage into it. The container has holes to permit water to escape into the drain. After each meal preparation, empty the container into your garbage pail.

See Bathtub Drain, Clogged, *page 32*
Clogging of Kitchen Sink, Preventing, *page 47*
Drains, Clogged , *page 81*
Kitchen Trap, Replacing, *page 194*

SINK STRAINERS ARE AVAILABLE IN DIFFERENT SIZES, STYLES AND SHAPES.

FIG. S -16

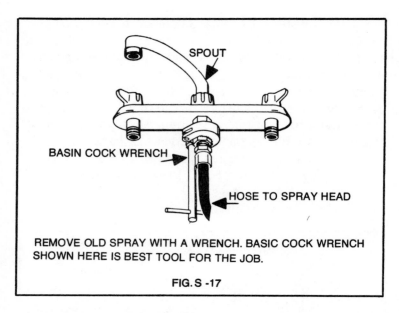

SPOUT

BASIN COCK WRENCH

HOSE TO SPRAY HEAD

REMOVE OLD SPRAY WITH A WRENCH. BASIC COCK WRENCH
SHOWN HERE IS BEST TOOL FOR THE JOB.

FIG. S -17

□ Sink Spray, Installing a New

To install a new *sink spray,* you will need to work in the close space beneath the kitchen sink. The sink spray is connected to the center spout. Using a wrench, loosen and remove the nut holding the spray hose in place.

It may be difficult to use an open end, crescent, or a monkey wrench because of the cramped space. An excellent tool for this purpose is a basin cock wrench (Fig. S-17). You can also use this tool for removing and installing faucets. However, do not buy the basin cock wrench until you have tried using other wrenches and find it impossible to turn the sink spray nut.

After you have removed the nut, mount the new spray terminal in place and tighten the nut. Since you are installing a new spray assembly, complete with spray head, it will not be necessary to work on the spray head itself.

Two possible conditions exist beneath the spout at the point where you want to connect the spray hose. The faucet may have a female thread, in which case you can simply screw in the male end of the spray hose (Fig. S-18). You may find, though, that the faucet is equipped with a *nipple.* Since

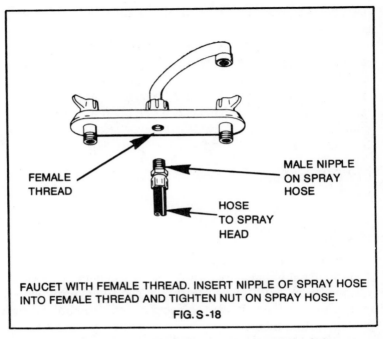

FAUCET WITH FEMALE THREAD. INSERT NIPPLE OF SPRAY HOSE INTO FEMALE THREAD AND TIGHTEN NUT ON SPRAY HOSE.

FIG. S-18

this nipple is pretty much like the nipple end of the spray hose, there is a problem of connecting the two. For this you can use an adapter. Screw the adapter onto the male end of the hose (Fig. S-19). Then screw it on to the nipple of the faucet. Spray head kits often include the adapter. If your faucet is equipped with a female thread end, you will not need to use the adapter.

See Sink Spray, Installing a New Head for, *page 311*

☐ Sink Spray, Installing a New Head for

To install a new sink spray head, turn off both hot and cold faucets. You will find your old spray head held in by a collar made of plastic. The collar is ribbed so you can get a good grip on it. Hold the collar with one hand and turn the spray head with the other. The spray head should then come off in your hand. When you do, you will see a rubber washer on top of the collar assembly. Remove this washer. Right beneath the washer is a retaining clip which holds the collar in position. You can take this clip off by prying it out with a flat blade screwdriver. Once you do so, the plastic collar will come out.

You can now put a new spray head in place of the old one just by reversing the procedure (Fig. S-20). Put the new collar on the hose and then keep it in place by using the clip. Slip a new washer over the top. All you need do now is to put on the new spray head. This screws right on to the threaded collar.

See Sink Spray, Installing a New, *page 310*

See Sink Spray, Installing a New, *page 310*

☐ Slip-Joint Pliers
See Pliers, *page 280*

☐ Soldering

A *soldering iron* is a useful tool for a number of repairs. You can use it to make electrically secure connections when you join wire. With a special tip you can remove hardened putty from windows when replacing panes. It is helpful for joining certain metals.

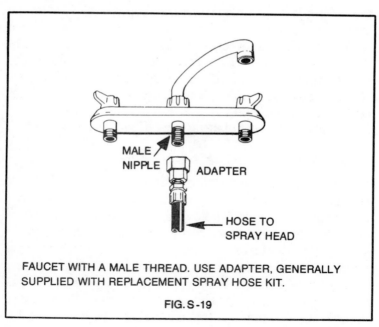

MALE NIPPLE

ADAPTER

HOSE TO SPRAY HEAD

FAUCET WITH A MALE THREAD. USE ADAPTER, GENERALLY SUPPLIED WITH REPLACEMENT SPRAY HOSE KIT.

FIG. S-19

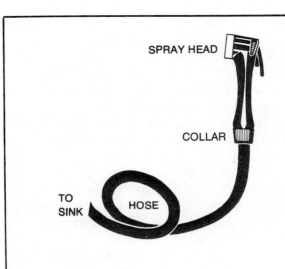

SPRAY HEAD

COLLAR

TO SINK

HOSE

YOU CAN USE EXISTING HOSE OF SINK SPRAY. REMOVE SPRAY HEAD BY TURNING IT WHILE HOLDING HOSE. REMOVE RUBBER WASHER, HOLDING CLIP, AND COLLAR WILL THEN COME OFF. REVERSE STEPS TO INSTALL NEW SPRAY HEAD.

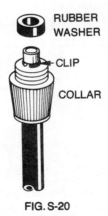

RUBBER WASHER

CLIP

COLLAR

FIG. S-20

There are two basic types: the *soldering iron* and the *soldering gun*. The gun has a number of advantages: it heats faster, it turns off automatically when you release the trigger, you do not need a soldering iron stand for it, and it is available with interchangeable tips. However, a soldering iron is less expensive. Its tips are bigger and heavier and last longer. If you do plan to use a soldering iron, get one that is rated at 100 watts or more. There are irons, lightweights known as *pencil irons* whose power is about 25 watts, but these are only suited for special work.

One of the problems in using a soldering iron or gun is that a film of oxide builds up very rapidly on the tip, a film that can prevent successful soldering. As a first step, mount the iron in a secure holder, such as a vise, and file the tip until the copper tip is shiny (Fig. S-21). Try not to round off the edges of the tip (Fig. S-22). If you will examine it, you will see it has four flat surfaces coming to a point. These surfaces supply heat to the joint to be soldered.

After the tip has been cleaned, remove the iron from the vise and connect it to an outlet. When the iron has become hot, apply some solder to the tip. You will probably get this effect: the solder will curl into a ball and will roll off. In the meantime the tip of the iron will lose its shiny appearance and become dark. Clean the tip with the help of a clean, dry cloth (Fig. S-23). Don't hold the cloth in your hand. Instead, put it on some flat surface and draw the tip of the iron across the cloth. Apply solder once again to the tip. As some of it

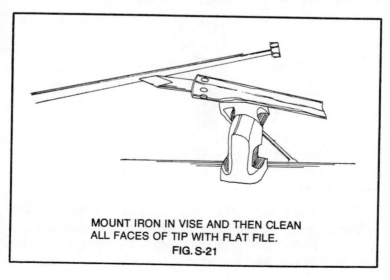

MOUNT IRON IN VISE AND THEN CLEAN
ALL FACES OF TIP WITH FLAT FILE.
FIG. S-21

begins to stick to the tip, once again draw the tip across the cloth. Keep repeating until you have a fine coating of solder on the tip. The soldering iron is then ready for work.

Use 16 AWG rosin-core solder, most suitable for home repairs.

The process of coating the tip of the iron with solder is known as tinning. Always tin the iron before using it. When working with an iron, clean the tip regularly. You will find it helpful to use a pot cleaning pad or steel wool (Fig. S-24). Without disconnecting the iron, draw the tip across the cleaning pad or the steel wool. Rotate the iron so that all faces of the tip become cleaned. To keep the pad from moving, tack it down to the work surface.

A soldering iron produces considerable heat and holds its heat for a long time. To keep from burning your work surface or bench, use a stand for holding the iron. You can buy a commercially made stand, or you can easily construct one of your own in various ways. Take a tin can and put a crimp in it large enough to hold the iron. Another method is to use a pair of large nails and hammer them into a block of wood so that the nails are crossed (Fig. S-25). You can also use a clamp made for holding papers together (Fig. S-26).

Using a soldering iron isn't difficult, but there are certain techniques which will make it easier for you. When soldering, hold the flat surface of the iron against the work or joint to be soldered. Then apply the solder to the work surface. The metal to be soldered must be hot enough to melt the solder. Do not put solder on the soldering iron tip and transfer it to the work. Instead, put the iron beneath the

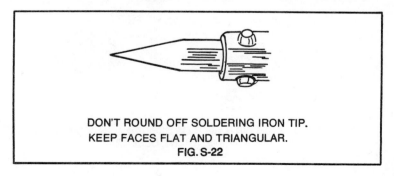

DON'T ROUND OFF SOLDERING IRON TIP.
KEEP FACES FLAT AND TRIANGULAR.
FIG. S-22

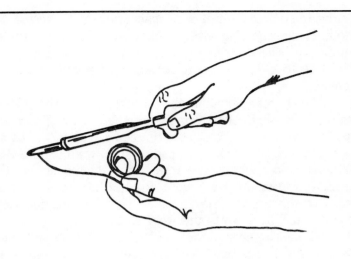

TO TIN THE IRON, APPLY SOLDER TO EACH FACE OF THE TIP, IN
TURN. WIPE THE TIP CLEAN WITH A RAG AFTER TINNING. THIS
WILL PUT A SMOOTH COAT OF SOLDER ON THE TIP.

FIG. S-23

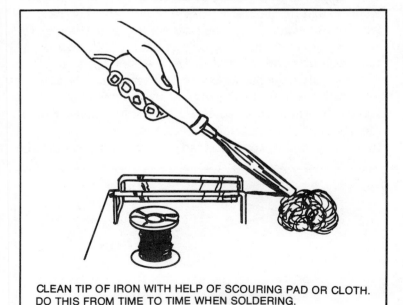

CLEAN TIP OF IRON WITH HELP OF SCOURING PAD OR CLOTH.
DO THIS FROM TIME TO TIME WHEN SOLDERING.

FIG. S-24

TWO CROSSED NAILS AND A BLOCK OF WOOD MAKE A PRACTICAL, INEXPENSIVE SOLDERING IRON STAND.

FIG. S-25

work—that is, the metals to be soldered. Heat with the iron while applying solder to the work. When the metal becomes hot enough, it will melt the solder, letting it flow. Once this happens, remove the iron but do not move the wires or metals that have just been soldered. Wait a few seconds to give the molten solder a chance to solidify.

Soldering iron tips are held in position in two ways. They may be threaded and thus screw into the end of the handle. Or they may be held in place by one or more setscrews. Remove the tip from time to time and clean out any dirt accumulation. If the threads of the tip corrode, it will become impossible to remove the tip.

Never dip a soldering iron into cold water to cool it. If you want to hasten the cooling process, put the iron on a flat metal surface. The metal should make maximum contact with the iron.

Do not use the soldering iron as a make-shift tool. It isn't a hammer or chisel.

A PAPER HOLDING CLAMP MAKES A QUICK, INEXPENSIVE SOLDERING IRON STAND.

FIG. S-26

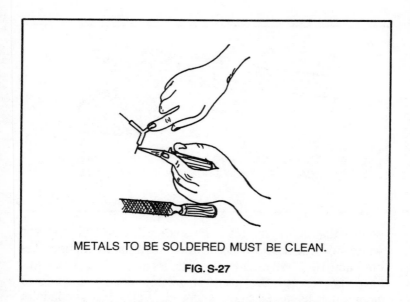

METALS TO BE SOLDERED MUST BE CLEAN.

FIG. S-27

Rosin Core And Acid Core Solder. There are two basic types of solder: *rosin core* and *acid core*. Acid core is easier to use for it helps keep the soldering iron tip clean and also cleans the metal being worked on. It is corrosive, however. You can also get an acid paste to help in soldering, but this is also corrosive. For certain metals, such as galvanized iron, acid core solder is necessary. Special solders are used for aluminum and stainless steel.

Before soldering, the work—metal or wires—must be thoroughly clean (Fig. S-27). Clean means more than the absence of dirt. The metal must be "shiny" clean, and that means any metallic oxide must be removed. To clean, use a file, sandpaper, emery paper, and steel wool. You may need to scrape with a penknife. Do not touch any part of the metal you have cleaned for natural body oils prevent soldering.

Flux. The purpose of *flux* is to let the solder make a bond with metal. Solder is supplied with flux built in as a core, with the flux either rosin or acid. You can buy flux separately in the form of a liquid or paste. You will need separate flux when using bar solder (solder that does not have a core of flux) or when doing a difficult soldering job. Liquid flux is convenient for you can brush it on. If you let

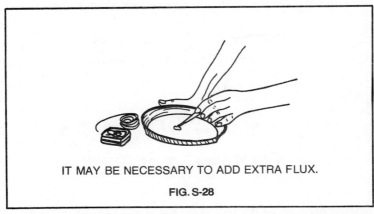

IT MAY BE NECESSARY TO ADD EXTRA FLUX.

FIG. S-28

solder remain on the tip of a hot iron, the flux will gradually boil away. You will need to add flux (Fig. S-28). Another advantage of separate flux, either as a paste or liquid, is that it improves the sticking capacity of solder. For surfaces that are difficult to solder, extra flux is helpful.

You cannot solder directly on to coated surfaces. If any surface has a coating, such as Teflon or enamel, remove the coating before soldering (Fig. S-29).

Making Electrical Connections. Soldering is extremely helpful in making electrical connections. Usually in home wiring, wires are twisted together and depend on the tightness of the twist for a good electrical connection. A soldered connection is much better. To solder wires, remove the insulation from the ends of the wire for a distance of

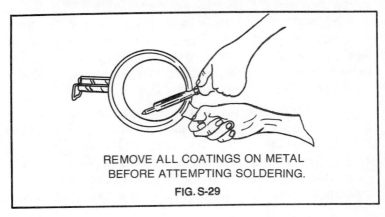

REMOVE ALL COATINGS ON METAL
BEFORE ATTEMPTING SOLDERING.

FIG. S-29

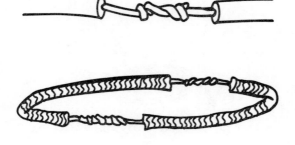

MAKE A GOOD MECHANICAL JOINT BEFORE SOLDERING WIRES.
IF SOLDERED WIRES ARE TO BE ADJACENT, MAKE SURE SOLDERED
JOINTS AREN'T NEXT TO EACH OTHER.
FIG. S-30

at least ½ inch. Scrape the wires clean with a penknife or rub
them with sandpaper. Twist the wires to be joined so they
first make a good mechanical connection (Fig. S-30). Then,
hold the hot soldering iron tip beneath the wire joint with the
joint resting securely on one of the faces of the tip (Fig.
S-31). Hold the wires and iron in this position for about a
minute. Then apply solder to the wires. Note that the solder
is applied to the work and not to the iron tip. In effect, the
joined wires must be made hot enough to melt the solder.

As the solder melts, let it flow into the joints formed by
the twisted wires. Do not use excessive solder. All you want
is a thin coating, not a large lump. Do not remove the iron.
First, stop feeding solder. Then take the iron away. Do not
let the joined wires move until the solder has cooled enough
to become solid. A good soldered joint has a smooth, silvery
appearance. A poor one is lumpy and dull.

A better technique is to tin each wire before soldering.
First, scrape each wire clean and then apply the face of the
soldering iron tip to one of the wires (Fig. S-32). Heat until
the wire becomes hot enough to melt solder. Coat the wire
with a layer of solder and then allow the wire to cool. Repeat
with the second wire. Then twist both soldered wires to-

gether. After you have done this, apply the hot soldering iron tip to the joined wires and apply some solder.

Don't try to solder wires together while holding them in your hand. Instead, mount the wires to be soldered in a vise. There are a few precautions.

Never shake the soldering iron. Solder can splatter and cause a painful burn.

Don't put so much solder on the joint that the solder runs off. When mounting wires to be joined in a vise, try not to have the jaws of the vise in contact with the bare wires. This may cause an excessive heat loss, making it difficult or impossible to solder.

If the wires you have soldered together are to be connected to some source of voltage, you will want to make sure these wires do not touch some other wire or ground accidentally, producing a short circuit. There are various kinds of insulation tape you can use such as friction tape or electrician's tape (Fig. S-33).

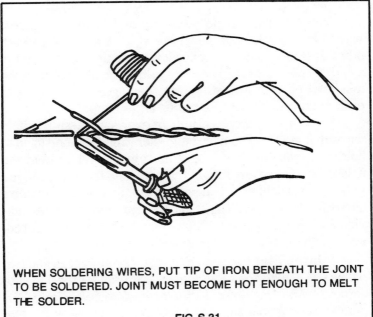

WHEN SOLDERING WIRES, PUT TIP OF IRON BENEATH THE JOINT TO BE SOLDERED. JOINT MUST BECOME HOT ENOUGH TO MELT THE SOLDER.

FIG. S-31

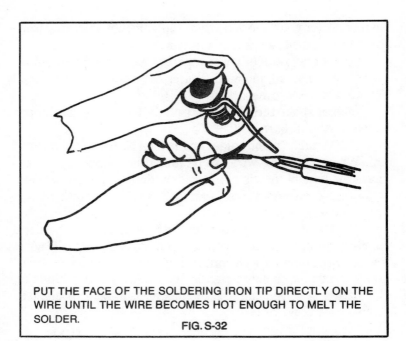

PUT THE FACE OF THE SOLDERING IRON TIP DIRECTLY ON THE WIRE UNTIL THE WIRE BECOMES HOT ENOUGH TO MELT THE SOLDER.

FIG. S-32

Sometimes it may be necessary to cut and join adjacent wires. In that case, do not make splices adjacent to each other. Instead, make one splice lower and the other higher to avoid any possibility of a short circuit. If you plan to cover the joined wires with insulating tape, having the joints next to each other will result in a rather large lump.

You can use a vise, a clamp, or even a clothespin to hold wires that are to be soldered together. You need one hand to hold and feed the solder and the other hand to hold the soldering iron, so any gadget that will hold the wires for you will do. You could even use a paper cup (Fig. S-34). Puncture opposite sides of the cup, near the top, and push the individual wires through the holes. When the wires are soldered, just cut the cup to free the joined wire.

Joining Flat Pieces Of Metal. If you want to join two flat pieces of metal, such as copper or tin, solder the opposite corners by putting down a thin layer of solder (Fig. S-35). Scrape the corners clean or use a file or polish with steel wool first. After the corners have been tinned, put the two

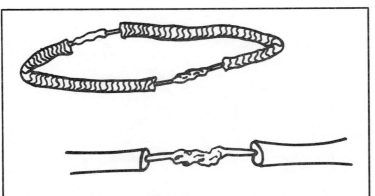

AFTER SOLDERING TUG ON THE WIRES TO MAKE SURE JOINT IS SECURE. TAPE WIRES TO PREVENT POSSIBLE SHORT CIRCUIT FROM NEARBY WIRES. FIG. S-33

pieces of metal face to face and apply the hot tip of the iron to one of the corners. Keep it there long enough for the solder beneath the corner to melt. The larger the piece of metal and the thicker it is, the more difficult this will be to do. Do not mount the metal being soldered in a vise since the vise will take away too much heat. A good method is to put the work on a brick. Using a wood surface means you run the risk of fire.

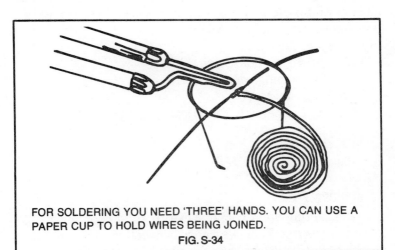

FOR SOLDERING YOU NEED 'THREE' HANDS. YOU CAN USE A PAPER CUP TO HOLD WIRES BEING JOINED.
FIG. S-34

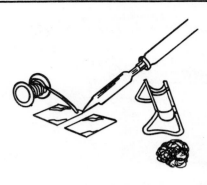

TO SOLDER FLAT PIECES OF METAL, TIN OPPOSITE CORNERS
OF EACH PIECE.

FIG. S-35

·If the metals you are soldering are very thin, they may tend to warp from the heat. To prevent this, hold a screwdriver down on the upper plate (Fig. S-36).

When you are finished with the soldering iron, remove its plug from the outlet. Before the iron has a chance to cool, wipe the tip with a rag or steel wool. You can use a tin can mounted on a wall as a soldering iron holder that will hold the iron safely until it cools (Fig. S-37). Use a large can since the handle of the iron may make it a bit top heavy. Make sure the interior of the can is clean , dry, and has no ragged edges.

See Aluminum, Joining, *page 21*
    Brazing, *page 34*
    Copper Pipe, Soldering, *page 60*
    Metals, Joining, *page 208*
    Welding, *page 376*
    Wires, Connecting Electrical, *page 385*

☐ Spackling Knife
See Putty Knife, *page 282*

☐ Splicing Wire

Connecting solid copper wire to solid copper wire is known as *splicing*. To make a good connection, remove about ¾ inch of the insulation from the ends of the two wires to be

WHEN SOLDERING A VERY THIN, FLAT PIECE OF METAL, HOLD IT DOWN WITH A SCREWDRIVER TO PREVENT WARPING

FIG. S-36

joined. You can do this with a sharp knife, a single edge razor blade or a pair of diagonal cutters. Whichever method you use, it is important not to nick the wire since this will weaken it.

Work your cutting tool in a circle around the insulation of the wire. Do so slowly and easily. After you have penetrated the insulation, you should be able to twist it off. Cut away any paper that may surround the wire. The bare copper wire should be clean and shiny. If not, scrape it with the knife or blade to remove any insulation that may be clinging to it.

Cross the wires and, using a pair of pliers, twist the exposed ends of the two wires together. Make the twist a tight one. You will find it helpful to use a vise to hold the wires in place while you twist the ends.

If the twisted wires are to be used to carry 117 V ac house current, the wires must be covered with some insulating material. The best and easiest thing to use is a solderless connector, available in electrical stores (Fig. S-38). Twist the connector on in a clockwise direction. If, after you have

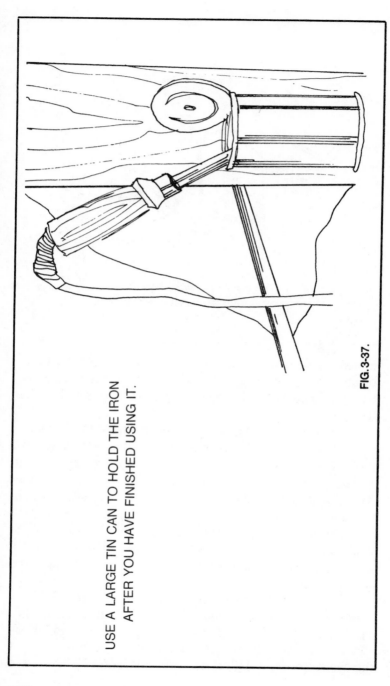

USE A LARGE TIN CAN TO HOLD THE IRON AFTER YOU HAVE FINISHED USING IT.

FIG. 3-37.

mounted the connector some of the bare copper wire is visible, remove the connector and cut the wires shorter. Then replace the connector.

You can also use rubberized or plastic electrical tape. Wrap the tape on as tightly as you can, and make sure that no part of the copper wire is exposed.

It is much easier to splice solid wire than to splice stranded wire. When removing the insulation from the ends of stranded wire, cut very carefully so as not to cut through one of the strands of the wire. After you have cut away the insulation, cut away any threads or insulating material that may be clinging to the wires. Twist the stranded wires together so that no loose wire strands stick out. The idea here is to make the individual wires of each as much like a solid conductor as possible.

Now cross the two wires, using a pair of pliers. After you have done so, solder the twisted pair. Heat the wires with the soldering iron until the wires are hot enough to melt the solder. It isn't necessary to form a lump on the wires, but the solder should flow down into any spaces between the wires.

The purpose of the solder is to make a good electrical connection, not to make the join physically strong. After soldering, wait a minute or two and tug on the wires to make sure that the joint is strong and well made.

You can insulate the joined ends with plastic electrical tape. Wrap tightly and make sure that no part of the copper wire shows through.

See Electrical Connections, How to Insulate, *page 94*

Electric Shock, How to Avoid, *page 107*

Soldering, *page 312*

☐ Spotlights (Spots)

See Floodlights, *page 134*

☐ Staples, Removing

There are several ways of removing staples, depending on the type of staple, how deeply it is embedded and whether

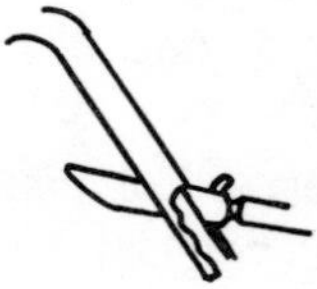

CUT INSULATION AWAY FROM SOLID WIRE

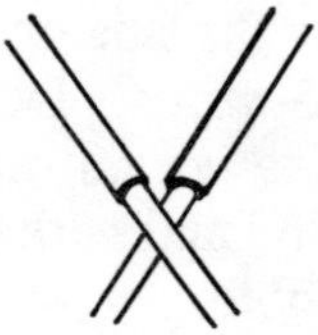

CROSS WIRES

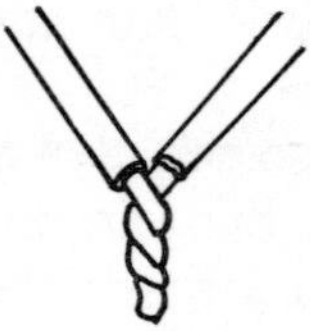

TWIST WIRES TOGETHER

PUT ON SOLDERLESS CONNECTOR

METHOD OF JOINING SOLID WIRES

FIG. S-38

or not the surface material, possibly plaster or wood, is to be protected.

If the staple is above the surface, you can use a pair of broad nosed pliers to grip the staple. Work with a rocking motion so that you apply force to one side of the staple, then the other.

Another method is to use a flat blade screwdriver and insert it under the staple. By lifting the handle of the screwdriver, you will be able to remove the staple. If you want to protect the plaster or wood surface, put a small section of scrap wood between the end of the screwdriver and the surface; otherwise, the screwdriver will leave a gouge mark.

If the head of the staple has been hammered in flush with the surface, you may be able to remove it by using a screwdriver and a hammer. Put the flat end of the screwdriver against the staple, and tap the handle end of the screwdriver with a hammer. After the staple head is above the surface, insert the end of the screwdriver beneath the staple and lift.

See Hammers, *page 163*

Nails, Types of, *page 214*

Nails, Removing, *page 223*

Pliers, *page 280*

□ Sweating Metal

See Brazing, *page 34*

Copper Pipe, Soldering, *page 60*

Metals, Joining, *page 208*

Soldering, *page 312*

Welding, *page 376*

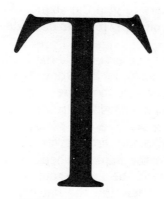

☐ Television Set—Quick Check

If your television receiver, whether black and white or color, doesn't work properly, the problem may be a simple one. A house call by a service technician can be avoided in such cases.

No Sound, No Picture. Make sure the line cord is plugged into its outlet. Check the outlet by connecting a lamp you know to be in good working order. Examine the prongs of the male plug of the television line cord. Spread them a bit to make better contact with the outlet. With the television set turned on, wiggle the plug in the outlet to see if this action restores power.

All Channels Come In Poorly, Snow On All Channels. Make certain that the antenna leads are securely connected to the antenna terminals on the back of the set. Twin-lead is most commonly used. Remove the connections and examine the ends of the wire. If any strands are broken or missing, cut the antenna wire directly across, and then strip the wires once again. You should have at least five wires, or possibly seven, for each of the two connecting leads. After stripping the wires of the twin lead, twirl them so they form a single conductor. Wrap the wires around the antenna screw in a clockwise direction. Tighten the screw using a screw-driver, and make sure that all the wires are under the screwhead. No strand of wire should reach across and touch the opposite antenna terminal.

Sound Normal, Picture Missing. Trouble may be at the television station. Tune in another channel to see if you get good sound and picture. If you do, go back to the original channel and adjust the fine tuning control.

Picture Normal, Sound Missing. Trouble may be at the television station. Tune in another channel to see if you get sound.

Color Missing. You may be watching a black and white picture. Try adjusting the fine tuning control. Adjust the color control. Turn the channel selector to a different channel. If you get adequate color, the set isn't at fault.

Wrong Color. Adjust the tint control.

Crackling Sound in Television Set. Trouble may be caused by some appliance in the home. Electric shavers are notorious. A fluorescent fixture can produce this problem. Disconnect electric appliances one at a time to determine their effect on television sound.

Streaky Picture. This can also be caused by a home appliance. Turn appliances off one at a time to determine which, if any, are offenders.

Picture Doesn't Seem Too Clear. High voltage on a picture tube causes the face of the tube to collect dust. Wash gently with window cleaner. Make sure the set is off. Dry thoroughly.

☐ Time Delay Switch

A time delay switch will keep a light turned on, possibly for about 30 seconds, after you turn the switch to its off position. The advantage is that it lets you walk from one house area to the next in light, rather than in total darkness, giving you an opportunity to reach a part of the house that is lighted. A two-way lighting system achieves the same purpose, but the time delay switch is easier to install.

You can install a time delay switch in exactly the same way as the usual electric wall switch. Remove the old switch and substitute the time delay switch for it. The wiring and connections are identical.

□ **Toggle Bolts**

If you have walls made of plasterboard or similar material, you will find it difficult to use the wall to support a moderately heavy object. If you drive a screw into such a wall, the screw will not hold.

A better method is to use a *toggle bolt*. A toggle bolt consists of two parts, a bolt and a toggle. The toggle can be made to fold. When the toggle is pushed through a hole in the wall, the toggle will open behind the wall. When the bolt is turned and tightened the opened toggle will grip the rear of the wall, acting as an anchor.

As a first step, drill a hole in the wall large enough to permit the toggle to go through. Remove the bolt from the toggle and pass it through the object to be supported. Then replace the toggle. Push the toggle through the hole far enough so the toggle will open behind the wall. All you will need to do now will be to tighten the bolt. As you do, the toggle will grip the rear of the wall. The bolt will support the object (Fig. T-1).

Despite its name, Sheetrock is quite soft. You can go through it quite easily with a hand drill. You can use an electric drill if you wish, but it isn't necessary.

If the hole you drill is too small to let the toggle go through, use a larger bit. If you do not have one, ream the hole with a screwdriver or a tapered reamer. Do not make

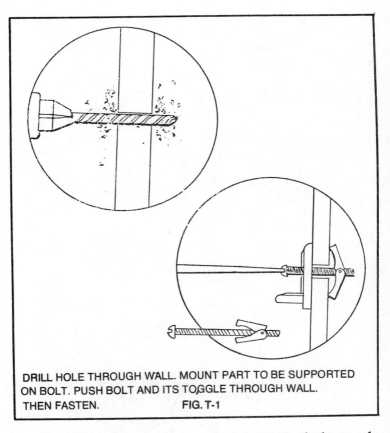

DRILL HOLE THROUGH WALL. MOUNT PART TO BE SUPPORTED
ON BOLT. PUSH BOLT AND ITS TOGGLE THROUGH WALL.
THEN FASTEN.   FIG. T-1

the hole larger than necessary. And do not push the toggle
through until you have previously mounted the part to be
supported on the bolt.

If at some future time you want to loosen the toggle bolt,
you can do so. However, it isn't possible to remove the bolt
completely since the toggle will fall behind the wall.

See Anchor Screws, Plastic, *page 22*

Molly Screws, *page 212*

☐ Toilets, Dimensions of

When planning an extra bathroom or possibly replacing
an existing toilet, it is helpful to have some idea about the
amount of space the toilet will occupy. Figure T-2 shows
some of the more commonly used toilets and their sizes.

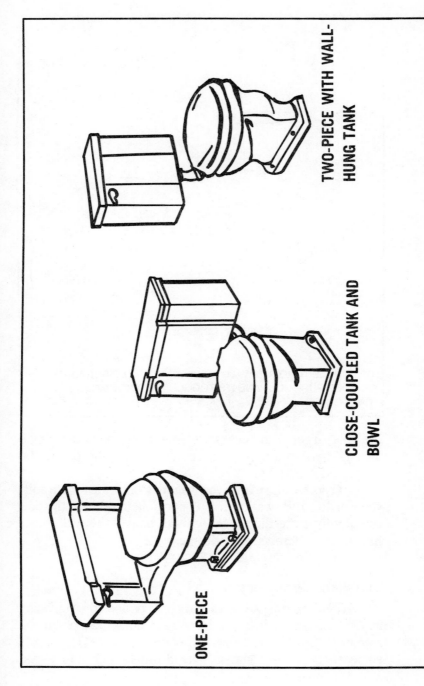

ONE-PIECE

CLOSE-COUPLED TANK AND BOWL

TWO-PIECE WITH WALL-HUNG TANK

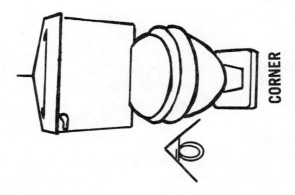

CORNER

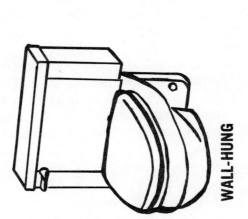

WALL-HUNG

FIG. T-2

These are not the only styles available. Toilets are also made in a number of different colors. At one time all toilets were white but now you can get them in colors to match the decor of the bathroom.

□ Toilets, Noisy

Inside the water tank of the toilet you will see a rubber object sometimes shaped like a ball or a sort of inverted cup. This flush ball or cup is attached to a thin metal rod held in place by a guide. Sometimes the setscrew holding the flush ball guide arm in place becomes loose, and the metal rod no longer holds the ball or cup in its proper position. When you flush the toilet, the ball or cup should drop right into the center of a rubber seat below it.

Sometimes there is some friction between the metal rod and its guide. Dry the rod thoroughly and coat it with some lubricant. A thin application of petroleum jelly will do. Adjust the setscrew holding the guide so the rod has a chance to fall through it easily.

If the flush ball doesn't seat properly, replace it. If you need to jiggle the handle used for flushing the toilet to get the water to stop running, adjust the guide and/or replace the flush ball. Complete replacement kits are available in hardware and department stores for the entire flushing assembly.

☐ Toilet Bowl, Clogged

If the toilet doesn't flush, try using a plunger. If repeated use of the plunger doesn't clear the drain, use a 10-foot auger having an adjustable crank type handle, a type of tool sometimes known as a *snake*. Be careful in handling it. The material of which the toilet is made, often vitreous china, can crack if the auger is handled carelessly. You can also try a commercial type liquid or powder made for unclogging toilet bowls.

There are two types of *plungers*. One of these is an open type, a *suction cup* plunger. While this type of plunger is suitable for removing sink and bathtub clogs, it doesn't work well with toilets. Instead, use a *force ball* plunger since this type can exert considerably more pressure.

If the regular auger doesn't work, try an auger made especially for toilets known as a *closet auger* (Fig. T-3). The closet auger lets the tool reach into the area where the clog is likely to occur.

See Bathtub Drain, Clogged, *page 32*
  Toilets, Noisy, *page 336*
  Toilet Repairs, *page 337*
  Toilet Tank Overflows, *page 346*

☐ Toilet Repairs

To see the mechanism that operates a toilet, just lift the toilet tank cover and look inside (Fig. T-4). The handle located at the upper left outside of the tank is connected to a lift arm which can be raised by the handle. The end of the lift arm has four or five holes, and going through one of these holes is a lift wire.

The lift wire consists of two separate pieces—the upper lift wire and the lower lift wire. The lower lift wire is attached to a stopper ball which fits snugly into a valve seat. When the two lift wires are raised, the stopper ball is pulled up from the valve seat. The water in the tank is allowed to flow into the toilet.

As the water in the tank rushes out, the float, a hollow copper or plastic ball, moves lower and lower. When the water gets near the bottom of the tank, a flush ball falls or

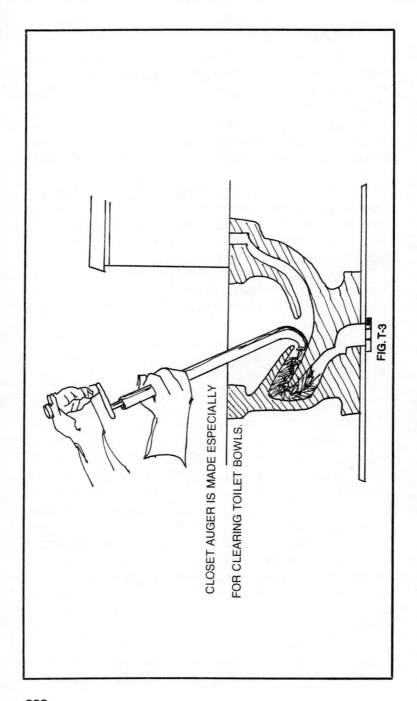

CLOSET AUGER IS MADE ESPECIALLY
FOR CLEARING TOILET BOWLS.

FIG. T-3

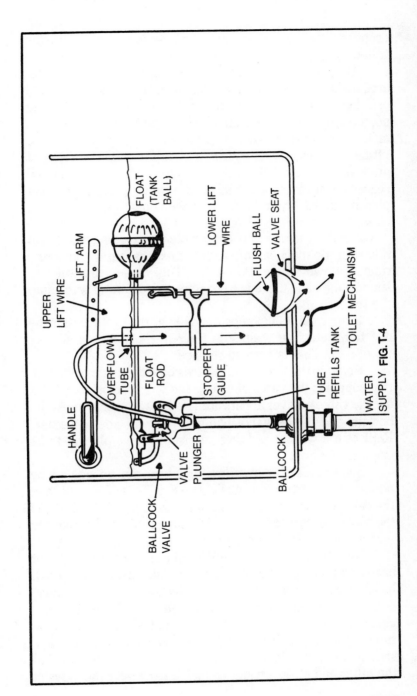

UPPER LIFT WIRE

LIFT ARM

FLOAT (TANK BALL)

LOWER LIFT WIRE

FLUSH BALL

VALVE SEAT

HANDLE

OVERFLOW TUBE

FLOAT ROD

STOPPER GUIDE

VALVE PLUNGER

BALLCOCK

TUBE REFILLS TANK

BALLCOCK VALVE

WATER SUPPLY

TOILET MECHANISM

FIG. T-4

339

drops into the valve seat, cutting off the flow of water into the toilet.

The float by now is near the bottom of the tank. The float arm attached to it is now pointing down at some angle instead of being horizontal. The float rod, in this downward pointing position, opens a valve plunger which lets water flow into the tank. As the water moves into the tank, the flush ball rises, lifting the float rod as it does so. As the float rod rises, it gradually shuts off the valve plunger. When the float rod reaches a horizontal position, the valve plunger is completely closed, shutting off all further flow of water into the tank.

A toilet can have various problems including a tank that fills with too much water, with the excess water constantly running down an overflow tube. This causes the toilet to sound noisy, and there is a constant movement of water into the toilet.

If the toilet tank keeps overfilling, the problem may be due to a defective washer in the *ball cock* valve assembly (Fig. T-5). This is easy to replace.

Remove the two thumb screws on either side of the arm that supports the valve plunger. You will then be able to lift out the valve plunger and its attached float rod or arm. At the bottom end of the valve plunger you will see a washer. Replace the washer and then return the valve plunger to its original position.

Sometimes the overflow problem can be solved by bending the float rod down slightly (Fig. T-6). This will have the effect of lowering the float. Since the float will be lower in the water, it will exert more pressure on the valve plunger that is part of the ball cock assembly.

Sometimes the water will keep running after the toilet has been flushed. This is due to the fact that the flush ball hasn't dropped properly into the valve seat, or that the flush ball or valve seat are worn. Sometimes the lower lift wire gets stuck. To remedy the problem, shut off the water to the toilet by its water control valve. If you cannot do this, tie a string around the float rod, connect a weight of some kind to the other end of the string, and let it hang over the sides of

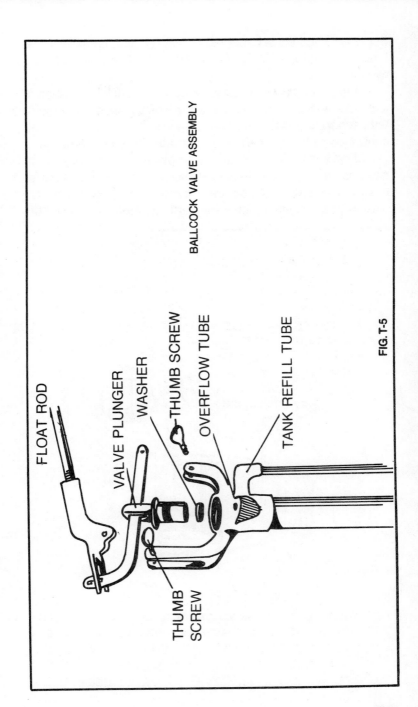

FLOAT ROD

VALVE PLUNGER

WASHER

THUMB SCREW

OVERFLOW TUBE

THUMB
SCREW

TANK REFILL TUBE

BALLCOCK VALVE ASSEMBLY

FIG. T-5

341

the tank. The idea is to keep the float rod held up to keep the tank from refilling. After you do this, raise the lower lift wire to empty the tank.

When the tank is empty, remove the flush ball which is just screwed onto the lower lift wire. Clean it thoroughly with scouring powder and water and replace. If the flush ball continues to let water flow past it into the tank, replace it.

The lower lift wire is held in place by a stopper guide and flush ball guide arm. Sometimes the guide moves out of position, constricting the free movement of the lower lift wire. Check to make sure the guide arm lets the lower lift

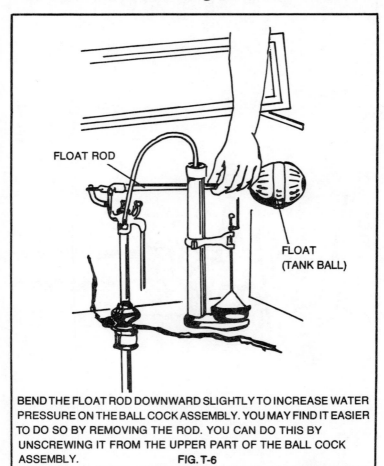

FLOAT ROD

FLOAT (TANK BALL)

BEND THE FLOAT ROD DOWNWARD SLIGHTLY TO INCREASE WATER PRESSURE ON THE BALL COCK ASSEMBLY. YOU MAY FIND IT EASIER TO DO SO BY REMOVING THE ROD. YOU CAN DO THIS BY UNSCREWING IT FROM THE UPPER PART OF THE BALL COCK ASSEMBLY.   FIG. T-6

wire move freely. You may find it helpful to coat the lower lift wire with a thin layer of petroleum jelly.

If water flows continuously into the overflow tube, bend the float rod down slightly. The float rod is solid and is threaded at both ends. Check the float by removing it. Shake it, and if you can hear the movement of water inside the float, replace it. If bending the float rod and replacing the float (tank ball) doesn't stop water from continuously pouring into the overflow tube, you will need to replace the entire ball cock assembly.

To do this, shut off the water supply. You will need to keep the float in a horizontal position, so hold it in place with a string as mentioned earlier, or put a suitable length of wood between the float rod and the bottom of the tank to keep the rod from moving down. Now remove the flush ball and all the water in the tank will empty, but it will not refill. Close the valve that supplies water to the tank.

Beneath the tank you will find a pipe that supplies water to it. This pipe is secured to the tank by a coupling nut and a locknut, plus a washer. When you loosen the nuts sufficiently, you will be able to lift out the ball cock assembly. Remove the float rod and its float.

The ball cock is supplied in the form of a kit and generally has two copper tubes. One of these is the tank refill tube and the other is a tube that connects to the overflow tube. Mount these on the ball cock assembly. Replace the ball cock assembly, following the removal steps in reverse order.

To replace the flush valve, shut the water off and remove the locknut beneath the bottom of the tank that holds the discharge tube in place. Remove its associated large washer and you will be able to move the valve seat out.

There are a number of different devices available that may work better than your existing flush valve assembly. They all work on the principle of having the water pressure in the tank close the valve. Some valve designs are better than others (Fig. T-7).

See Condensation, Toilet Tank, *page 49*
Drains, Clogged, *page 81*
Toilets, Dimensions of, *page 333*

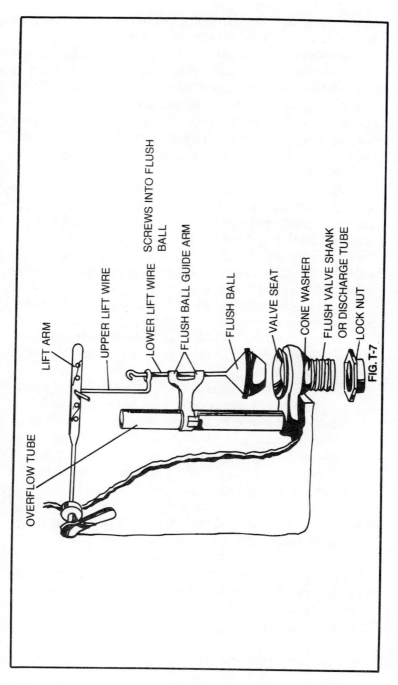

LIFT ARM

OVERFLOW TUBE

UPPER LIFT WIRE

LOWER LIFT WIRE

SCREWS INTO FLUSH BALL

FLUSH BALL GUIDE ARM

FLUSH BALL

VALVE SEAT

CONE WASHER

FLUSH VALVE SHANK OR DISCHARGE TUBE

LOCK NUT

FIG. T-7

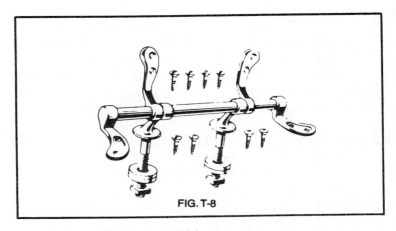

FIG. T-8

□ Toilet Seat Problems

A toilet seat should provide a firm, unmoving support. There are rubber bumpers on the underside of the seat which provide a cushion effect. Eventually the bumpers become hard and brittle, ultimately corroding. When they do, the toilet seat no longer positions properly. You can buy a bumper set to replace the old ones (Fig. T-8). Bumper sets are either screwed or glued into position. The screws may have become rusty. If you cannot take them out with a screwdriver, cut away as much of the bumper as you can to expose the screws. Then use a pair of pliers to turn the screws.

Pressure and age sometimes makes bumpers adhere to the toilet seat surface. If some of the bumper material remains after you have made efforts to remove it, use a wood scraper until you reach the flat undersurface of the toilet seat.

If the toilet seat and its cover are in good condition, but the hinge has become unsightly, rusty, and corroded, you can buy a replacement kit. It is sometimes difficult to remove this hardware since it has a tendency to rust. The hardware is held in position by nuts on the underside of the toilet. You will need to use a wrench or similar tool to remove them. In very stubborn cases you may need to use a hacksaw.

If the toilet seat or cover, or both, are cracked, get a replacement. Don't try to patch. A damaged toilet seat can not only be awkward but dangerous.

☐ Toilet Tank Overflows

Suspect your toilet tank of overflowing if you hear the sound of running water coming from the toilet tank, and if there is a steady flow of water into the bowl. If the overflow tube in the toilet tank cannot carry the water away fast enough, the tank will spill over and flood the bathroom.

As a first step in repair, turn off the water valve. This is generally located near the floor on the left side as you face the toilet. If the valve is stuck and will not turn, remove the top of the toilet tank and pull the float rod up toward you. Then reach in and lift the flush ball off its valve seat. This will let the water out of the tank.

Slowly lower the lift rod so that the tank starts filling. At some point during the filling procedure the tank ball will drop and close the opening leading to the toilet bowl. Quite often the ball is worn and doesn't seat properly, permitting water to flow past it into the bowl. You can assume this to be the trouble if you must jiggle the handle of the toilet bowl regularly to get the water to stop flowing.

Sometimes the valve that permits water to flow into the tank is defective. In that case replace the entire assembly. Replacement kits complete with instructions are available in department and hardware stores.

☐ Underwriters' Laboratories

Buy electrical materials only that are UL (Underwriters' Laboratories, Inc.) approved. This is not a guarantee of quality, simply that the material has been tested and has been found to meet certain minimum standards. The UL insignia can be a label, a stamp, and a tag (Fig. U-1). It can be printed on a label or impressed on a metal disc.

The UL stamp of approval has no relationship to price. An inexpensive item may be UL approved; a more costly, similar item may not be.

Underwriters' approval does not mean you can overload an electrical appliance or abuse it. It has no relationship to a warranty. All it does mean is that the appliance, wire or electrical apparatus has been checked by an independent testing laboratory. Manufacturers do make their own tests, but these can be self serving.

VARIOUS TYPES OF UL TAGS AND LABELS.

FIG. U-1

☐ **Varnish, Removing**

See Paint Removing, *page 238*

☐ Wallboard, Holes in Sheetrock or Plaster

Longitudinal cracks often develop in walls of new homes after these homes have had a chance to "settle," generally after about six months. You can also get a hole in an old wall for a variety of reasons. You may have had a water leak, or you may have accidentally pushed the edge of furniture into it. Whatever the cause, it is easy to patch.

For making a plaster patch all you need is some plaster and spackling compound or vinegar (Fig. W-1). Plaster dries rather quickly, often so fast it is impossible to put in a patch unless you are experienced. By mixing either spackling compound or vinegar with the plaster, it is possible to keep the plaster from drying so rapidly. You won't need much of either substance.

You can also use a vinyl or acrylic base spackling compound available in ready mixed form. These pre-packaged compounds cost a little more than making your own plaster patching mix, but they do save the bother of trying to estimate the proper proportions of plaster and spackle or vinegar. They work better and give you a chance to do a better patching job. There is also less waste since you will be able to estimate more accurately the amount of patch required for the hole.

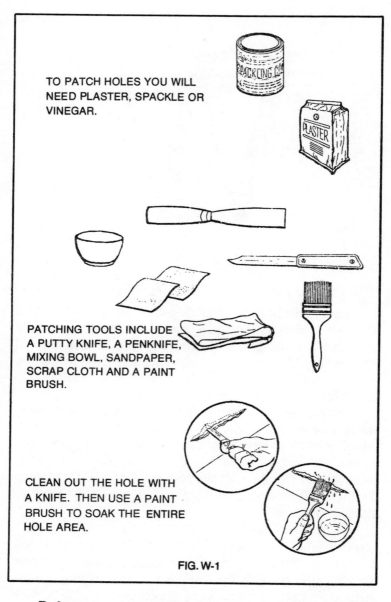

TO PATCH HOLES YOU WILL
NEED PLASTER, SPACKLE OR
VINEGAR.

PATCHING TOOLS INCLUDE
A PUTTY KNIFE, A PENKNIFE,
MIXING BOWL, SANDPAPER,
SCRAP CLOTH AND A PAINT
BRUSH.

CLEAN OUT THE HOLE WITH
A KNIFE. THEN USE A PAINT
BRUSH TO SOAK THE ENTIRE
HOLE AREA.

FIG. W-1

Before you prepare the plaster, use a knife and clean along the edges of the crack. Scrape out plaster until the back of the crack is wider than the front.

Using a sponge or cloth, thoroughly dampen the interior

walls of the crack and also the front surface. A paint brush is even better since it will let you reach all parts.

To prepare the patching plaster, mix the plaster with about a ratio of 4 to 1—that is, four parts of plaster to one part of spackle. Mix just a small amount. First, mix the plaster and spackle thoroughly, and then gradually add water in small amounts, stirring all the time. Do not put in too much water. If you do, add a small amount of plaster but keep mixing. Continue until you get a smooth paste.

With the help of a putty knife, fill the hole or crack with the plaster mix. Press in so that the mix fills the hole completely. Use the putty knife to get a smooth surface and to remove any excess plaster. If you dip the putty knife in water before you do this, you will be able to get a smoother finish.

Putty knives are available with blades that range from about 1 to 4 inches. The best kind to use for patching is one that is springy, not stiff, is made of polished steel and has a smooth, sharp edge. Don't bother trying to use a putty knife that has been previously used as a substitute for a paint scraper, and is nicked and has a dull blade. The larger the width of the blade, the better. The reason for this is that the wallboard will be able to support the blade of the knife on both sides. Thus, when running the blade over the patch, you will be able to make its surface absolutely flush with the wallboard or Sheetrock. This means less sanding when the job is finished.

After the patch has dried, sand it with a fine grade of sandpaper. You can make a sanding block using a sandpaper square and a small, scrap block of wood. The block will enable you to get a smooth, uniform surface.

If the hole you want to fill is large, you can still do a repair, but do one step at a time. Clean out any dirt or scrap plaster. Using a sponge or paint brush, wet the area to be plastered. Start at the edge of the hole and plaster all around, but don't try to fill the entire hole all at one time. Let this patch dry and then add more plaster, once again working in a circle around the edge. Do this until the entire hole is filled. After it is filled sand it using a sandpaper block (Fig. W-2).

If the hole is very large, you can avoid using an excess amount of plaster by filling the hole with newspaper or cardboard.

When the patch is completely dry and has been sanded, paint glue sizing over it. If the wall is one that is painted, you can try covering the patched area using the same paint applied to the wall originally. Usually, however, the entire wall has to be repainted. If the wall is papered, all you need do is cut a small section of wallpaper to cover the patch.

If you have any plaster mix left over, don't try to salvage it. Once the plaster has dried, you will not be able to mix it with water again. To dispose of dried, leftover plaster, let it dry and then put it in with your garbage. Don't use your sink or toilet as a waste disposal for plaster for it will simply clog the drain.

Clean all tools immediately after using them with plaster. If you let plaster dry on tools, you will find it difficult to remove. A good technique is to keep a bucket handy, partially filled with water, into which you can put tools as soon as you have finished using them.

If you need to drive nails into plaster, drill a small pilot hole first using a small bit and a hand or electric drill.

Plaster bricks make an excellent, economical, and highly practical wall decoration. You can make your own plaster bricks by buying flexible plastic molds made for that purpose. It isn't necessary to fasten the bricks with glue or paste. Just drill two holes at opposite ends of the brick and small finishing nails to hold each brick to the wall. Use plaster as a mortar around the four sides of the brick, and you will find that the mortar will hold the brick securely to the wall. The bricks will also be held in by the nails. You can countersink the nails by tapping them in with a small metal rod or a large nail. Cover the nail heads with a bit of plaster, and they will never be seen.

See Nails Types of, *page 214*

    Paint, Tips On How to *page 250*

    Putty Knife, *page 282*

    Screw Holes, Repair of, *page 297*

MIX PLASTER WITH SPACKLE OR WITH
VINEGAR. ADD ENOUGH WATER TO MAKE
A SMOOTH PASTE. FORCE PLASTER INTO
CRACK WITH PUTTY KNIFE.

USE SANDPAPER BLOCK TO GET SMOOTH
PLASTERED SURFACE.

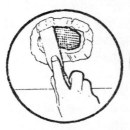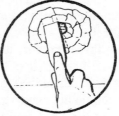

FOR LARGE HOLES, PLASTER AROUND
THE EDGE. WAIT UNTIL PLASTER HAS
DRIED, THEN REPEAT UNTIL HOLE IS
FILLED.

AFTER PLASTER HAS DRIED, SAND
PLASTERED AREA.

FIG. W-2

☐ Wallboard, Nailing

Casing nails and finishing nails aren't suitable for fastening wallboard against a wall. The diameter of the heads of such nails is too close to that of the diameter of the shank of the nail, and the wallboard has a tendency to "pop" or spring away from the nail. There are special nails made for attaching wallboard (Fig. W-3). The nails do not depend on the nail's serrations for holding power, but have rings around the body of the nail. They are shaped so as to permit entry of the nail, but also to resist movement of the nail in the opposite direction. For this reason they aren't easy to remove once they have been driven into position. The heads of these nails, called wallboard nails, are circular and large enough to hold against the wallboard, preventing popping.

See Nails Types of, *page 214*

Paint, Tips on How to, *page 250*

Putty Knife, *page 282*

Screw Holes, Repair of, *page 297*

☐ Wall Fixtures, Installing

You can install a wall lighting fixture anywhere you have access to an in-home ac voltage line (Fig. W-4). Thus, if you have an outlet near a floor baseboard or an easily reached electric box having power, it shouldn't be too difficult to tap the ac voltage from that outlet or box to supply electrical power for a wall fixture. Since the outlet is mounted between studs, you should be able to have a fairly clear path between the outlet and the new wall fixture.

To set up a wall fixture, you will need to install an electric box. Use the box itself as a template and outline its dimensions on the wall. Score this outline with the point of a sharp knife. Keep making the score marks deeper. If the wall is made of plasterboard or some equivalent material, drill a large hole in the outline. Use a small saw to cut away along the outline of the electric box. Follow the same routine if the wall has been paneled.

Measure a length of Romex or BX cable and, using a box connector, attach it to the electric box, allowing about 6 inches of wire to extend into the box. Make sure the BX or

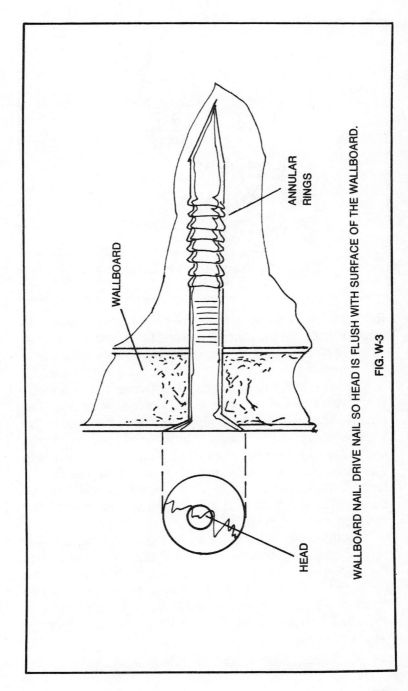

WALLBOARD

ANNULAR
RINGS

HEAD

WALLBOARD NAIL. DRIVE NAIL SO HEAD IS FLUSH WITH SURFACE OF THE WALLBOARD.

FIG. W-3

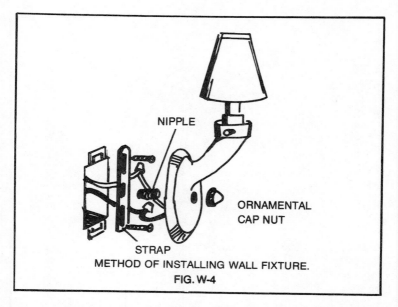

NIPPLE

ORNAMENTAL
CAP NUT

STRAP

METHOD OF INSTALLING WALL FIXTURE.

FIG. W-4

Romex is long enough to reach the power outlet. Snake the cable through the wall until it reaches the power outlet, first shutting off all power to that outlet by removing its fuse.

Screw the electric box for the wall fixture to the wall. As part of your wall lamp mounting kit, you will have a metal strap with a threaded center hole. Mount this strap on the electric box, and insert the nipple in the center hole of the strap. Coming out of the lamp fixture you will see two wires, one coded white and the other black. Connect these wires to the corresponding white and black wires of the BX or Romex, using wire nuts (Fig. W-5). Mount the wall lamp on the nipple, and hold it in place with an ornamental nut supplied with the lamp.

At the outlet connect the white wire of the cable to the corresponding white wire screwed to the outlet receptacle, the black wire to the black wire of the outlet. The wires of the outlet are held in place by machine screws. Loosen these screws a bit, and they will be able to accommodate the wires of the cable. After completing, turn the power on again and test the fixture.

See BX Cable, Cutting and Installing, *page 38*

☐ Wall Switches

See Electric Switches, Installing, *page 111*

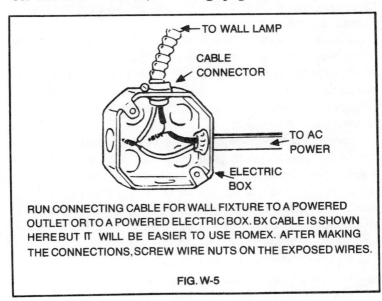

TO WALL LAMP

CABLE
CONNECTOR

TO AC
POWER

ELECTRIC
BOX

RUN CONNECTING CABLE FOR WALL FIXTURE TO A POWERED
OUTLET OR TO A POWERED ELECTRIC BOX. BX CABLE IS SHOWN
HERE BUT IT WILL BE EASIER TO USE ROMEX. AFTER MAKING
THE CONNECTIONS, SCREW WIRE NUTS ON THE EXPOSED WIRES.

FIG. W-5

☐ Water Hammer

Water pipes will sometimes produce a hammering sound when a faucet is closed suddenly. Hammering is not only a noise nuisance, but it can cause pipes to vibrate, loosening them and also separating pipe joints that results in water leakage.

Water hammer is caused by the fact that moving water has kinetic energy, and the water must find some way to dissipate this energy. Water doesn't simply flow through pipes of its own accord; it is pushed. Every moving body, and water is no exception, has energy. It takes energy to stop a car, and it takes energy to stop water. Water hammer is the energy of moving water being dissipated.

To prevent water hammer, install an air chamber ahead of a faucet or appliance. You can usually learn which faucet or appliance is responsible just by listening. Hammer is caused by water being turned off and on suddenly.

The air chamber need be nothing more than a length of pipe or tubing, mounted vertically. One end of the pipe is sealed, and the other end is incorporated into the water line. The simplest air chamber can be a section of tubing about 2 feet long (Fig. W-6). To conserve space, the chamber can be wound in circular form.

Sometimes water hammer may be due to an air chamber that has become filled with water instead of air. If you notice water hammer in conjunction with a faucet or appliance that has an air chamber, shut off the water supply, remove the air chamber, and let the water drain out of it. You can then replace the air chamber.

Sometimes a condition similar to water hammer exists which is simply due to pipe vibration. Examine all fresh water pipes to make sure they are securely fastened. Have someone turn faucets on and off or watch when a washing machine is operating. Secure any pipes that may be loose by strapping the pipe to a beam or by using a wedge between the pipe and a beam.

See Copper Pipe, Cutting, *page 54*
Copper Pipe, Soldering, *page 60*
Copper Pipe, Types of, *page 64*

Hacksaws, How to Use, *page 160*
Pipe, Cutting, *page 274*

□ Water Leaks

A faucet leaking at the rate of 60 drops a minute, not at all unusual, will waste 2,299 gallons of water a year. The average family uses about 60 gallons of water per day. For a family of four, this will be approximately 18,000 to 20,000 gallons every three months.

Water leaks are of two types: those which can be readily seen, such as a dripping faucet, and those which aren't readily noticeable. To check if you have a water leak, turn off all faucets and all appliances that use water. Check your water meter and make a note of the reading. Wait at least an hour and then take another water meter reading. The second should be identical to the first. If the leak is a substantial one, you may be able to see one of the meter pointers moving. The difference between the two readings is the amount of water you are losing.

Faucets are the most common causes of water leaks, so check all of them. If any one must have strong pressure to shut off water flow, then that faucet is ready for repair or

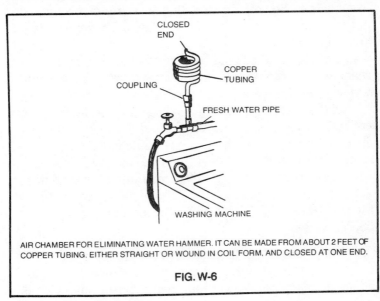

AIR CHAMBER FOR ELIMINATING WATER HAMMER. IT CAN BE MADE FROM ABOUT 2 FEET OF COPPER TUBING. EITHER STRAIGHT OR WOUND IN COIL FORM, AND CLOSED AT ONE END.

FIG. W-6

replacement. Usually the problem is due to the need for a new washer. If the washer requires frequent replacement, the valve seat requires dressing or replacement. Valve seat dressing tools are available in hardware stores.

Examine all toilets. You can easily remove the top cover to the toilet tank. If the water shutoff mechanism isn't working properly, there will be a constant flow of water into the overflow pipe. You can verify this by looking into the toilet bowl, for you will see a movement of water down the sides of the bowl. Another symptom is the presence of air bubbles in the toilet bowl.

If your home uses steam heat radiators, examine all valves to make sure that none of them drip water. If you have access to exposed piping, examine all joints to make sure none of them are leaking.

See Damp Basements, *page 71*

Gutters and Downspouts, Maintaining and Repairing, *page 154*

Water Pipes, Leaky, *page 364*

☐ Water Meter, How to Read

Water meters measure water flow directly in gallons or in cubic feet. You can check with your water company to find out what kind of water meter you have. To determine just how much water you are using, take a reading of the meter, wait a week, and then take another reading. Subtract the first reading from the second, and you will have the amount of water you have used for that week.

If the meter supplies a reading in cubic feet, you can convert to gallons by multiplying by 7-½ since there are about 7-½ gallons of water in one cubic foot. If your water meter does read in cubic feet, then you can easily convert to gallons by multiplying the difference in meter readings by 7-½. If your first reading is 10,727 and the second is 18,494, then $18,494 - 10,727 = 7,767$ cubic feet. So $7.767 \times 7-½ = 58,252$ gallons.

☐ Water Pipes, How to Protect from Freezing

When water freezes, it expands, and if permitted to do so inside pipes can cause them to burst. Not only does this lead to an expensive plumbing repair, but when the temperature rises above the freezing point, water flow from a burst pipe can flood your home.

If you must leave your home during cold weather, set your heating plant to about 40°F to maintain this level of temperature throughout. This is the most convenient and least troublesome method. You can also drain all the water from your pipes by opening the drain valve located at the low point of the fresh water supply coming into your home. Drain any water storage tanks, hot water tank, toilet tanks, and water treatment system. Pour antifreeze into all kitchen and bathroom sinks and into bathtub and shower drains and toilets. While the drain valve will remove water from pipes, water will still remain in the traps associated with your water fixtures.

Be sure to drain your hot water and steam heating system. When you decide to put your plumbing system back into action again, fill all pipes slowly. Turn the main water valve just a little and let the water trickle back into the pipes. Turn faucets just slightly. You may hear the pipes hammering at first, but this will stop when they fill with water.

If you have an outside water faucet, turn it off if your outside temperature will drop below 32°F. First, locate the valve that controls the water flow to the outside faucet. Turn this valve off. Then open the outside faucet until all the water drains out of the line. Once no more water comes out of the faucet, close it and keep it closed during the winter season.

In some instances water pipes may be located where there is no heat to protect them, as in an unheated garage or basement. Insulation around the pipes will help, but if there is a protracted freezing period the pipes may burst.

Wrap the pipes with electrical heating tape. This tape contains special resistance wires which become heated when a current of electricity flows through them. Wrap the electrical heating tape directly over the pipes and then cover the heating tape with insulation. The electrical tapes are supplied with a thermostatic control so that electrical current flow is turned on only when the temperature drops close to 32°F or 0°C.

☐ Water Pipes, Leaky

There are several ways of repairing a leak in a water pipe if the leak isn't at a joint and is caused by a small hole in the pipe. One way is to force a round head self-tapping screw into the hole. Put a fiber or lead washer under the head of the screw, but do not use a screw that is too long. This will interfere with the free flow of water in the pipe. Preferably, use a brass or galvanized screw. While a repair of this kind is "temporary," it should last for several years. Don't use an iron or steel screw since it will rust quickly.

You can also cover the hole with clamping patches. These are available in various diameters in plumbing supply stores. To measure the diameter of the pipe you want to repair, use a length of string and make one complete turn of the string around the pipe. Measure the length of string required and then divide by 3.14. Thus, if the string is 6-⅛ inches long or 6.125 inches long, then 6.125/3.14 is 1.95 inches. A clamping patch with a diameter of 1-¾ inches will do well for this repair.

The clamping patch is supplied with screws to hold it tightly in place (Fig. W-7). Remove these screws. Put the two sections of pipe clamping patch around the pipe so that the hole is in the approximate center of the patch, and then replace the patch screws. If the clamp is too loose, remove it and cover the hole with a flexible square of rubber. Replace the patch.

You can also use iron patching cement. Turn the valve controlling water flow through the pipe to its off position. Make a paste of the iron cement with water and, using a scraper or knife blade, force the paste into the hole. Make sure the hole is filled completely. Let the patch dry, preferably overnight, before turning the water valve on again.

CLAMP FOR REPAIRING LEAK IN WATER PIPE.
FIG. W-7

☐ **Water Pipes, Noisy**

If water pipes are loose or aren't adequately supported, the flow of water through them can cause them to vibrate. Noise is caused by the vibrating pipe striking a nearby material. Sometimes pipe supports work their way loose or else fall off.

You can get water tube straps for any type of pipe material whether the pipe is made of plastic, copper, or any other metal. Pipe straps are available in various sizes such as ⅜-inch, ½-inch, and ¾-inch sizes. You can get an approximate idea of the diameter of the pipe by measuring and then dividing that circumference by three. To measure the circumference, put a single turn of string around the pipe and then measure the length of this turn. If, for example, the circumference is 2 inches, divide two by three. And you will have two-thirds. A ¾-inch pipe strap would be suitable. The dimensions of the pipe strap should be a little larger than the diameter of the pipe.

You can avoid measuring by using perforated pipe strap. The sample shown in Fig. W-8 is made of 20-gauge steel with a copper finish. It is ¾-inch wide and 10 feet long. The advantage of straps is that you can make any size support. You can also use it to fasten pipe to supports that may be a few inches away.

See Pipes, Protecting, *page 279*

Water Pipes, Leaky, *page 364*

☐ Water Pressure, Low

Speak to your neighbors to learn if they also have the problem of low water pressure. If they do, then check with your water supply company or the water supply division of your municipal government. However, if the problem has existed for some time, it is much more likely that the cause of low water pressure is in your home.

Check all water shutoff valves and make sure they are in their fully turned on position (Fig. W-9). Do this by turning

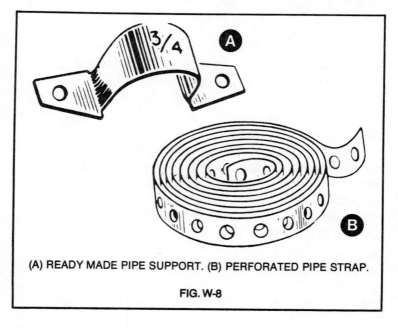

(A) READY MADE PIPE SUPPORT. (B) PERFORATED PIPE STRAP.

FIG. W-8

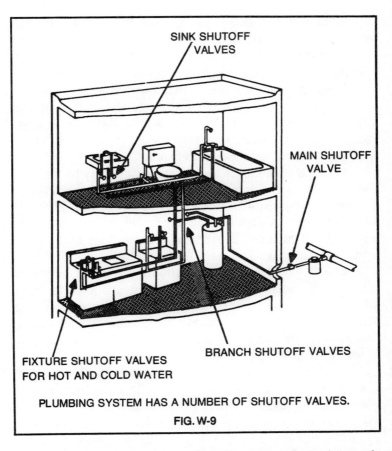

SINK SHUTOFF
VALVES

MAIN SHUTOFF
VALVE

BRANCH SHUTOFF VALVES

FIXTURE SHUTOFF VALVES
FOR HOT AND COLD WATER

PLUMBING SYSTEM HAS A NUMBER OF SHUTOFF VALVES.

FIG. W-9

all valve handles to their maximum counterclockwise position.

Check aerators used with faucets, shower heads, and washing machines. These use fine mesh screening which may have become partially clogged. If low water pressure is associated with just a single faucet, then the problem is in the water line going up to and including the faucet. If just hot water flow is sluggish, but not cold, then the hot water heater is probably clogged. If this is the case, turn the hot water heater off and wait at least a day for the water in the heater to cool. Using a bucket, open the hot water heater's drain valve. This will help remove any clogging material in the heater's exit pipe.

If the water from the heater contains rust and sediment and the exit water continues to show such rust and sediment after repeated flushings, then the heater may be badly corroded and will require replacement.

When buying a replacement hot water heater, the best is one having a large capacity. For gas heat, use at least a 40 gallon unit. For electric heat, use a 60 gallon unit. A large capacity unit will allow multiple use of hot water outlets—shaving, bathing, and washing dishes.

Low water pressure at one faucet only may be due to a defective faucet. The faucet valve seat may be corroded or the washer may be out of shape. If the washer is an old one, it can crumble and pieces can clog the faucet. Sometimes if the valve seat is corroded it will bend inward, restricting water flow.

Check all exposed water piping. If the piping is deeply pitted, if it shows white spots or there are pinhole leaks which have been repaired, the pipe or pipes may be filling with corrosion. Pipes may also develop mineral buildup. For this you can use a water softening powder. Mineral clogging is usually a problem in horizontal pipes.

Water pressure is associated only with the fresh water system of your home. It has nothing to do with other parts of your plumbing system, such as drains or vents.

See Aerator, How to Install, *page 16*
Faucets, Compression Type, Leaking, *page 121*
Faucets, Repairing Non-Compression or Single Lever Types, *page 122*
Water Pipes, Leaky, *page 364*

☐ Water Rings or Marks on Tables or Other Furniture

Wet glasses left on furniture tops can result in a white water ring. Remove with *camphorated oil*, obtainable in drug stores. Rub gently with the cloth or with a very mild abrasive pad. The idea is to remove the stain without damaging the finish. Wipe clean when stain disappears and then polish with wax. You can try using denatured alcohol if the camphorated oil doesn't work. Do not let water stains on furniture remain too long; they become more difficult to remove. If stain is dark, it indicates that water has penetrated finish and has reached the wood surface. In that case the remedies indicated here won't work.

☐ Weather Stripping

Most of the heat in a home is lost through windows and doors. Single pane windows are poor insulators since a large outside surface area is subjected to low temperatures, while the same large sheet of glass is reached by the much higher inside temperature. As a result, there is a constant transfer of heat from the inside to the outside through the glass.

Double windows, windows consisting of two separate panes of glass, are better since the air between the two panes works as an insulating medium. There are various arrangements possible. One is to use storm windows, thus providing the effect of a double pane. There are also special types of insulating glass, consisting of two closely adjoining sheets of glass with air in between. The advantage of a sealed double window instead of a storm window is that less maintenance is required. With a storm window four panes of glass must be cleaned, with a sealed double window just two.

Storm windows and double sealed windows are useful in summer as well as in winter. They can reduce the amount of hot outside air coming into a house by as much as 50%.

Heat coming into a home does so in two basic ways. One is via the air that is heated outdoors and the other is by sunlight. Sealed double glass is no more effective against solar heat than single glass. Solar heat can be kept out only by window shades and some of these, quite expensive, are made specifically for that purpose.

For protection against cold, weather stripping is fairly inexpensive and can be used to make strong reductions in home heat loss. There are various kinds of weather stripping including spring bronze, foam rubber, sponge edged wood strips, gaskets made of vinyl, felt, and caulking materials.

Caulking is one way of keeping winter cold where it belongs—outside. Caulking not only helps keep a house airtight but weathertight as well. Caulking is needed where windows and doors butt up against siding, where the chim-

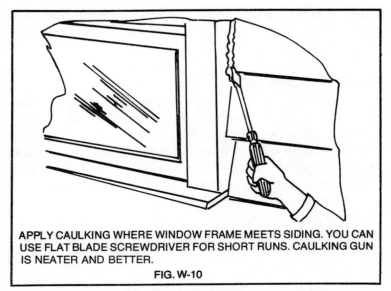

APPLY CAULKING WHERE WINDOW FRAME MEETS SIDING. YOU CAN USE FLAT BLADE SCREWDRIVER FOR SHORT RUNS. CAULKING GUN IS NEATER AND BETTER.

FIG. W-10

ney meets the roof, and where any two walls meet (Figs. W-10 and W-11).

Examine both sides and bottom and tops of windows to make sure caulk hasn't dried out and that there are no possible air spaces. Caulk is a putty-like substance, and you can apply it with a putty knife for small repairs or with a gun (Figs. W-12 through W-14).

The least expensive caulk is oil based but is suitable for temporary repairs only as its life expectancy is just a few months. Silicone caulk will last longer, but may not adhere well to painted surfaces. It is also difficult to paint over. Butyl rubber caulk is a good material but is very troublesome to work with.

Acrylic latex caulk is long lasting and can be used on either dry or damp surfaces. It is fast drying and will accept an oil base or latex paint. It will not discolor a covering of paint—that is, it will not "bleed" through the paint.

Caulking compounds are available in a variety of colors—white, light, and dark gray. You can apply caulk around windows and door frames, chimneys, or any area that shows a crack. You can use it instead of putty for puttying glass and, unlike putty, it doesn't eventually get hard and

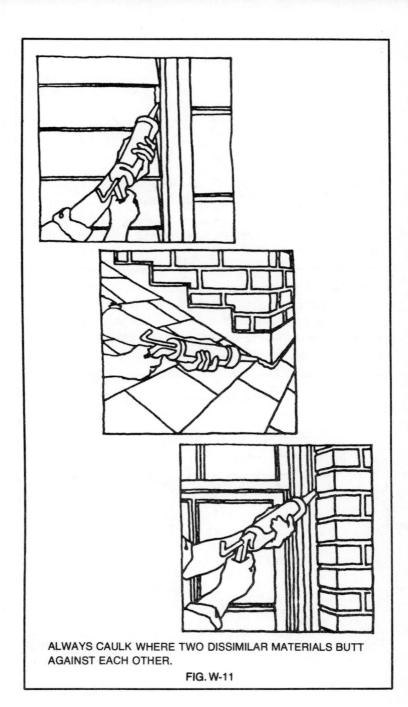

ALWAYS CAULK WHERE TWO DISSIMILAR MATERIALS BUTT
AGAINST EACH OTHER.

FIG. W-11

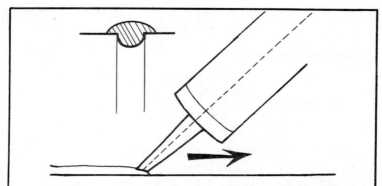

USING A CAULKING GUN TAKES SOME PRACTICE. MAKE SURE THE CAULK OVERLAPS BOTH SIDES, FOR EXAMPLE, A WINDOW FRAME AND ITS ADJOINING SIDING.

FIG. W-12

crumbling. If you buy caulk in a can, cover the surface with water, close the lid tightly, and the caulk will be ready for use again when you need it. You can also use caulk as a seal in place of mortar where mortar between bricks has become loose and has fallen out.

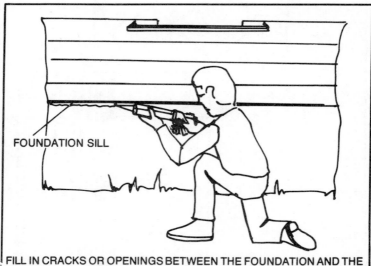

FOUNDATION SILL

FILL IN CRACKS OR OPENINGS BETWEEN THE FOUNDATION AND THE LOWER EDGE OF THE SIDING. YOU CAN USE OAKUM, GLASS FIBER OR INSULATION STRIPS. FINISH THE JOB BY CAULKING WITH A GUN.

FIG. W-13

To check areas inside the home where weather stripping could be useful, use a lighted candle as a testing tool. Move the candle up and down and across the windows. Strong flickering indicates a movement of air. You can also use the palm of your hand in the same way to detect cold air movement. Air can come through a window area even if there are no holes or cracks in the wood frame or in the wall around the frame. Air very often finds its way into the home through the window channels. A channel is the groove in which the sides of the window slide up and down. Use thin spring metal and nail it into place into the casing (Fig. W-15). You will need to move the windows, upper and lower, so they are together.

The bottom or top of a window that rests on the sash is called a *rail*. Install an insulating strip on the bottom rail of the lower sash and on the top rail of the upper sash (Fig. W-16). You can use adhesive back foam strips for this.

To weather-strip a door, apply adhesive backed foam to the inside face of the door jamb. Alternatively, you can nail rolled vinyl with an aluminum channel backing snugly against the door on the casing. Or you can nail spring metal along the inside of the door frame and the outside edge of the door. When the door closes, the faces of the spring metals mesh,

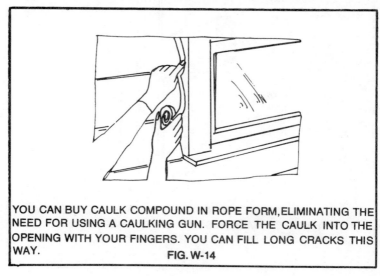

YOU CAN BUY CAULK COMPOUND IN ROPE FORM, ELIMINATING THE NEED FOR USING A CAULKING GUN. FORCE THE CAULK INTO THE OPENING WITH YOUR FINGERS. YOU CAN FILL LONG CRACKS THIS WAY.   FIG. W-14

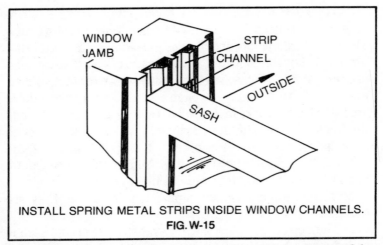

INSTALL SPRING METAL STRIPS INSIDE WINDOW CHANNELS.
FIG. W-15

effectively sealing the door. You can lift the outer edge of the metal strip with a screwdriver. This will help supply a better seal.

Mount a sweep across the bottom of the door (Fig. W-17). The sweep consists of a strip of aluminum holding a material such as fiber or rubber. The sweep is suitable if the

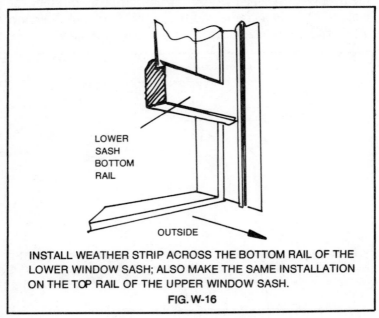

INSTALL WEATHER STRIP ACROSS THE BOTTOM RAIL OF THE LOWER WINDOW SASH; ALSO MAKE THE SAME INSTALLATION ON THE TOP RAIL OF THE UPPER WINDOW SASH.
FIG. W-16

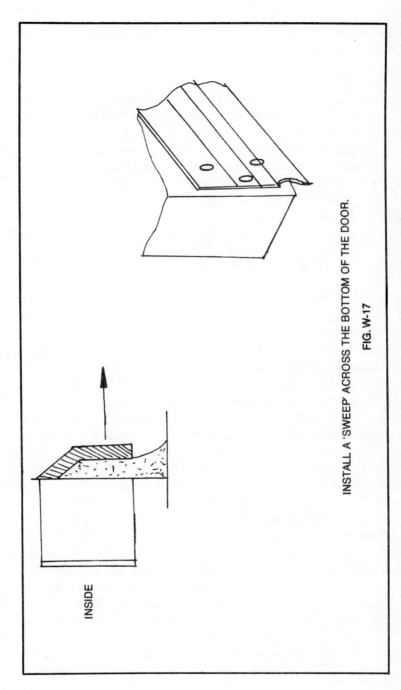

INSIDE

INSTALL A 'SWEEP' ACROSS THE BOTTOM OF THE DOOR.

FIG. W-17

375

floor is vinyl, ceramic, or linoleum, but not too good where the floor is covered with a rug.

☐ Welding

The strongest bond you can get between two metals, whether alike or dissimilar, is by *welding*. This is the process of heating the two metal parts to the melting point and making them flow together. Because the tremendous amount of heat is required, this is a complicated process and is a job best done by a professional welder.

See Aluminum, Joining, *page 21*
     Brazing, *page 34*
     Copper Pipe, Soldering, *page 60*
     Metals, Joining, *page 208*
     Soldering, *page 312*

☐ Windows, Stuck

There are many things that can cause a window to get stuck. But the two most common causes are paint and dirt, in that order. Paint forms an incredibly strong bond between the sash and the adjacent window molding. The sash consists of tracks on either side of the window, which are wooden grooves that may or may not be lined with metal.

To free the window from paint, use a sharp, single edge razor blade and try to insert it between the sash and molding. Work down, not up. Use short strokes and don't try to cut away too much paint at a time. Go over the entire sash/molding. That includes the full length of both sides, across the edge of the upper window and the lower horizontal edge of the bottom window. Even a small strip that remains stuck because of paint will keep you from moving the window. If you don't have a razor blade, use a penknife. The razor blade is preferable because it is thinner and sharper. A single edge blade is better than a double edge type because the backing of the single edge blade lets you get a good grip. Also, a single edge type will not bend as much as the double edge type. A razor blade holder is very helpful.

If the paint doesn't yield to this treatment, you may need to use sandpaper, especially if the paint is an accumulation of several paint jobs, one on top of the other. You might also try using a small block plane. A wood chisel will also do, but unless you are experienced in the use of this tool, you may find yourself gouging the sash and molding rather than removing the paint.

Still another method is to apply paint remover. Using a small brush, apply paint remover to the entire length and width of the window. Give the paint remover an opportunity to soften the paint, and then remove the paint with the help of a scraper.

After all this, you may find that the window still remains stuck. If you can work from the outside of the window, use a prying tool of some kind. You can get a tool of this kind from your local hardware store. Put the sharp edge of the tool under the bottom of the window and, pressing down on the tool, try to force the window up. Don't put the tool near the center of the window. Instead, work near one edge for that will apply the strongest force nearer a stuck edge. Work back and forth between the edges of the window.

Still another method you can try is to use a small block of hard wood and a hammer. Put the end of the block against the window frame, near the top, and tap the other end of the block with the hammer. Move across the top of the frame, while continuing the tapping process. Move down one side of the frame and then the other. The disadvantage of this method is that the block may damage the paint finish. If you want to protect the finish, put a soft cloth between the frame and the block. You will find it more convenient to fasten the cloth to the block. You can do this by tacking the cloth to the sides of the block. If you try to tap the frame by using the head of a hammer, you will definitely mar the paint. Even if you plan to repaint direct hammer blows may indent or gouge the wood.

Sometimes a window is stuck because the latch on the inside center has been locked and painted into position. Here you have two choices. You can scrape away enough paint by chipping away at it, or by using paint remover, until you can force the latch open. However if successive layers of oil paint cover the latch, probably the best method is to remove the latch completely. The screw heads holding the latch in position are probably covered over with paint. Scrape away the paint over the screw heads. If the screw head slot is filled with paint, and it probably is, you can chisel the paint out by using a thin flat blade screwdriver and a hammer. After you've removed both screws, don't expect the latch to fall off. It won't. But if you tap it repeatedly with a hammer, you will be able to work it loose.

A window can also be stuck because the humidity or rain has caused the wooden frame of the window to swell. This means the wood has expanded and is making an extremely tight fit in the track. To solve this problem, you will need to widen the track to free the window. Cut a small block of hard wood and force it into the track with the help of a hammer. Still using the hammer, make the block of wood travel up and down the track. This should widen the track enough to free the window. If this method doesn't succeed, try sanding the inside edges of the track. Of course, if you have paint on the inside edges of the track, this will also keep the window from moving. Use a paint scraper or a paint scraper plus paint remover. A small plane is also helpful, except that with a plane you cannot get near the top and bottom edges of the track.

After you have freed the window, you will probably find that while you can move it up and down, it does so only if you exert considerable effort. You can help by lubricating the track in which the window slides. You can use *graphite powder*, available in home supply or hardware stores, or other commercially prepared lubricants. As an interim measure, try hard soap. Don't wet the soap, but use it as it is. Rub the entire track with it, and that means all sides of the track. Paraffin is also helpful.

Sometimes the effort to free a stuck window means that the window frame and sash must be repainted. Unless you are careful, you will be back in the same position of having a window but being unable to open it. Immediately after you paint the window, keep moving it up and down. Do this every 10 minutes or so to keep the paint from forming a bond between sash and molding. With quick dry paints, this won't take as much of your time as you might think. A better arrangement is to use self stick paper tape. Cover the sash with the tape and paint the molding. After the paint has dried, cover the molding with tape and paint the sash.

☐ Window Glass, How to Replace Broken

A cracked window pane is not only unsightly but can be dangerous. Further, such a pane eliminates the prime function—to protect you and the inside of your home against weather.

As a first step in putting in a new pane, you must remove every bit of the old one. Broken glass can have razor sharp edges, so be sure to wear gloves. If the old glass is shattered, you will probably be able to remove the glass a section at a time. Work the glass section back and forth until it comes loose. Then put it in a double lined paper bag—that is, one bag inside another, or else use a shopping bag. Try to work without an audience, particularly if that audience is small children (Fig. W-18).

If the pane is simply cracked, you can attack the problem in two ways. You can remove most of the putty holding the glass in place with a sharp knife. A quicker way, but a bit on the risky side, is to tap the pane with a hammer until the pane shatters. If you select this option, hold the hammer at the far end of the handle. Wear a jacket whose sleeve is long enough to completely cover your arm. Wear safety goggles or at least shatterproof glasses.

Still another safety measure would be to crisscross the damaged pane with masking tape. This will help keep pieces of glass from flying about. Or you could cover the pane with a sheet of soft, flexible cardboard. Just make sure that the cardboard is larger than the pane and extends beyond its borders.

After you have all pieces of glass out, remove old putty from the window frame. You can do this with a screwdriver, a wood chisel, and a putty knife (Fig. W-19). The idea here is to work one step at a time. Don't try to remove long sections of putty but break the putty into small sections. Your purpose is to remove putty without damaging the groove or channel used to hold the pane.

IT IS SAFER TO WORK FROM THE
OUTSIDE OF THE WINDOW FRAME.

FIG. W-18

You can remove old putty by working under it with a flat blade screwdriver and by tapping the screwdriver lightly with a hammer (Fig. W-20). You can also use a brazing torch with a small tip. Play the flame onto the old putty, and follow with a sharp scraper to work out the old putty as it softens. Be careful not to let the flame strike the glass since it can cause the glass to break.

After you have removed the old putty, apply a coat of linseed oil or outside primer, which will fill the pores of the dried out wood and make a good bond for the new putty.

As you remove the putty, you will notice small metal triangles. Known as *glazier's points*, they are used to hold the glass pane in place (Fig. W-21). In some cases, the putty to be removed will have become extremely hardened with age. You may not be able to pick out small sections. In that case, use a soldering iron. The heat will soften the putty and make it easier to get out. Allow a few minutes for the iron to reach its maximum heat, and then run it just slightly ahead of the tool you are using for removing the putty.

REMOVE PIECES OF BROKEN GLASS
WITH PLIERS. WEAR GLOVES WHILE
WORKING.

FIG. W-19

REMOVE OLD PUTTY WITH THE HELP OF A SCREWDRIVER.

FIG. W-20

Putty sometimes forms long sections which will fall out easily. Yet you may also find some sections that are stubborn. Be patient; work slowly and easily.

After all the old putty is out, run a screwdriver blade or knife through the window pane channel on all four sides. Remove any rough spots. Examine each channel carefully to make sure no obstructions are left over. Remove any that remain, for unless you do it will be difficult or impossible to put in the new glass.

With the help of a small, clean paint brush, apply a heavy coating of linseed oil to every part of the window pane channel. The purpose of the linseed oil is to keep putty from drying out or from doing so too quickly. One of the problems with putty is that as it gets old, it dries and cracks. This means it forms a less effective window seal and can result in window pane rattling and the letting in of drafts of cold air.

Put a layer of fresh putty into the window pane channel on all four sides (Fig. W-22). The putty you are using should be very soft and malleable. Avoid any putty lumps. If the top layer of putty seems to have dried out, remove it, throw it

REMOVE GLAZIER POINTS WITH PLIERS.

FIG. W-21

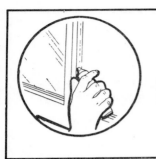

PUT A THIN RIBBON OF PUTTY IN THE FRAME.

FIG. W-22

away, and work with the softer putty beneath. If necessary, mix some linseed oil in with the putty to make it softer. When putting in the new putty, don't make the layer too thick. The new putty base should have a thickness of about 1/16 inch.

Putty has several purposes. It acts as a cushion for the glass. It prevents the glass from vibrating and rattling, and it stops the leakage of air.

Fitting The Glass. The new pane of glass should be exactly the right size. This means it is a fraction of an inch smaller, both in width and height, than the window area. It should fit in easily and smoothly, without forcing. It is always a good idea to test for size by putting the new pane into place before you apply the putty just to see if the glass size is right. Hold the glass in position with your fingers and then examine all four sides. Make sure that there are no open areas between the glass and its wood frame.

After you have made sure the glass will fit correctly, and after you have puttied the frame, insert the window pane into the frame area and press against the glass firmly. Don't worry about oily finger marks or dirt on the glass. You can clean these later.

Now push against the four edges of the glass. Do this by running a finger along each of the sides (remember, you are still wearing gloves). This will eliminate any air pockets between the glass and putty and will provide a tight seal all around (Fig. W-23).

Holding the glass in position with one hand, insert a glazier's point near the center of one side. If the frame is extremely hard or resists positioning of the point, apply pressure with a small block of hard wood. A small block of metal will also do. Then insert a glazier's point on the side opposite the first one. Finally, put glazier's points completely around on all four sides, spacing them about 4 inches apart (Fig. W-24).

Inserting glazier's points is easy once you have acquired a little bit of experience. Put each point flat against the glass. You will find it helpful to apply a chisel against the side of the glazier's point away from the window. Keep the chisel as flat against the window pane as you can to avoid damaging the glass. Tap the chisel lightly with a flat block of wood. It doesn't take much pressure to get the points into the window frame. Once the points are in place, you are ready to apply new putty.

Applying Putty to a Window. There are several ways of applying putty to a window. You can use a wide blade putty knife. The wider the blade, the more putty you can handle at any one time. Another technique, but this does take some practice, is to form the putty into pencil-like strips. If you have an old pane of glass, use this as a kneading board. Take some putty out of the can. Work it back and forth with your bare fingers on the glass until the putty is extremely soft and pliable. Add linseed oil if necessary. Then roll the putty back and forth until it assumes the shape of an unsharpened pencil. Take the putty, start at one corner of the window frame, and lay the putty in place. As you do, don't worry about its unevenness. When all the putty is in place, hold your putty knife at an angle, and make it smooth with long, even strokes. Dip the putty knife blade into linseed oil,

PUT THE GLASS INTO POSITION. MAKE SURE IT PRESSES AGAINST THE PUTTY.

FIG. W-23

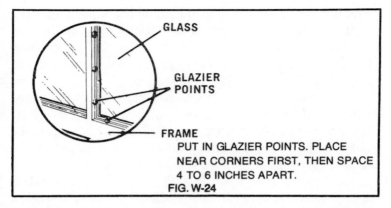

GLASS

GLAZIER POINTS

FRAME

PUT IN GLAZIER POINTS. PLACE
NEAR CORNERS FIRST, THEN SPACE
4 TO 6 INCHES APART.
FIG. W-24

and you will find the strokes making the putty much smoother. When you are finished, the putty should be completely smooth, without lumps, and with all glazier's points completely covered. You should not be able to see the putty from the opposite side of the glass (Fig. W-25).

After you have finished, use a scraping tool or a single edge razor blade to clean away any putty that may have touched other parts of the glass accidentally. Remove any excess putty along all four sides of the frame. If the window seems smeared or dirty, don't try to clean it at this time.

Fresh putty doesn't take paint very well, Wait about three or four days to give the putty a chance to set. For a good paint job, use a high-quality paint, preferably a type made for outdoor use. Wait for the first coat to dry thoroughly, usually about a full day, and then apply a second coat. To keep the paint from smearing the glass, buy a metal shield, available at low cost in any paint store. Any scrap bit of thin, flat metal you have around the house will do as well.

Once the second coat of paint has dried, you can start cleaning the window. You may need to use linseed oil to remove any traces of putty on the window. Keep the oil away from your freshly painted surface. Finish the job with a commercial window cleaner. A mixture of water and ammonia is also an effective cleaning agent.

Not all panes use putty. If you have a glass door inside the house, you will probably find the glass held in place by wooden strips. Pry out a single strip, and you will find the others will come out much more easily. Getting out the first strip can be a bit tricky. Since the wood strips are usually thin, they are easy to break. They have often been painted into place, so you may need to use a razor blade or knife to cut away the paint between the strip and the door frame.

The strips are held in place by small nails. If you can locate these and manage to pull them out with pliers, it will be much easier to get the wood strips out.

You will probably find, in replacing a window pane, that you have used relatively little putty. Putty can last a long time if it is kept away from air. If the putty comes in a can or jar, make sure the cover is sealed tightly. Before closing the can or jar, however, put in a small amount of linseed oil, enough to barely cover the surface of the putty. If you want to really make sure the putty will remain airtight, try the jar within a jar trick. Put the can or jar of putty into another jar. This second jar should be barely large enough to accommodate the first. Make sure the covers on both jars are absolutely tight. If the jars are equipped with cover washers, so much the better.

See Glass, Cutting, *page 153*

□ Wire Nuts

See Electrical Connections, How to Insulate, *page 94*

□ Wires, Connecting Electrical

When connecting a wire to a screw on an electrical device such as a switch or receptacle, bend the wire into a

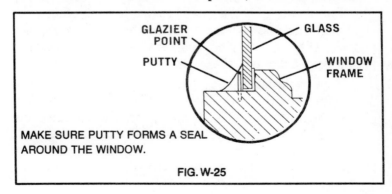

GLAZIER POINT

GLASS

PUTTY

WINDOW FRAME

MAKE SURE PUTTY FORMS A SEAL AROUND THE WINDOW.

FIG. W-25

loop so it is in the same direction as the screw when it is fastened. If the wire is mounted the wrong way on the screw, the action of closing the screw will push the wire out of position. On the contrary, if the wire loop is in the direction of the screw when it is closed, the screw head will tighten its grip on the wire.

Some screws are captive types and cannot be completely removed. In that case just wrap the wire around the shank or body of the screw. Again it is important to make sure the wire is wrapped in a clockwise direction. When connecting stranded wire to a screw, twirl the strands so that the total number of wires resembles a solid conductor as much as possible.

If you have a wire which must be fastened to a screw terminal, and that wire is to continue on to some other switch or outlet, you can make a good connection by scraping away some of the insulation on the wire and then forming the exposed wire into a loop. The loop can then be forced around the threads of the screw (Fig. W-26).

See BX Cable, Cutting and Installing, *page 38*
Electrical Connections, How to Insulate, *page 94*
Electrical Wire Color Code, *page 102*
Electric Shock, How to Avoid, *page 107*
Romex Cable, Cutting and Installing, *page 287*
Soldering, *page 312*

□ **Wood, Fastening at Right Angles**

Two pieces of wood at 45° angles to each other or at right angles can be fastened to each other using *corrugated fasteners* (Fig. W-27). The fasteners have a sharp edge to permit easy entry into the wood.

If the two wood pieces are to be joined to form a corner, use a miter box to cut the ends at 45° angles. The two cut pieces should form a smooth butt joint. Do not drive the corrugated fasteners too close to the edge as this may split the wood. One fastener at each joint may be adequate. For larger pieces it may be necessary to use a pair of fasteners.

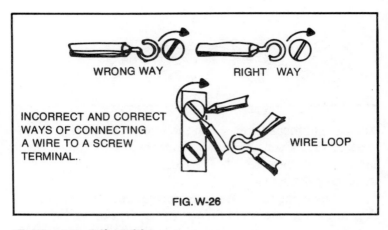

WRONG WAY   RIGHT WAY

INCORRECT AND CORRECT
WAYS OF CONNECTING
A WIRE TO A SCREW
TERMINAL.

WIRE LOOP

FIG. W-26

☐ Wrench, Adjustable

The *adjustable wrench*, also known as a crescent wrench, can be adjusted to fit different sizes of nuts (Fig. W-28). If a nut is difficult to turn or loosen, apply some penetrating oil or kerosene (Fig. W-29). Various anti-rust liquids for this purpose are also available. Let the oil, kerosene, or other liquid remain on the nut for several hours.

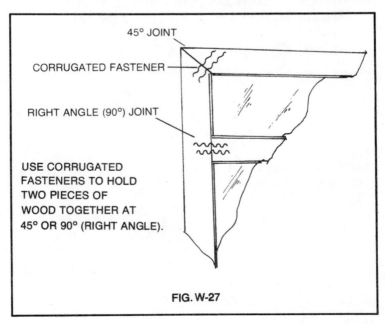

45° JOINT

CORRUGATED FASTENER

RIGHT ANGLE (90°) JOINT

USE CORRUGATED
FASTENERS TO HOLD
TWO PIECES OF
WOOD TOGETHER AT
45° OR 90° (RIGHT ANGLE).

FIG. W-27

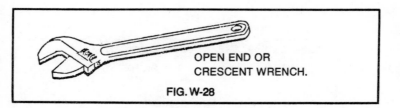

OPEN END OR
CRESCENT WRENCH.

FIG. W-28

You can get more leverage on the wrench and apply a much greater force if you slip a 1 foot length of pipe (or longer) over the handle of the wrench. The danger here is that too much force may damage the tool.

When using the adjustable wrench, position the jaws so they are at the bottom of the nut and so that the nut is as far into the jaws as it can go. If the wrench has a tendency to slip off, try turning it over. If the sides of the nut aren't flat, the wrench will have a tendency to slip. Sometimes filing one or more of the flat surfaces of the nut will help. The filing action will also make the surfaces of the nut somewhat rougher and will let the wrench get a better grip.

See Wrench, Box End, *page 389*
    Wrench, Combination, *page 390*
    Wrench, How to Use Adjustable, *page 391*
    Wrench, Monkey, *page 393*
    Wrench, Open End, *page 395*

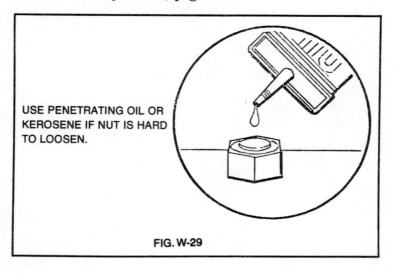

USE PENETRATING OIL OR KEROSENE IF NUT IS HARD TO LOOSEN.

FIG. W-29

☐ Wrench, Allen

Sometimes known as the *hexagonal* or *hex wrench* (because it has six sides), an *Allen wrench* is used for removing setscrews (Fig. W-30). Faucet handles are sometimes held in place by setscrews or with slotted head screws which can be removed with a small flat blade screwdriver. The faucet handles may be force fit types which use no screws at all. Allen wrenches are available in different sizes and are sometimes sold as a complete kit or set.

☐ Wrench, Box End

A *box end wrench* fits completely over the nut or bolt it is to turn, and it is easier and safer to use than fixed or adjustable open end wrenches (Fig. W-31). This tool generally has 12 points or notches arranged in a circle. Six and eight point wrenches are intended for heavy duty work, with 12 point wrenches for medium duty work and 16 point types for light work only.

The two openings of the box end wrench are at opposite ends of the handle and are designed to fit different sizes of nuts and bolts. The wrench can be used with square head nuts or bolts or those that have hexagonal heads. To get maximum turning power, hold the tool at the end that is farthest from the nut or bolt being turned.

If, in using a box end wrench, a nut or bolt is fastened so firmly in position that you are unable to turn it, you can get extra turning power by tapping the end of the wrench with a hammer. Short, tapping strokes are better than heavy hammer blows which could damage the tool. Once the nut or bolt

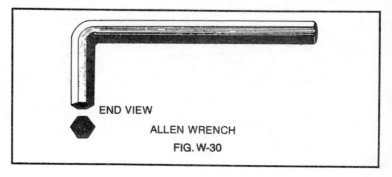

END VIEW

ALLEN WRENCH

FIG. W-30

starts to move, discontinue the use of the hammer and try turning with the box end wrench only.

Sometimes a nut or bolt may be "frozen" into place, a condition that occurs when the threads of the nut or bolt have rusted. Liquids are available in hardware stores which can be used to help remove some of the rust, making it easier to turn the nut or bolt.

See Wrench, Adjustable, *page 387*
    Wrench, Combination, *page 390*
    Wrench, How to Use Adjustable, *page 391*
    Wrench, Monkey, *page 393*
    Wrench, Open End, *page 395*

☐ Wrench, Combination

A *combination wrench* is a two-tool-in-one arrangement with an open end and box wrench at opposite ends of the handle. Sometimes the box end of the wrench is offset by an angle of about 15° to let the tool clear adjacent bolts or nuts (Fig. W-32).

When working with a fixed wrench, whether box, open, or combination, always pull on the free end of the wrench. This will not only give you better control over the tool, but will keep you from hurting your hand if the tool should slip. When using any kind of wrench, there should be minimum play between the tool and the nut or bolt to be turned.

See Wrench, Adjustable, *page 387*
    Wrench, Box End, *page 389*
    Wrench, How to Use Adjustable, *page 391*
    Wrench, Monkey, *page 393*
    Wrench, Open End, *page 395*

BOX END WRENCH IS DESIGNED TO TURN TWO DIFFERENT
SIZES OF NUTS AND BOLTS.

FIG. W-31

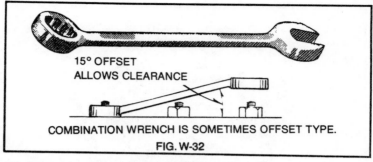

15° OFFSET
ALLOWS CLEARANCE

COMBINATION WRENCH IS SOMETIMES OFFSET TYPE.

FIG. W-32

☐ Wrench, How to Use Adjustable

You can make your in-home repairs easier and faster by doing two things: using the right tools and using them correctly. One of the most misused tools is the adjustable open end or crescent wrench (Fig. W-33). When used improperly, it can damage the hand.

Wrenches are used for loosening and tightening nuts. Don't expect a single wrench to be able to do it all. If you must open a wrench to its maximum, then the wrench is too small. You should not need to open the jaws of the wrench to more than about 50%.

The jaws of the wrench must fit smoothly over two faces of the nut. Do not try to fasten the wrench on the apex or joining line of the faces of the nut. If the flats of the nut are sloped or corroded, try to select a pair that are in reasonably

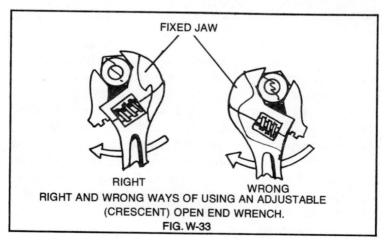

FIXED JAW

RIGHT   WRONG
RIGHT AND WRONG WAYS OF USING AN ADJUSTABLE
(CRESCENT) OPEN END WRENCH.
FIG. W-33

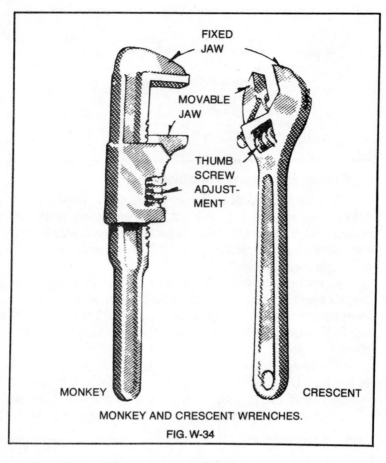

FIXED JAW

MOVABLE JAW

THUMB SCREW ADJUST- MENT

MONKEY

CRESCENT

MONKEY AND CRESCENT WRENCHES.

FIG. W-34

good condition. Make sure the jaws of the wrench are over as much of the flat area of the nut as possible. It is usually better to have the wrench as far down on the nut—that is, as close as possible to the bolt to which the nut is fastened.

Always position the wrench so you will turn it in the direction of the adjustable jaw of the wrench. The reason for this is to keep the adjustable jaw from springing open. You will get maximum leverage if you keep your hands as close as possible to the handle of the wrench. If a nut is "frozen" in position, possibly by rust, apply "rust remover liquid." Commercial preparations are available in hardware and home supply stores.

You can get greater leverage, and more turning power, by slipping a small section of iron pipe over the handle of the wrench. However, too much force could break the handle of the tool.

See Wrench, Adjustable, *page 387*
      Wrench, Box End, *page 389*
      Wrench, Combination, *page 390*
      Wrench, Monkey, *page 393*
      Wrench, Open End, *page 395*

☐ Wrench, Monkey

Like the crescent wrench, the *monkey wrench* is an adjustable type and is available in sizes ranging from about 4 inches to 2 feet (Fig. W-34). A 6-inch monkey wrench is suitable for most in-home uses. The correct opening of the wrench jaws is about 50% of maximum. If you must open the jaws to or near maximum capacity, then the wrench size is too small.

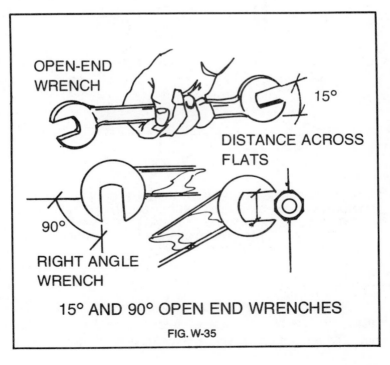

OPEN-END WRENCH

15°

DISTANCE ACROSS FLATS

90°

RIGHT ANGLE WRENCH

15° AND 90° OPEN END WRENCHES

FIG. W-35

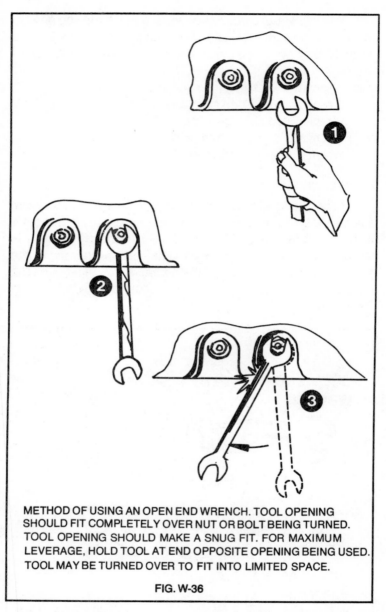

METHOD OF USING AN OPEN END WRENCH. TOOL OPENING
SHOULD FIT COMPLETELY OVER NUT OR BOLT BEING TURNED.
TOOL OPENING SHOULD MAKE A SNUG FIT. FOR MAXIMUM
LEVERAGE, HOLD TOOL AT END OPPOSITE OPENING BEING USED.
TOOL MAY BE TURNED OVER TO FIT INTO LIMITED SPACE.

FIG. W-36

When tightening or loosening a hexagonal (hex) nut,
make sure the jaws of the wrench are across the flats of the
nut. Tighten the thumb screw adjustment of the tool so that

the tool will remain firmly in place even if you remove your hand. Make sure the nut is as deep as possible into the jaws of the wrench.

When you pull the wrench, do so with the handle moving in the direction of the side having the adjustable jaw. This will keep the adjustable jaw from opening, preventing the tool from sliding off the nut that is being turned.

See Wrench, Adjustable, *page 387*
　　　Wrench, Box End, *page 389*
　　　Wrench, Combination, *page 390*
　　　Wrench, How to Use Adjustable, *page 391*
　　　Wrench, Open End, *page 395*

□ Wrench, Open End

Open end wrenches, often made of vanadium steel, are non-adjustable tools used for turning nuts or bolts. The tool is supplied with openings at both ends, with these openings at some angle to the body of the tool. An open end wrench whose end is at right angles to the handle or body is called a *right angle wrench*. The typical angle, though, is 15 degrees (Fig. W-35). The purpose of having the head at an angle is to permit use of the tool in space where there isn't enough room to make a complete turn.

Open end wrenches are often sold in sets of six to 10 wrenches with head openings ranging from 5/16 to 1 inch. Usually, the larger the head opening, the larger the tool.

The head opening of the open end wrench must fit the nut or bolt it is to turn (Fig. W-36). If the head opening is too small, you will not be able to use the tool. If it is too large, there will be too much "play" between the nut or bolt and the end opening of the tool.

The body or handle of the open end wrench is usually straight, but it can be curved. Such tools are called S wrenches. Some open end wrenches have an offset body, letting the head reach nuts or bolts that are below a surface.

See Wrench, Adjustable, *page 387*
　　　Wrench, Box End, *page 389*

☐ X-Acto Tools

X-Acto manufactures a variety of tools which are useful for household repairs. Items include knives, tweezers, saw blades, files, compasses, pliers, C-clamps, a cordless power drill, planes, and other tools (Figs. X-1 through X-8). Figure X-9 shows a set of good files. If you get a set like this from X-Acto, you will have the shape of file you will need for almost any job. The miniature tools from X-Acto are ideal for small jobs. If you cannot obtain these tools at your local hardware store, consult a hobby shop.

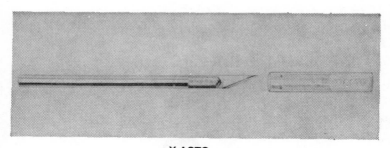

X-ACTO
NUMBER 1
KNIFE

FIG. X-1

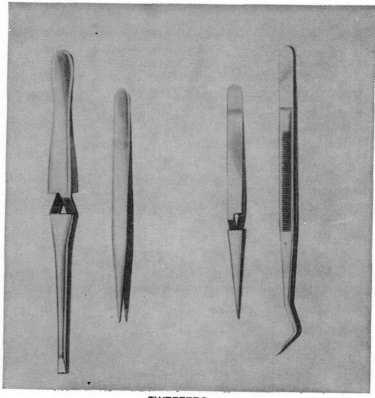

TWEEZERS
FIG. X-2

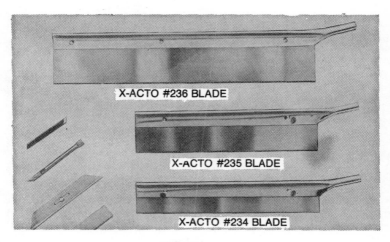

X-ACTO #236 BLADE

X-ACTO #235 BLADE

X-ACTO #234 BLADE

FIG. X-3

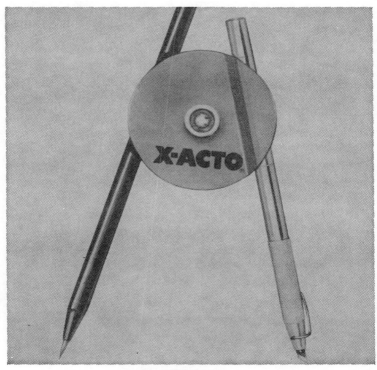

X-ACTO COMPASS
FIG. X-4

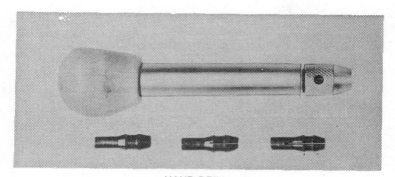

HAND DRILL

FIG. X-5

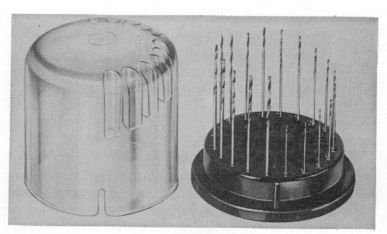

DRILL BITS

FIG. X-6

MITER BOX

FIG. X-7

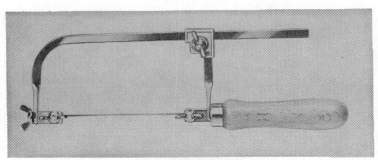

JEWELER'S SAW

FIG. X-8

X-ACTO FILES
FIG. X-9

☐ Yardstick, Using a

See Glass, Cutting, *page 153*

□ **Zinc Chromate Primer**
See Exterior Metal Surfaces, Painting, *page 119*